SMOOTH OPERATOR

Geoff Andrews was educated at Ruskin College, Oxford and University College, Cardiff. He has taught in adult education for many years, mainly for the Oxford University Department for Continuing Education and The Open University, where he is Senior Lecturer in Politics. A historian with wide interests, his previous books have been on the history of British communism, Italian politics, and the Cambridge Spies.

BY THE SAME AUTHOR

Agent Molière: The Life of John Cairncross, the Fifth Man of the Cambridge Spy Circle

The Shadow Man: At the Heart of the Cambridge Spy Circle

The Slow Food Story: Politics and Pleasure

Not a Normal Country: Italy After Berlusconi

Endgames and New Times: The Final Years of British Communism 1964–1991

SMOOTH OPERATOR

The life and times of
Cyril Lakin, editor,
broadcaster and politician

GEOFF ANDREWS

PARTHIAN

Parthian, Cardigan SA43 1ED
www.parthianbooks.com
First published in 2021
This edition 2022
© Geoff Andrews 2021
All Rights Reserved
Hardback ISBN 978-1-913640-18-7
Paperback ISBN 978-1-914595-54-7
eISBN 978-1-913640-85-9
Cover design by www.theundercard.co.uk
Typeset by Syncopated Pandemonium
Printed and bound by 4edge Ltd
Published with the financial support of the Welsh Books
Council.
The Modern Wales series receives support from the Rhys
Davies Trust

the RHYS DAVIES TRUST

British Library Cataloguing in Publication Data
A cataloguing record for this book is available from the British
Library.

Contents

Preface

In 2016, while looking through George Orwell's BBC correspondence for something else, I came across a 1943 entry for Cyril Lakin, whose surname connected me to family on my mother's side. Orwell, who was then working in the BBC Talks department, had recommended Lakin, a politician with previous broadcasting experience, as a possible presenter for a forthcoming radio programme. At the time I had only a vague recollection that he was a distant relative (my uncle's uncle) and that he had been an MP during the war. I began to learn more about him and embarked on the trail that took me to his daughter Bridget (then aged eighty-nine and living on the Isle of Wight), gradually assembling the disparate components of what I came to realise was an unlikely and, in many ways, extraordinary life.

Who was he? Where was he from? The very English circles in which he moved, and the culture and institutions that he thrived on and fully embraced, belied quite different origins. Born in Barry (where I spent my early years), he shared the

seemingly obscure background of others from that modern
port that had emerged abruptly and unannounced on the back
of the South Wales coal industry. One of my first discoveries
was that his father Harry, a native of Birmingham who had
moved to South Wales in the early 1890s, had been one of
the pioneers who helped make the new town; a butcher in
Cadoxton when that district was beset by disease, poverty and
crime, he served as a councillor on several of the committees
that shaped Barry's modern infrastructure.

Beyond that, there was very little to go on. An inaccurate
Wikipedia item describes him as a farmer while another
listing seemed to confuse him with a nephew (also called
Cyril) who *had* been a farmer as well as a local councillor.
He has no entry in the *Dictionary of Welsh Biography*, nor has
there been much written about him in secondary accounts of
Welsh politics and history. I could see that the enigma was
partly explained by his humble beginnings in that new Welsh
urban settlement, comparable in some ways to an American
frontier town. Aspirational Barry was a stepping stone for
him as it was for his contemporaries and the generation
that followed, among them the politicians Barnett Janner
and Gwynfor Evans, composer Grace Williams, journalist
Gareth Jones, the cartoonist Leslie Illingworth, the historian
John Habakkuk, and United Nations diplomat Abdulrahim
Abby Farah. Lakin's journey by South Wales standards took
a different route, facilitated by a doting mother, inspiring
headmaster and influential High Anglican vicar who helped
get him to Oxford with the prospect of a career in the Church.

As I pieced together the different fragments of his life
from scattered Welsh archives, old BBC scripts, letters from
the 1920s that had remained in my cousin's attic at Highlight

Farm, regular conversations with his daughter, and the editorial correspondence of the *Sunday Times* and the *Daily Telegraph*, it was evident that the life-defining connections that transported him to Fleet Street, the BBC and Westminster also had distinctive Welsh origins. The story of William and Gomer Berry (later Lords Camrose and Kemsley), the two powerful press barons from Merthyr Tydfil, has never been told in full (least of all in Wales). It was their influence (which at its peak matched that of Rothermere and Beaverbrook) that made Lakin's rise possible and helped establish his roles in both the literary world and the appeasement debate (and an ill-judged meeting with Hitler), a wartime broadcasting career and, finally, a return to Barry as its MP.

Chapter 1

A Man from Somewhere

In common with many of the families who helped to build modern Barry, the Lakins had their origins in England. In their case it was the Midlands. Cyril Lakin's father Henry ('Harry') was born in what is now the Birmingham suburb of Erdington (then classified as Warwickshire) in 1870, the son of James Lakin, a wire drawer, and Eliza Jones, born in Herefordshire to a farmer originally from Cardigan, West Wales: Farmer Jones, Cyril Lakin's great-grandfather, was in fact his sole Welsh ancestor. James's father Joseph was an agricultural labourer who set up home with his wife Elizabeth and their seven children in Bell Lane, then part of a hamlet where most of his neighbours worked on local farms. In the late 1860s Bell Lane was renamed after the huge orphanage built there by Josiah Mason, the self-educated industrialist and philanthropist, who also constructed almshouses nearby as a further contribution to the well-being of the poor. At the top of the orphanage was an enormous 250-foot tower, from which Sir Benjamin Stone, a notable documentary photographer and later Conservative MP, compiled his panoramic images of the surrounding area. Stone, who would become the first mayor of Sutton Coldfield, embodied the civic and entrepreneurial spirit of Victorian Birmingham that had a lasting influence on Harry Lakin.

After Joseph's death in 1860, Elizabeth worked as a registered nurse while her children supported the family through their work as labourers and dressmakers. James found regular work in local industry and, after his marriage to Eliza, moved a couple of streets away to Easy Row, Sutton Road, a working-class thoroughfare in Erdington village where their neighbours were a mixture of skilled and semi-skilled labourers and small shopkeepers. Here Harry Lakin was born, their only son among six children. His upbringing suggests an importance given to a stable family life, with religion playing an important part in the shadow of St Barnabas Church (where he was baptized). His schooling was brief but adequate in its basic instruction to enable him to decide on a trade as a butcher. Beyond his trade he had wider ambitions, including an early interest in civic affairs inspired by the example of Joseph Chamberlain, whose tenure as Birmingham's Liberal mayor had brought a range of municipal reforms such as slum clearance, libraries, parks and museums, and encouragement for local artisans. Nineteenth-century Birmingham was at the centre of transformations in local government, though by the time Harry Lakin had begun work Chamberlain was already an MP, representing the Liberal Unionist wing and disaffected with Gladstone and the Home Rule legislation. From Harry Lakin's subsequent brief political career in Barry it appears that Chamberlain's evolution from entrepreneur to civic champion had left a marked impression on him, though he did not share Chamberlain's Nonconformity, earlier 'gas-and-water socialism', or support for the temperance movement. He was proud that his first apprenticeship was in the butcher's shop patronized by the Chamberlain family, a story that he would later recount in his appeal to the Barry electorate. The Chamberlains would continue to hold significance for his family: many years later, in the turbulent years of interwar British politics, Cyril Lakin would get to know Joseph's sons Austen and Neville, who were then on opposite sides of the appeasement debate.

Harry Lakin's horizons were broader than Birmingham, however, while his shrewd business sense, an attribute that would bring many advantages to his family, was already evident. His decision to move to South Wales was a recognition of the transformational impact of the coal industry, and informed by both an awareness that the prosperity of the communities depended upon on the migration of new tradesmen, and an optimism for the new business opportunities presented. At the beginning of the 1890s he moved to Tredegar, South East Wales, then in the county of Monmouthshire, and one of the early centres of the Industrial Revolution. The Circle was the heart of the town, with its central core – a meeting point for businesses – leading out to adjoining streets, and it was here (at number 10) that he took up employment as an apprentice butcher for Enoch Woodward. The same building would later be a local landmark as the home of the Medical Aid Society, so inspirational for Aneurin Bevan – Tredegar's most famous resident and the founder of the National Health Service – who served on the committee that provided health assistance to the town. When Harry Lakin moved there as a live-in servant and apprentice it had different concerns, however. The master butcher and head of the house, Enoch Woodward, was a Wesleyan Methodist, a member of Tredegar Council, a Poor Law Guardian and a strong supporter of local charities and temperance causes. He was keenly involved in the life of the town, including its literary and musical societies, and as a notable local figure and entrepreneur was likely an early mentor for Harry Lakin.

After his apprenticeship in Tredegar, Harry Lakin was ready to establish himself as a butcher. Convinced by now that the coalfields of South Wales afforded new opportunities to ambitious tradesmen, he sought to be at the heart of it. He made a very wise choice in Barry, which was already heralded as the most significant emerging industrial town in South Wales, often compared with American frontier towns where new migration settlements laid the basis for new urban communities and civic cultures. When he arrived in 1891 to live at 11 Vere Street, Cadoxton, Barry was in the process of merging its three villages – Cadoxton, Barry and Merthyr Dyfan – to form an industrial centre founded on the docks, which had been opened just two years earlier. After much parliamentary and legal wrangling, The Barry Dock and Railway Act in 1884 had finally been approved by Royal Assent on the grounds that the nearby Cardiff and Penarth docks were insufficient to meet the rising demand for coal following the construction of new pits in the Rhondda Valley. The opening of Barry Dock in 1889 was the culmination of a campaign launched by the big colliery owners, notably David Davies – or David Davies Llandinam as he was known – and John Cory, who wanted to extend the facilities for transporting and exporting their coal. Both Cory and Davies were major coal owners in the Rhondda who held other extensive business interests, and their influence extended to politics, a host of philanthropic causes, temperance and Wesleyan Methodism. They received the backing of other prominent businessmen, including Archibald Hood, another Rhondda coal owner, and J. O. Riches, the president of the Cardiff Chamber of Commerce, who had first pursued the Barry Dock scheme in 1881 (though David Davies is credited with leading the battle to get legislation through Parliament).[1] Initially, they had faced local opposition from the Windsor estate, the owners of Barry Island, who were concerned about protecting their business at Penarth Dock, fearing that the island, rather than Penarth, could be the prosperous Cardiff suburb; at one point the Windsors even closed Barry Island to deter tourists. However, after Penarth was established as the retreat for the Cardiff bourgeois, and the Windsors saw increased profits in the unrelenting demand for coal, there was a volte-face and they went into business with David Davies and the other coal owners.[2] Moreover, the siting of Barry Dock was enhanced by the island being situated in an area that was thought to be ideal for loading coal.

In 1881 the combined villages of Cadoxton, Barry and Merthyr Dyfan had shared a population of 478; as small agricultural communities they were isolated from each other in an area still defined by the big landowners, notably Windsor, Romilly, and Jenner. After the Barry Railway Company succeeded in achieving Royal Assent to build the docks, railway stations were opened at Cadoxton and Barry Dock in December 1888 (Barry Station was opened in February the following year) along the Cogan line, with the first coal delivered in July 1889. The opening of the docks – to great fanfare and approximately 2,000 spectators – precipitated an enormous migration into Barry from other parts of Wales, and particularly from England (including many from the West Country), with Irish and Scottish immigrants moving south. The influx of navvies to work on the docks and railways provided the strong working-class core of the town. By 1896 it had grown to a population of around 20,000, only a quarter of whom were of Welsh origin.[3] As a result, the population underwent significant social and cultural transformation, with the task of building its infrastructure – including its civic and political institutions – still in its early stages when Harry Lakin arrived. Urbanization had been so rapid that the living conditions were chaotic, crime was endemic and disease common. Initially, Cadoxton was intended to be the main hub of the new town and received the majority of the first inhabitants and building work, and this may have been the reason he chose Vere Street, which together with Main Street was one of two principal centres of trade. In addition to commercial premises – butchers, drapers, chemists, confectionery and newsagents were starting up – by the mid-1890s Vere Street also accommodated two banks and the Royal, Cadoxton and Wenvoe Arms hotels as well as the Cadoxton Conservative Club.

One of the consequences of the influx of dockworkers and railway workers was that it turned previously rural Cadoxton into a working-class district. The Barry Trades Council had been founded in 1891 amid the turmoil of labour insecurity and dangerous working conditions. Inspired by the new unionism of the late 1880s (which, among others, had led to the London Dock Strike of 1889) under the leadership of J. H. Jose, a future councillor colleague of Harry Lakin, it helped organize serious campaigns for improved wages and conditions. This was strengthened by the formation of the Navvies' Union and the proliferation of meetings and gatherings in the reading rooms, temperance halls and coffee shops of Cadoxton and Barry.[4]

The mixture of agitation and ambition characterized the growth of Barry in the 1890s. As a purposeful twenty-one-year-old tradesman Harry Lakin had arrived in a town that was 'booming' with aspiration. 'No port in the kingdom,' the *South Wales Daily News* declared in the year of his arrival, 'exhibits a more marvellously thriving record, or views the future with more confidence than this latest *protégé* of fortune'.[5] But it also had significant social problems in its early years that affected in one way or another all its inhabitants. In Cadoxton, unfinished roads and pathways amounted to 'mud lakes' and 'quagmires' at times of inclement weather (leading to the nicknames of 'Mudoxton' and 'Slushoxton'), with open sewage causing stench, disease and sanitary problems, including an outbreak of typhus fever shortly before Harry Lakin moved in. The initial overcrowding caused by the rapid migration of dockworkers co-existed with derelict or unfinished houses and illegal drinking dens ('shebeens'), and Cadoxton became a fertile area for speculators. Crime was a perennial problem with prostitution, petty theft and violent assaults stretching the resources of the Cadoxton police, whose limited manpower amounted to stationing one of its three police constables at each end of Vere and Main Streets to quell Saturday night revellers.[6]

This all contributed to a difficult settling-in period and meant an even more testing time following Harry Lakin's marriage to Annie Palmer in 1892. They were married at Cardiff Registry Office, but they most likely met in the Midlands when he was serving his first apprenticeship. Annie had endured a tough childhood in Bewdley, Worcestershire. From a farming family, she had lost both her parents when very young after they had contracted typhoid from drinking well water, and was brought up by her elder sister Lizzie. Despite the difficulties in her early years, Annie held firm aspirations, which she took with her to Barry – ones she shared with her husband and would later invest in her eldest son. Ambitions aside, building up a butcher's business and establishing a presence in a rapidly growing and at times hazardous environment meant long hours and constant vigilance to property and person. Not long after their marriage Harry had to appear as a witness in the 'Cadoxton Assault and Highway Robbery' case at Barry Dock Police Court after a woman was assaulted by a local fireman who had followed her from the nearby Wenvoe Arms Hotel. After refusing him money, the woman (in a drunken state, according to Harry Lakin's testimony) was struck in the chest outside his butcher's shop. After refusing the man's demand to pick up a dropped sixpence, she was then hit again in the ribs and fainted. The charge was amended to 'assault' (presumably as no money was taken) and 'the ruffian' sentenced to a month's imprisonment with hard labour.[7]

These were the conditions in Cadoxton when Cyril Henry Alfred Lakin was born on 29 December 1893. While he was not a product of the classic proletariat, his early life as the son of a young, enterprising butcher making his way in the chaotic world of Barry Dock was shaped by the class character and industrial demands of the South Wales coalfield, which was rapidly turning Barry into a major coal exporting town – a second dock was opened in 1898, with the imposing Barry Dock Offices completed by 1900. Modern Barry was founded in the years immediately prior to and following his birth and saw its biggest changes during his childhood. Some individuals continued to exercise disproportionate influence on the development of the district. These included John Cory, who as director of Cory Brothers and Co shipping and coal export business had earlier been central to the decision to build Barry Dock and subsequently became Barry's first county councillor. As first chairman of the Barry and Cadoxton Local Board, which preceded the Barry Urban District Council, he was a prominent figure who used his status as one of the richest men in Wales to support local causes. Like many of the Liberal politicians and industrialists of that time, he was a strict Methodist and teetotaller, which clearly imbued him with a certain sense of moral and civic responsibility, though he was not a regular attender at council meetings (or a notable contributor on his rare appearances) and soon resigned his chairmanship.

Many of the founders of the new town were, like Harry Lakin, immigrants from England. Some of its members would go on to be stalwarts of the town. Its chairman in 1891, the year of Harry Lakin's arrival, was John Claxton (J. C.) Meggitt, a timber merchant from Wolverhampton, who in 1884 was one of the first businessmen to move to Barry and had been a member of the Cadoxton Parochial Committee (until its succession by the Local Board) and a Poor Law Guardian. In the first Local Board election in 1888 he had come top of the poll and by 1891 was already a 'dominant figure' through his capacity to introduce new ideas and turn them into plans for action. He was 'business-like, curt and practical' and a man of 'strong opinions', but also able to compromise when necessary, if it was to the benefit of his adopted town. As a speaker he was clear and precise without the passion and oratory of some of his Welsh counterparts, but in the view of the electorate and

fellow board members, any lack of imagination was made up
for by his common sense and 'sound administration'. Like many
others on the board he was a 'Progressive Liberal' and a 'firm
congregationalist'.[8] Meggitt, like the younger Harry Lakin,
had also been heavily influenced by Joseph Chamberlain,
while he had been impressed after hearing Prime Minister
William Gladstone in Birmingham's Bingley Hall. The two
Midlanders and their families would know one another for
the next half-century.

Dr Peter Joseph O'Donnell, a native of Tipperary, was
another of modern Barry's founders lured by its appeal as a
land of promise, enterprise and industry. In 1886 he may have
had some doubts as he first entered the town after a precarious
five-hour journey from Cardiff in an old furniture cart, years
before the building of the railways and properly constructed
roads. At that time Barry only had Dr George Neale, its long-
serving medical officer, to cater for the health requirements
of its growing population, and Dr O'Donnell, as he settled
into his new Cadoxton home (a former 'navvy club') with his
young wife, quickly established himself not only as a doctor
but as a forthright and outspoken figure, whose honesty and
sense of purpose won him respect. The 'Hibernian doctor'
was less inclined than Meggitt to compromise (particularly,
as a Catholic, on questions of religious education), but was
respected for his conscientious manner and loyalty to the
town.[9]

The political consensus on the Barry and Cadoxton Local
Board came to favour the Liberal and Progressive cause, but
also influential in the early years was the Cymru Fydd ('Young
Wales') movement, whose first branch in Wales was founded
in Cadoxton, mainly due to the energies of W. Llewellyn

Williams, who was then editor of the *South Wales Star,* the local newspaper. Founded by Tom Ellis, a Liberal Party associate of David Lloyd George, Cymru Fydd had held its first meeting in London in 1886 (attended by Welsh residents of the capital) and was partly inspired by similar gatherings of Irish nationalists. In 1892 in Cadoxton, the 'Young Wales Society' agreed to hold weekly classes and discussions in English and Welsh on alternate Tuesday evenings, normally in the Philadelphia Welsh Baptist chapel or the vestry of the Court Road Methodist chapel. Their founding proposals were radical and included similar objectives to those proposed by the wider movement that was then influencing Welsh Liberalism, namely disestablishment of the Church of Wales, Home Rule for Wales, reform of the land system, appointment of Welsh-speaking government officials for Wales, the use of the Welsh language in elementary schools, and a national system of education for Wales.[10] Williams, as president of the society, clearly believed in the early 1890s that Barry would follow the radical directions of Welsh Liberalism under Lloyd George. The pages of his newspaper were filled with sympathetic columns and letters, and he urged Barry's Young Wales Society to 'organise Welsh opinion in the district'.[11] That he and others had underestimated the cosmopolitan nature and aspirations of the new town would only become clear later.

Politics was some way from Harry Lakin's mind as he and Annie struggled to build the business in Vere Street, in competition with five other butchers' shops, including the Colonial Meat Company next door. In their first years in the shop they were always 'exhausted' and after a long day at work just 'flopped', with little time for anything else.[12] It did not help that Harry and two other Cadoxton butchers were among the first to fall foul of the Barry and Urban District Council Act, which outlawed the exposure and sale of blown meat (an old practice that 'plumped up' the meat to give it a healthier appearance). In his defence he argued that as he had killed his own animals, he could not understand why it was wrong to have the meat blown, but along with the others was fined a nominal charge of ten shillings.[13]

Despite the difficulties, their efforts were rewarding and necessary as they raised a family. Cadoxton School was just a ten-minute walk away, situated on the edge of Cadoxton Common, and Cyril Lakin was first entered there in April 1898 to attend its nursery classes at the age of four years and three months.[14] His admission to the school coincided almost exactly with the desperate coal strike of that year, which would last six months and leave families suffering, including all those in Barry who depended on the mines for work. By this time Barry had established some strong labour representation, with its Trades Council now prominently active in local affairs. The arrival in 1895 of John Spargo, a Cornish stonemason, further increased the political agitation in the town. Spargo, later one of the first biographers of Karl Marx and a prominent public intellectual in the US, set up the Barry branch of the Social Democratic Federation (SDF), and this, together with his leading role in the Trades Council and his position as a prominent opponent of the Boer War, for a while made him an influential figure in Barry. The strength of the SDF in the navvies' lockout of 1896–7 illustrated the potential power of union organization and the dissemination of socialist ideas, which extended beyond improved wage rates to the provision of medical, social and cultural resources.[15]

This meant that there was strong support for the strikers.

In addition to the dockworkers affected, around a hundred sailors were stranded for a time at Barry Dock. Free teas were given out to hundreds of poor children in the town and Harry Lakin, mindful of the town's dependency on the industry, regularly contributed free meat to the soup kitchens that sustained the community over the five-month duration of the strike. At the beginning of July, the *Barry Dock News* reported that 'destitution in the town is becoming more and more pronounced' and further appeals had to be made for charitable contributions, with Cadoxton School helping to distribute the proceeds to families.

Cadoxton School had opened in 1879 (with a new building added in 1887), and was housed in a typically imposing Victorian building at the top of a hill, situated in what was still an agricultural village at the time it was built. In 1898 the building was still incomplete, with school walls in need of paint, 'badly constructed' galleries, and with backrests missing from some of the seats, but Miss Carr, the headmistress of the infant school, was praised for her 'intelligent grasp of the work of the school' and for the supervision of her staff: a combination of certified teachers, trained assistants and pupil teachers. When Cyril Lakin was admitted there were in excess of 400 pupils in all, though attendance and punctuality was a matter of concern. It would have been a relief for his parents to leave him in capable hands for much of the working day, while Annie took his education very seriously even from an early age. They were attentive parents, and if in his early years their working hours meant they sometimes had to miss out on pantomimes and shows, Harry Lakin would read him stories before bed, with *Aladdin*, the classic rags-to-riches tale, a particular favourite in his son's memory.[16]

Despite the obvious restrictions and limited resources of Victorian education as he moved through the school, he and his Cadoxton classmates were encouraged to make the most of their environment and pursue nature studies on Cadoxton Common and the surrounding area, with occasional visits to Barry Island. They were introduced to clay modelling, bead shredding and drawing, in which Thomas Ewbank, the headmaster of the main school, took a keen interest.[17] Ewbank was a central presence in Cyril Lakin's early life as an active and benevolent participant in Cadoxton activities. He was on the ward committee of the local Conservatives and a district master of the Cardiff Oddfellows, as well as a prominent promoter of many other cultural and educational initiatives in Cadoxton, presiding at lectures on astronomy and hosting musical evenings at Barry's Theatre Royal. He was a founder member and treasurer of the Allotment Holders and Cottage Gardeners, which was instituted to encourage the 'mutual improvement of the working man'.[18] As a long-standing member of the local school board (local education authority after 1902), he was at the centre of some important decisions over school finances and staffing and sometimes embroiled in battles with religious figures such as the Baptist minister Ben Evans, the Reverend Pandy John and Dr O'Donnell. He was often asked to explain the high levels of truancy and variable attendance as well as acts of vandalism when some of his boys had been stoning trains or smashing windows. At the same time, he was proud to present to the committee examples of outstanding attendance and other school achievements. His commitment and loyalty to the school was evident to his pupils, even if at times he appeared as a strict custodian of rules and procedures. With limited resources he did his best to instil in his charges some sense of responsibility and to introduce new experiences for them, whether by establishing the Cadoxton School Fife and Drum Band or instructing them in singlestick drills. At the time of the coronation of King Edward VII, he was chief marshall at the celebration at Buttrills fields that was attended by 7,000 local schoolchildren. When Cadoxton was facing particularly difficult times of distress during the coal strike and in the early years of the new century, he supervised on the school premises the provision of food and beverages for those in most need.

The efforts of Mr Ewbank and the other teachers offered some security for Cyril Lakin as he made his way up to the school from Vere Street, through Main Street, or the slightly longer but more pleasant journey up Little Moors Hill. Here he could cast an eye at the relatively salubrious Belle Vue Terrace, a set of villas inhabited by Dr Edward Treharne, a prominent surgeon, former rugby union player (who had played in Wales's first ever international against England in 1881) and leading Conservative; and Miss Small's Belle Vue School for Girls, which catered for the children of Cadoxton's more affluent residents.

Cyril Lakin's early schooling was important, but his parents, regular churchgoers, also sent him to attend the Sunday school run by St Cadoc, Cadoxton's ancient village church. Renowned for its architectural distinction and sheltered by yew trees, it had undergone significant restoration in the 1880s. At the time of their arrival in Barry, the rector was Ebenezer Morris, well known in Cadoxton as 'Parson Morris', who cut a distinctive figure around the district in his wide-brimmed black hat.[19] A Cambridge graduate who married the daughter of the local 'gentleman' of nearby Buttrills, Morris was the father of nine children. Regarded as 'conscientious' and a 'genuine friend of the poor',[20] he enjoyed the respect of his parishioners as 'one of those Anglican clergyman whom [Thomas Babington] Macaulay must have had in mind when he declared that the Establishment was worth preserving even if only for the guarantee of the presence of one gentleman in every parish of the land'.[21] Parson Morris was wise enough, however, to adapt to the needs of the new population as Cadoxton underwent transformation from a rural village to a working-class port suburb. Though St Cadoc experienced the same chaotic upheaval as other religious bodies and was barely able to accommodate the new arrivals in a church building in need of updating, his sermons would have offered some spiritual reassurance to the Lakins as they started out.

It was Morris's successor, the Reverend John Smith Long-don, who was the main influence on Cyril Lakin's early life. Longdon, who took up his position in December 1902, was a Welsh-speaking Oxford graduate from Clydach in the Swansea Valley who had earlier practised at Aberdare and Hirwaun. A talented sportsman who had played rugby for Oxford University, Swansea and London Welsh, he and his wife Zoe ('a model Rector's wife'[22]) brought more energy into the activities of the parish. Longdon had played a pivotal role in building the Sunday school movement among Anglicans, and in Barry his classes were often packed and in need of additional accommodation. Aware of Longdon's background, status and influence, Annie Lakin was determined to put her son in his charge. Cyril Lakin was not only one of his young parishioners, he also delivered meat to the rectory on his bike as part of his weekly delivery run. He was a willing participant in the sports programmes, sang in the choir and was ever-present at bible-reading classes. More than that, he saw Longdon as an early mentor, whose encouragement in his education and sporting activities was crucial to his formative development. Longdon nourished Lakin with an early ambition to follow him into the Church. His interest and commitment evidently impressed, as did his amiable disposition, which many of his elders took as indicative of his personal charm. Like her husband, Zoe Longdon saw the potential of their young protégé and kept a keen eye on the progress of this 'dashing/beautiful young subaltern'.[23]

The Reverend Longdon was the last lay parson in the parish before disestablishment and disendowment of the Church in Wales, and he had to compete with the strong Nonconformist denominations that had spiralled in the new town. As a preacher he was admired for clarity and lucidity of expression rather than emotional rhetoric, though his adherence to unfamiliar rituals and ceremonial practices got him into some serious difficulties with some of his own parishioners, who found his endorsement of the Oxford High Church movement unpalatable and some divergence from what they had been accustomed to under Parson Morris.[24] However, the Lakins stood by him and their involvement with the church endured, and Harry and Annie remained regular attenders at church events and functions.

By this time Harry had acquired bigger premises for his Vere Street business, directly opposite at number 53. His neighbour was newsagent Thomas Fairbairn, widely thought to be the district's oldest resident having moved from Scotland thirty years before. As the new district emerged from the early social upheavals, a growing community helped provide mutual support. When his finances were low, Fairbairn's son,

J. Clark Fairbairn, a talented artist, would offer his paintings to Harry Lakin in lieu of cash payment for meat.[25] The Lakins themselves in their early years in Cadoxton struggled to make ends meet and had a larger family to support following the arrival of brothers Stanley (1900) and Harold (1903). However, it was the firstborn who continued to receive most attention. Annie 'doted on him and saw and nurtured his talents',[26] and Cyril formed a strong emotional attachment to his mother that extended well into his adult life. Her encouragement of him was driven by her desire to get him out of Cadoxton and move on to better things. Beyond his school and church commitments, she arranged regular singing lessons with Professor W. H. Shinn. Shinn, who would later have a distinguished career in Canada (lending his name to a conservatory of music), taught voice and piano and was an enthusiastic promoter of Barry's musical talents, registering students for nationally recognized music awards – Cyril Lakin was among the 1903 cohort who passed London College of Music examinations – conducting local choirs and championing Barry's case to be given the national eisteddfod. He felt it was better suited than other 'less important and less attractive' places that had recently hosted it and would be a 'first-rate advertisement for the town', as well as bringing educational and cultural benefits.[27] In fact Barry would not host a national eisteddfod until 1920, by which time Shinn had emigrated to Canada. He was a well-respected figure in Barry and aspirational parents sought his services.

It was probably in this group that he first met Barnett ('Barney') Janner, who with his older sister Rachel ('Ray') also showed early musical promise under Shinn's tutelage. The Janner family had moved to Barry from Lithuania via the

United States in 1893 (when Barney was nine months old), with his father Joseph Janner opening a house furnishing store in Holton Road, the main thoroughfare in Barry Dock. The Janners were one of the first Jewish families to arrive in modern Barry, and his father gave Barney daily lessons in Hebrew. As with the Lakins, life was hard in the early years, and made worse after the Janner family was struck by tragedy in 1902 when Barney's mother, very religious and learned like her husband, and conversant in several languages, died giving birth to twins, who also died shortly after. His father's business acumen did not match that of Harry Lakin (he had trouble retrieving unpaid debts from sailors), and Joseph was forced to start another temporary business.[28] After the Janners settled, they helped establish a very small orthodox Ashkenazi Jewish community in Barry – Cardiff by contrast had a Jewish population of approximately 1,500 and two synagogues at the turn of the century – but once the first Yamim Noraim (High Holy Days) had been held in 1904, they were at the forefront of organizing activities, with Barney involved from a young age.

The Janners and the Lakins shared the difficulties and deprivations of Barry at this time, but also saw the opportunities of making a life and improving the prospects of their children. This they shared with many others in the increasingly cosmopolitan town, which had drawn in young families from across Britain and been diversified further by the comings and goings of workers from all parts of the world, some of whom continued to live in desperate circumstances in accommodation arranged by seamen's missions, such as The Priory in Barry Dock. In running small businesses their story was a different one from the working-class dockworkers and labourers, but there were common experiences too. By 1901

Barry was exporting more coal than Cardiff, with significant effect on the economy of the town. At the beginning of the new century the Lakins were making their mark in Barry, and other family members, encouraged by Harry's endeavours, followed him to the town. Three of Harry's five sisters moved from Birmingham to Barry and they were later joined by his father and mother, as well as a Bewdley nephew of Annie. Julia, the eldest of the sisters, was the first to arrive after Harry, marrying Edwin Williams, a butcher from Aberdare who ran a business in Pyke Street. Shortly after, two younger sisters, Edith and Ethel, both of whom had worked as dressmakers, married grocers in Holton Road. Edith's husband, Frank Bee Wilkins, a native of Tewkesbury in Gloucestershire, quickly absorbed the entrepreneurial ethos of the district, which he was keen to convey to his customers:

> Mr Frank B Wilkins of the Central Stores 147 Holton Road, Barry Docks, is one of the most enterprising and go-ahead young tradesmen in the town. The latest addition to his already up-to-date establishment is a Raisin Seeder which stones the fruit absolutely clean. In order that the public may test the quality of his fruit, he undertakes to stone all raisins FREE OF CHARGE. Under his own personal supervision, by stocking and selling only the best quality, Mr Wilkins has worked up one of the best businesses in the town, which he conducts on the very latest and most modern principles.[29]

Harry Lakin, like his brother-in-law, was looking to get ahead, and by the early 1900s he had established himself as a master butcher and a leading participant in the activities of the Barry and District Butchers and Cattle Dealers Association.

Each year, along with fifty or so other butchers, he attended its annual dinner at superior venues like the Barry Hotel or the Royal Hotel in Cadoxton, dressed in a dinner jacket adorned with the national emblem (leek) to enjoy a feast and musical accompaniment, and to toast 'kindred associations'. The butchers would share their worries over infected animals, complain about the cattle inspectors, lament the Urban District Council's continual disregard for their concerns and look forward to another year of increased trade. He was a steward on its annual competitive walk to Aberthaw and exhibited his horse and cart at the Barry May Show and Horse Parade. In future years he would become the association's president and help promote their cause on the council.

However, it was becoming initiated as a Freemason that was of greater value to his standing among fellow tradesmen and the route to prominence taken by many leading figures in Barry. Freemasonry, a movement of ideals and influential patronage, both secretive and ubiquitous, was central to the making of modern societies. That 'fellowship of men, and men alone . . . bound by oaths to a method of self-betterment . . .'[30] was instrumental in disseminating the new values that would sustain public life in emerging towns like Barry. Barry Free-masons Lodge had been consecrated in 1890 at Dunraven Hall, opposite Cadoxton Station, soon after the opening of the docks. The founder members of the lodge reflected their status within the new town. Its first Worshipful Masters were J. Jewel Williams, landlord of the Royal Hotel in Cadoxton, and Dr Neale, the town's medical officer, while Dr Treharne took on the same role in 1895. Other early members included John Alexander Davies, proprietor of the Barry Hotel, Parson Morris, and several tradesmen and schoolteachers, including

Thomas Ewbank. In 1900 it moved its meetings from the Royal Hotel to the palatial rooms of the Barry Hotel, centrally situated on Broad Street. Six years later, they would open their own Masonic Hall in new premises alongside the hotel.[31] Freemasonry was taken seriously in Barry as a measure of local esteem as well as an obvious vehicle for benefits and privileges, and Harry Lakin would have judged it worthwhile to invest in the ten guineas required for initiation into its ranks. In doing so he agreed that 'whatever his trade . . . in all his social and business transactions [to] deal honestly and squarely with his neighbour'.[32]

When Dr Treharne died unexpectedly from a heart attack in 1904 at the age of forty-two, a mile-long cortège in Cadoxton slowly made its way down Vere Street, enabling his patients and fellow dignitaries to pay their last respects. After the funeral ('confined to gentlemen'), Harry Lakin joined others at the graveside, where

> for fully half-an-hour the large assemblage filed round the open grave to obtain a last glance at the coffin of one who was respected and beloved by all, rich and poor alike, and as one by one the freemasons passed the same affectionate tribute over the grave of their departed brother, each dropped on the lid of the coffin a sprig of acacia, as the particular token of love and of sorrow prescribed by the craft for use on such occasions.[33]

Treharne's death left a gap in the Conservative presence in Cadoxton, which a few months before had, along with the rest of Barry, returned a Progressive majority to the Urban District Council. Cymru Fydd and the Welsh nationalist Home Rulers had waned in influence since the 1890s and

Llewellyn Williams, its strongest advocate in Barry, had by now moved on to seek a parliamentary seat. Despite this earlier reversal, David Lloyd George was entering the formative influence of his political career, leading a 'Welsh revolt' against the Conservative government's Education Act of 1902, which in shifting power from school boards to local education authorities had privileged the funding of Church of England (and Roman Catholic) 'voluntary' schools. In galvanizing opposition, he reignited the radical Nonconformist tradition and revived the case for disestablishment and disendowment (though it was nearly twenty years before that became law). The Act was generally unpopular, and on the back of this strength of feeling the Progressives in Barry prepared an electoral committee for the 1904 local elections, which included representatives of the Radical Institute, Liberal Association, Labour and Progressive Association, the Protestant Five Hundred and the Free Church Council. Their candidates ranged from J. C. Meggitt, Nonconformist ministers Pandy John and Ben Evans, to Fred Walls, a former member of the Marxist SDF. Although John Spargo had moved to the USA in 1901, the pressure from Labour campaigners had continued with the formation of the Labour Representation Committee in 1900, which would become the Labour Party in 1906.

It was into this cauldron of Nonconformist radicalism that Harry Lakin – a supporter of the Education Act – ventured two years later to make his appeal as a Conservative to the Cadoxton ratepayers. He had put a lot of time into establishing his presence in the district, was well respected among his neighbours and been accepted into some of the circles helpful to advancement. His family was proud, too, that their eldest son Cyril had made excellent progress at Cadoxton School, aided

in these endeavours by the Reverend and Zoe Longdon and
Mr Ewbank. He had won a place at Barry County School and
received the news in September 1905 that he had come fifth in
the scholarship examinations, with the highest score among the
Cadoxton boys. (Cadoxton girls, in a 'remarkable' set of results,
did even better, sending ten pupils on a scholarship to the
county school, at this time still co-educational.[34]) His parents
had always understood that their son had some academic
ability, but it still needed a sacrifice on their behalf to enable
him to continue his schooling, and the scholarship was a
crucial supplement in that regard.

Barry County School had been set up in 1896 after a
sustained campaign by local councillors, who had to convince
the Glamorgan County Council that Barry deserved its own
secondary school rather than having to send its pupils to
Penarth. Three years after its foundation it came under the
influential headship of Edgar Jones, who, after being shocked
by the state of the buildings and the absence of a main hall,
instigated large-scale refurbishment of the site with the help
of Dr O'Donnell (now on the county council). While the
school took up temporary accommodation in hotels in the
town, a new lecture room was built along with chemistry and
physics laboratories, and a new block to accommodate the
gymnasium, dining rooms and the caretaker's lodgings. These
were all completed by the time Cyril Lakin was admitted, and
as he emerged from the playground of Cadoxton School for the
last time and looked down beyond the familiar streets of his
childhood to the docks and the Bristol Channel, he had good
reason to imagine that better prospects were on the horizon.

Chapter 2

The Lakins: Making a Mark in Barry

Harry Lakin's decision to stand for the council in 1906 seems to have owed less to the burning ambitions of a politician and more to the conviction that his status in the community would be enhanced by his election. His candidature was promoted on the back of his sound business sense, as someone who would serve the ratepayers faithfully without being directed by a political caucus. He may have taken on board the advice of one of his predecessors as Cadoxton representative, B. G. Davies, who had earlier offered to would-be candidates his summary of the ideal councillor. Warning them that they should not 'humiliate' themselves by canvassing door to door and 'begging for votes', he suggested that the best councillors were those unconstrained by the close trappings of political associations. Though Harry Lakin, at thirty-six, was younger than Davies's recommended minimum age of forty, he shared some of the latter's core councillor criteria. For example, as someone already established in business he had 'proved he can manage his own affairs successfully ... [and] could with some degree of confidence ask his fellow townsmen and ratepayers to repose some trust and confidence in him arranging their affairs'.[1] Davies's further recommendations that councillors should have acquired an aptitude for public speaking, be aware of the 'rules of debate', could exercise the 'art of logic' and be able to talk eloquently on a subject for half an hour, might have stretched Harry's experience on the butchers' committees and at church gatherings, though they were skills that his son would later pick up and perfect.[2]

However, Harry Lakin's election had wider political overtones locally. It came shortly after the election of nearly 400 Liberal MPs (together with the first group of Labour Party MPs), which established the reforming 1906 government at the beginning of the high point of Edwardian Liberalism in Britain, with David Lloyd George's Nonconformist radicalism the main driving force of change. In Barry, where 'Lib-Labism' incorporated Welsh Nonconformity, aspects of Victorian radicalism and the new labour interests – a vibrant branch of the Independent Labour Party had been formed in 1905[3] – under the umbrella of 'progressivism', William Brace, vice president of the South Wales Miners' Federation (SWMF) and a prominent figure in the 1898 strike, was elected for the South Glamorgan parliamentary constituency. His claim to represent the 'Progressive forces'[4] bolstered his support in Barry, where Progressives already controlled the Urban District Council and were defending their seat in Cadoxton. As in 1904, they advertised strong endorsements of support from their numerous affiliated groups. The incumbent councillor, Thomas Walters, a Cadoxton grocer, sensed his position was under threat from Lakin and inserted several notices in the local press before polling day urging voters to consider his record and reminding them that he was standing at the 'unanimous invitation of the Progressive Electoral Committee'. Education featured strongly in the election campaign, with the question of Church disestablishment high on the priorities, and this, combined with the realization that the Progressives were an organized grouping with a majority on the council, meant 'an unusual amount of partisan feeling was aroused'.[5] Pandy John, the Baptist minister from Holton Road whose candidature for re-election on the Progressive list was questioned by some who felt his increased council commitments had diminished his church duties, had been particularly vociferous on the question of religious education. He had gained a reputation for intervening on a range of social and moral issues – including trying to prevent boys from playing football on Sundays – and had begun to irritate some of his electorate. His claims that Barry was being turned into a Roman Catholic district and that High Church ministers were part of a secret society extended beyond the election and embroiled him in a public dispute with the Reverend Longdon, which was only resolved by the intervention of the Bishop of Llandaff and Pandy John's public apology.[6]

Harry Lakin, in the weeks up to the election, cut a fine, confident figure around Cadoxton, immaculately turned out in suit and collar, with his impressive moustachioed features prominently displayed on the badges worn by family and supporters. His campaign seems to have been mainly confined to informal gatherings among the public and fellow tradesmen. His candidate press statement merely noted the success of his business while reminding voters that as 'a large rate-payer' himself, he would have their interests at heart.[7] In the event, Cadoxton went against the tide of progressivism and his moderate entrepreneurial message prevailed: Harry Lakin defeated Walters by ninety votes. The other notable defeat for the Progressive candidate was in the Castleland Ward where Mr J. Marshall, another butcher (originally from Stratford-upon-Avon) comfortably defeated Pandy John. The other five seats were retained by the Progressives but the high interest in the contest brought a big crowd to Holton Road School for the announcement of the results, with the candidates paraded before the public to a mixture of cheers and jeers.[8]

Harry Lakin's victory was greeted enthusiastically in the ward, while for his twelve-year-old son it was both a proud moment and an early introduction to the workings of politics in a constituency he would later represent. As a newly elected councillor he was introduced as one who had 'succeeded, by dint of energy and perseverance and straightforward conduct in building up a large and successful business so that his election to a seat on the District Council comes as a natural sequence to the respect and esteem in which he is held by his fellow townsmen'.[9] His standing as a councillor complemented his business reputation, and in the post-election notices he was able to remark on his Birmingham apprenticeship to Joseph Chamberlain's butchers (while elevating his father from wire drawer to wire manufacturer). Although he did not fight a particularly political campaign, he was given a generous reception by Cadoxton Conservatives in a meeting at Dunraven Hall dedicated to opposing disestablishment of the Church of England within Wales. He and other Conservative councillors, including James Lovat-Fraser – who would later become a Labour MP and loyal supporter of Ramsay MacDonald's national government – denounced the proposed Education Bill of 1906. This would end public support of all religious schools – thereby breaking the hold of the Church of England – while, under Lloyd George's influence, establishing a separate education committee for Wales. As the political face of the Anglican Church, Conservatives saw the legislation as threatening the Church of England and church schools in Wales. The meeting declared that Lloyd George and his supporters must be repelled and the House of Lords needed to be strong in resisting the 'treacherous' bill. (In the event, that is exactly what happened.) Harry Lakin, in his closing remarks, told fellow Conservatives that the Education Bill would have extremely dire consequences and fair-minded citizens needed to be aware of its implications.[10] Though it would be several years before the Welsh Church Act became law the issue remained a burning topic locally.

The Progressives maintained their majority on the council, and two of its representatives – J. H. Jose and W. R. Lee – were members of the newly founded Labour Party. On the same ticket, Dr Charles Sixsmith was a radical further to the left and a contrarian who frequently derided others on the council for failing to keep their private interests out of politics. At the first meeting of the new council there was much argument over who should be the new chairman and the extent to which 'hole-and-corner' gatherings had been organized by factions ahead of the meeting. After the sharp exchange of views, membership of the key committees was decided and Harry Lakin found himself on the Licensing Committee, the Health Committee and the Hospital Committee, while along with other councillors he was required to attend the long sessions of the education authority. He had hoped to be chairing one of the committees, and the other Cadoxton councillors complained that they did not occupy the same positions of influence as those in Barry Dock and other wards.

Nevertheless, his membership of those committees ensured that he had an important role in influencing decisions that would help to shape Barry's long-term development as a town. The Licensing Committee had to decide on the provision of licences to the burgeoning number of hotels and other premises that had grown to meet the demands of an expanding working population. It was a contentious issue, not only because of the rapid spread of unlicensed drinking 'shebeens' but also because of the strong temperance movement in the town that had grown on the back of the Nonconformist Liberal surge. Five years before he became a councillor, Harry Lakin had been a witness in one of the Barry Licensing Committee hearings, which went on for over five hours before a packed magistrates court. Applications for the granting and renewal of licences had been submitted by the expanding number of hotel businesses in Cadoxton, and as a local tradesman he was called on to demonstrate the need for more hotel accommodation and give evidence in support of hotel owners. Leading the opposition to the provision of hotel licences was Lady Jenner, a leading landowner in the district, and Donald Maclean, a Cardiff solicitor and prominent representative of the Temperance Party who would later become a Liberal MP and president of the Board of Education (and the father of the future Cambridge spy). In positioning himself as the representative of temperance supporters and residents, Maclean was part of a movement – popular among local Liberal and some Labour politicians – that sought to reduce the influence of alcohol in the new business environment. Barry had many temperance bars and billiard halls, which offered alternative facilities to hotel bars and pubs. For many Liberals and Progressives, deprivation and inequality were moral as well as economic problems and extending licences for the sale of alcohol was a prime cause of them.[II] By 1906 Harry Lakin, a 'beer-and-bible' Tory, was encouraged that more hotels had become established, but along with fellow committee members he was now required to recommend action against boarding houses that had allowed illicit drinking, prostitution and other 'immoral' behaviour.

The same committee had responsibility for issuing licences for various modes of transport, including a single-deck motor bus service and brakes, and among the contentious issues the committee had to deal with was a controversy that had arisen following a petition instigated by brake drivers who objected to the awarding of a licence to a Greek driver. The committee decided that the attitudes were driven by jealousy and antipathy to a 'foreigner'; nationality should not be an issue in cosmopolitan Barry and the driver concerned deserved the licence as an experienced, long-term resident of the town from its earliest days who was known to work long hours in all weather. The less serious matters taken up by the Licensing Committee – though still contentious for some – included a decision taken at a meeting in the Barry Island cloakrooms to require every bather to wear regulation bathing costumes, in place of the traditional bathing drawers.

As a member of the council's Health Committee – after an unsuccessful attempt to take the chairmanship away from Dr O'Donnell – Harry Lakin was made aware of the most serious illnesses inflicting the town, including a scarlet fever outbreak in 1907, a 'plague' brought in on a vessel from Karachi and, in 1908, Asiatic cholera, all of which demanded the full attention of Dr Neale. The sanitary conditions of the port were a constant cause of concern and the possibility of typhoid fever being brought in from different ships was a continual threat. Patients were often quickly moved to hospital in Cardiff, prompting concern among the town's councillors regarding whether Barry had the health resources to cope with the problem. At the same time, there was underlying resentment at what they felt was a lack of recognition by their bigger neighbour of health problems resulting from the town's rapid growth and development. 'What has Cardiff done for Barry?' Dr Sixsmith, another member of the Health Committee asked. 'Nothing at all,' he continued. 'But Barry has done a great deal to make Cardiff what it is today.'[12] Harry Lakin was also concerned that health and welfare facilities in Barry did not match those in Cardiff, particularly when it came to the care and slaughter of animals. He was also obliged to point out to the committee that many houses in Cadoxton were still unconnected to a sewer. He pressed them to agree proposals for a firehose cart and ambulance for the district in the case of emergencies. Outbreaks of whooping cough, measles and chickenpox were more mundane matters in comparison with some other diseases (though serious enough if untreated), but the general health of the town was good according to the regular reports provided by Dr Neale. Given the overcrowding still prevalent in the town, news that Barry's birth rate was lower than average (even comparable with France) was not overly concerning. 'A case of economy,' Harry Lakin concluded. 'A case of economics,' Sixsmith, his radical colleague, corrected him.[13]

Education was taken very seriously in the early days of Barry, and indeed remained an issue of vital importance for an ambitious, forward-thinking town. Salaries for teachers were some of the highest in the country (with women teachers being particularly well remunerated). The education authority had to address many contentious issues, notably the battles between different denominational groups over the provision of resources. In 1906, when the staffing at St Helen's Roman Catholic School was thought to be 'inadequate' (with a high pupil-per-teacher ratio and poor discipline), disputes between Nonconformist Ben Evans and Catholic Dr O'Donnell reflected deeper tensions between the Nonconformist and Church establishments. There were differences over whether religious instruction should be compulsory in schools and when, and in what ways, the education authority could be expected to intervene. At one point, priests were accused of interfering by attempting to cajole Gladstone Road School students to move to St Helen's; at another point the condition of St Helen's was (in the words of O'Donnell) 'a disgrace to the authority' – a view rejected by Ben Evans.[14] More widely, Harry Lakin and colleagues discussed the performances of teachers and the content of the curriculum. Some made the case for the compulsory teaching of Welsh, while others asked if too many subjects were taken at the expense of basic reading and writing skills. Opportunities afforded by education were accompanied by strong approaches to discipline, raising complaints over excessive forms of punishment. The inability of poorer parents to pay for school visits or photographs were also raised. The most serious question of ensuring that hungry schoolchildren were adequately fed was driven by campaigns of some councillors and by the members of the Independent Labour Party.

In April 1908 a very proud moment for the town (and for Harry Lakin and his family) arrived with the opening of the

Town Hall in the central square at the end of Holton Road.
An enormous crowd turned up for the formal ceremony and
to see the new building, which in its spatial rooms and offices
would house council employees and officials, including the
medical officer, the sanitary inspector and school attendance
officers, with separate offices for clerks and accountants. A
large committee room dominated the first floor, with the rates
section and surveyors on the ground floor and strongroom and
stores in the basement. The public library had been built two
years earlier, and the extensive buildings designed by architects
C. E. Hutchings and E. Harding Payne made for an impressive
spectacle: a new landmark for the town, complete with clock
tower at the front looking out from what was first known as
Town Hall Square and then (from 1910) King Square. After
being presented with a gold key, W. J. Williams, chair of the
Urban District Council, entered through the outer door and,
to loud cheers, declared the building open. He provided a brief,
timely lecture on the 'ends and purpose of government', while
hoping that the earlier bitterness and rancour on the council
would now give way to purposeful cooperation between 'all
nationalities'. Using the occasion to ask if Barry councillors
had thus far 'maintained the rights and secured the welfare of
the people of Barry', he concluded: 'I feel that I can honestly
say, and I am inclined to believe that you will agree with me,
that local government in Barry has on the whole been a great
success, and that its successes have overwhelmingly outweighed
any blunders which it may have made.' He ended by reassuring
the public that 'the true seat of government is in the people
themselves'.[15] Among other dignitaries, the Reverend Longdon
was present to deliver a solemn prayer composed with suitable
reverence for the new offices and its inhabitants:

Let all things be done herein with wisdom and healthfulness of spirit, unto virtue and strength, guide and govern the minds of all who shall use it, that being called to be councillors on behalf of the people of this place, they may understand the sacredness of the trust committed to each one.[16]

That evening Harry and Annie Lakin and the other councillors, wives and dignitaries attended a banquet for around 200 townspeople at the Masonic Hall. Over the sumptuous meal of fillet of sole, sirloin of beef and roast turkey, washed down with wine, champagne, sweets and liqueurs, they might have considered their good fortune in choosing Barry as their adopted town. They would have concurred with W. J. Williams's comments in his after-dinner speech when he praised his 'cosmopolitan' town, composed, he reminded the diners, of a 'happy combination of all nationalities'.[17]

Harry Lakin's involvement in a prestigious moment in the history of the new town – its coming of age as a civic authority – was not the family's only cause for celebration. At the same time, Cyril Lakin was beginning to distinguish himself at Barry County School, enabled by his sixpence-a-week scholarship. Here, once he and Barney Janner, 'filled with awe ... walked over the threshold of the school and saw for the first time the begowned staff',[18] his days became very occupied. After his daily cycling route up the steep Buttrills Hill, he encountered new ideas, stimulating subjects and more mentors, notably in the form of its long-serving headmaster Edgar Jones. Jones was a tall, handsome man with an athletic build and a keen eye for talent. Still in his early years as headmaster, he was a formative influence on staff and pupils alike through his educational philosophy and his appreciation of arts and culture, and as a keen sportsman (he was an excellent runner and footballer) he regularly cheered on his pupils from the touchline. Among the teachers, he was known for his collegiate manner and for treating his staff as equals by enabling them to carry on their own work without interference. There was no 'exhibition of superiority', as one of his former teachers put it to him on retirement. 'The schoolmaster in you has been dominated by the man.'[19] Among pupils, he had the ability to excite in them an interest in classic works of literature and to instil in them the confidence that they should go out into the world equipped with a strong sense of civic responsibility as well as individual accomplishment. As an MP, Lakin later acknowledged his debt to Edgar Jones, 'one of the most enlightened headmasters Wales has ever produced', for teaching him 'the true spirit of service to the country and to one's fellows'.[20] Particularly evocative for his pupils – boys and girls – were the early morning assemblies where, every Tuesday and Friday, he would cite whole passages from A. E. Houseman, Alfred Tennyson, Rudyard Kipling, Walter Raleigh and Francis Drake, while introducing his pupils to the 'bold and free' ethos he thought necessary for young people in search of principles to live by.[21]

Early Friday evenings were given over to the Literary and Debating Society, where Barney Janner first excelled as a speaker. Despite showing academic prowess, Joseph Janner had wanted to take his son out of education when he had reached fourteen in order to help in his furniture shop, and it needed a visit from Edgar Jones to persuade him otherwise. Jones told Janner senior that he could make him work in the shop all night so long as he stayed on at the school.[22] Jones had evidently seen some indication that Janner – who became a senior prefect and house captain – had potential as a future public figure or civic leader, and saw him as a protégé worth nurturing with his own brand of progressive Liberalism. Many caught Jones's eye in that era of Liberal government before the First World War. Illtyd David, the tenth child of a Nonconformist Methodist father who was the postmaster of Nantymoel, a mining village on the River Ogmore, near Bridgend, was another impressive young orator. Under the influence of his father, David moved to Barry to complete his schooling and lodged with Edgar Jones and his family, where he discussed the government's social and welfare reforms with some prominent Liberal figures. Edgar Jones's Liberalism was an important influence on David, who would go on to be a socialist and a significant figure in the adult education movement as tutor-organizer for the Workers' Educational Association and a staff tutor in Swansea University's extramural department.[23] Like David, Howard Ingli James, a future Baptist minister, outspoken pacifist and conscientious objector, also first developed his political interests in the school hall. James would have been a match for Janner, whose maturity was evident in his involvement in the activities of the Barry Dock Jewish community, where he was treasurer from his early teenage years. But it was in politics that Janner would distinguish himself and, as with David, Ingli James, Lakin and the others, the future Labour MP first honed his debating skills under the critical eye of Edgar Jones. Like David, Janner's first political sympathies were with the Liberals – he stood first as a Liberal parliamentary candidate – and it is not difficult to see the influence of the headmaster in the development of his political outlook.

If by night and at the Friday evening debates Edgar Jones espoused radical progressive Liberalism, in his day-to-day running of the school he was a traditionalist, indulging in the classics, teaching them civics and personal responsibility. Lakin developed a keen interest in Classics, while his values of loyalty and patriotism – for Britain – were first conceived within the school buildings. It was here, as he remarked later, that he 'donned his first uniform' in the outfit of the Cadet Corps, under the command of Senior Master H. P. Lunn. Edgar Jones's influence on Lakin was therefore of a broad nature, primarily through inspiring an interest in ideas and the importance of leadership in civic affairs. While Lakin never had the oratorical skills of Janner – who would become a powerful speaker – he would become adept at addressing meetings, chairing events and handling the procedural aspects of public meetings.

Lakin's friendship with Janner continued and they would often cycle part of the way home together, an adventurous journey which included 'reckless rushes downhill on a bone shaker'.[24] However, of more enduring significance for his later life and career was the friendship he formed with Frank Webber. Webber was the younger brother of Robert Webber, who had been a pupil at Barry County School a decade earlier. After a spell as a clerk at the Barry Railway Company, Robert Webber took a job as private secretary to George Riddell (Lord Riddell), chairman of the *News of the World* and a shareholder in the *Western Mail*. Subsequently, on the recommendation of Riddell, Robert Webber would become general manager of the *Western Mail* and part of its board, which was under the ownership of the Berry brothers, the press barons from Merthyr Tydfil. Frank Webber himself would become manager and director of the *Western Mail*, and his friendship with Lakin would prove to be vital for the latter in subsequent years as he sought connections to Fleet Street journalism.

School work was hard and relentless. Headmaster Jones and his begowned colleagues had high standards and expected their pupils to achieve good results as they progressed through the Central Welsh Board examinations. Frank Webber recalled much 'cramming' late at night or in the early hours of the morning; a strong scholarly atmosphere prevailed to channel the attention and priorities of the pupils.[25] In Lakin's Barry County School notebook, the extensive reading lists and summaries of key works included William Warde Fowler's *The City-State of the Greeks and Romans,* a key accompanying text to the classics, while politics and government was covered in some depth with the help of Sir J. R. Seeley's *Introduction to Political Science*, Dicey's *The Law of the Constitution* and Bagehot's *The English Constitution*. An enthusiasm for history was most evident in Lakin's notes, which featured commentary on the essays of Macaulay and Morley alongside Frederic Harrison's *The Meaning of History* and various works of Thomas Carlyle. Pupils at Barry County School were given a broad grounding in classic literary works, with a liberal tone: Matthew Arnold, Leo Tolstoy and John Ruskin were all required reading.[26]

Despite the intense demands of their schoolwork, there was much opportunity for sport and recreation. A Dramatic Society organized regular productions of Shakespeare's plays, the casts enriched by the co-educational nature of the school. Some distinguished women were contemporaries of Lakin, among them the actress Flossie Prichard, while many others went on to have notable careers in education. Frank Webber thought 'the girls had a civilising influence on the young barbarians'.[27] Lakin had an interest in amateur dramatics but a keener passion for football, rugby and cricket. In 1908, according to school contemporaries Barry County School had one of its best football teams, and his fast, nimble footwork may have caught the eye there, as he did later with the oval ball as a member of its rugby XV during his last year at the school. His long interest in cricket may have been cemented here too, helped by the passion for the sport from several teachers, including H. P. Lunn, and enhanced by the presence of one of his contemporaries, Frank Pinch, who would later play for Glamorgan, becoming their first batsman to score a century on his first-class debut. He maintained his sporting interests at Oxford and was the first in a long line of Lakins to demonstrate some sporting ability – his great nephew, Robert Lakin, became a back-row forward for Cardiff and the Barbarians in the 1980s. The school also had some notable athletes, and Lakin, like his headmaster, was a keen runner who regularly turned out at school and town athletics events.

Though his schoolwork now took priority, Lakin continued to participate in church and family events, such as the annual Whit Monday sports day, which brought together up to 10,000 children from Sunday schools of different church denominations and was normally officiated by the Reverend Longdon. Here Lakin, as well as his cousin Bernard Tolley, generally performed well. The cousins, along with Lakin's younger brothers Stan and Harold, were also obliged to attend the annual summer trips organized by the Barry butchers, which normally involved being transported by the Barry and Great Western Railway, supplemented by brakes and charabancs, for a day out in Abergavenny or along the River Severn in Gloucestershire. A good lunch would be followed by an afternoon of sports and finished off by a big tea. Lakin was usually among the prizewinners over his preferred distance of 440 yards, while his parents invariably joined in the entertainments by competing in the 100-yard pipe-and-tobacco race (Harry) or the thread-and-needle race (Annie). At church events he still performed in the choir, and on special church occasions his lucid recitations were admired by the local hierarchy.

On the council, Harry continued to share responsibility for important decisions in the building of the town, whether dealing with legislative matters to do with the Barry Railway Company or education policy, while within his own ward he helped to oversee the development of Cadoxton Common – whose unsafe barren fields had previously concerned him – into Victoria Park, complete with bowling green (he was a founder member of Cadoxton Bowling Club). He remained active in local Conservative Party politics, addressing meetings and presiding over 'Conservative Conversazione' occasions or Primrose Day in commemoration of the Earl of Beaconsfield (Benjamin Disraeli). Annie Lakin was a stalwart at such events, serving on committees, presenting prizes, running a whist drive or organizing the tea and cakes.

However, he seemed jaded by the divisions and tensions between rival factions on the council, which, despite W. J. Williams's hope that political rancour on the Urban District Council was in the past, had resurfaced over his re-election as chairman. Harry questioned the re-election of Williams, an experienced politician, suggesting that a Progressive caucus had met in advance of the meeting to ensure that particular outcome. Harry himself had not been present at any 'hole-and-corner' business, nor was he 'in the know' about such matters. Dr O'Donnell, part of the Progressive group on

the council, denied this. 'What I said last night was that Mr
Williams would probably be re-elected unanimously,' he
maintained. 'There was no "probably" about it, doctor,' Harry
replied, before arguing for a Conservative (David Lloyd) to
be chairman. Eventually, the meeting decided by a majority
that W. J. Williams be re-elected for a further year, with
Lakin (who accused one of his adversaries of talking 'rot' and
regarded the whole affair as 'shameful') in a minority of two to
vote against.[28] The infighting presumably took its toll on this
slightly gruff but clear-thinking and down-to-earth Brummie
tradesman, and was probably behind his decision not to seek
re-election for the Cadoxton Ward in 1909.

He had shared the excitement – as well as the risks –
of other Barry pioneers and was a good example of the
'entrepreneurial *bravura* which had created the town'.[29] In his
own way he had contributed to Barry's cosmopolitan nature,
which became a defining feature of the town. His involvement
in Conservative politics was reduced to the more social side
after this time, though he remained involved in campaigns
such as galvanizing support for Tariff Reform, one of the
last causes of his old hero Joseph Chamberlain, by now over
seventy and in declining health.

For his son, politics was still a long way off, though no doubt
he picked up some insight on the machinations of committee
work as well as the belief that local representatives can bring
change to their communities. He was more drawn to the
Church, where the influence of the Reverend and Zoe Longdon was still significant. No doubt encouraged by Longdon,
he had his sights on Oxford. Headmaster Edgar Jones's vision
for the school went beyond that of a conventional grammar
school, and without the normal matriculation procedures

Barry County School did not then have an established route to Oxford University.[30] Barney Janner and Frank Webber were among the many who chose to go to university in Wales. To get into Oxford Lakin needed a stronger grounding in Latin and Greek in order to pass Responsions, the first under-graduate examination Oxford students were required to sit either before or soon after matriculation. For this he decided to apply for a short scholarship to Ystrad Meurig Grammar School, located in a remote village community in Ceredigion, east of the Cambrian mountains, for an intense term of study in the autumn of 1911. The school had been founded in 1734 by Edward Richard, who initially taught boys in the village's parish church, offering a free education in Latin and Church of England doctrines. Subsequently it gained a strong repu-tation for classical scholarship, with many pupils using it as preparation to enter Oxford, Cambridge or the University of Wales. In all probability it was not just Ystrad Meurig's position as a route to Oxford, where he intended to study jurisprudence, that appealed to Lakin. His Barry upbringing had planted in his mind the idea of a career in the Church, and the long train journey along the Carmarthen and Aber-ystwyth line (alighting at Strata Florida Station) was also a useful step in the furthering of that ambition. He was one of fifty-eight 'Edward Richard scholars', and the small, intimate surroundings would have been conducive for the rigorous preparation he needed before taking the entrance examination at the end of term.

The head of the school during his short stay was the Reverend John Jones, himself a former pupil, who had studied Classics (Greats) at Jesus College, Oxford before returning firstly as assistant master and then from 1870 as master, while combining his teaching with a role as vicar of Ysbyty Ystwyth. This would presumably have resonated with Lakin's idea that he might become a 'literary parson' himself, and no doubt the Reverend Jones offered him wise counsel for his future.

> It was probably due to the independent spirit of John Jones and his unwillingness to sacrifice sound Church principles in the interests of purely secular education that Ystrad Meurig continued to make its peculiar and invaluable contribution to the Welsh Church by preparing succeeding generations of young men for entry to the ancient universities and to St David's College, Lampeter.[31]

A term at Ystrad Meurig, where he was 'nurtured on the "hard food"' of classical studies, was a slog, though it brought its reward of a place at St John's College, Oxford from the 1912 Michaelmas term.

Chapter 3

Oxford

On the completion of his intense studies at Ystrad Meurig Grammar School, and after a successful interview in the winter of 1911, Cyril Lakin went up to St John's College, Oxford in October 1912. If the early part of his life in Barry had been shaped by the economic expansion of the coal industry, then the years in which he left it behind coincided with some of its most difficult and bitter disputes. The Tonypandy riots of 1910–11 had erupted after miners had been locked out by the Cambrian Combine (a coal owners' association with controlling interests in South Wales collieries) as they sought to control prices and wages. Disagreements over the rate of extraction of a new coal seam provoked the dispute and miners went on strike in protest. The coal owners employed strike-breakers, which led to serious clashes with police and the army, the latter deployed by Winston Churchill, then Home Secretary. In April the following year, when Lakin was awaiting confirmation that he had got a place at Oxford, the industry encountered its first national strike over the demand for a minimum wage to replace the existing arbitrary wage structure (the main grievance that produced the conflict in Tonypandy). As with previous strikes, the dispute had social and economic consequences for Barry given its dependence on the coal industry.

Lakin, however, had now departed for better things, though his later career direction would place him in the vicinity of the leading South Wales coal owners. His choice of St John's and not, for example, Jesus College, which had a long affiliation with Welsh students, was consistent with his religious convictions and early intentions to follow a career in the Church. Though founded in 1555 by a Roman Catholic, Sir Thomas White, master of the Merchant Taylors' Company, for long periods it had been notable for its Tory–High Anglican traditions and included prominent clergy among its alumni. At the time of his application to the college he would have been encouraged by the imposing presence of its president, Herbert Armitage James. The son of a Monmouthshire vicar, James was a Welsh Anglican cleric as well as an academic. Previously headmaster at a series of leading public schools, notably Rossall and Rugby, he was an influential figure in Oxford at the time. As a young man he had been a fellow of St John's as well as being ordained as dean of St Asaph. A strong personality who was 'equally effective and esteemed in the class-room and the pulpit',[1] he had the background and authority that would have held some appeal for Lakin, who had been inspired equally by teaching and sermons.

Herbert James's appointment as president, three years before Lakin went up to Oxford, had been the result of a hotly contested election. His predecessor, Dr James Bellamy, a shrewd administrator who never published any scholarly articles, was the leading Conservative figure in Oxford. He remained president of the college into his ninetieth year, while his unyielding defence of the college's traditions had earlier prevented married men from taking up fellowships. One of those affected by that policy was Sidney Ball, who had to resign his fellowship on his marriage in 1891, before being re-elected as a fellow in 1902. It was Ball, the college's senior tutor, and a leading Fabian socialist, social reformer and enthusiastic supporter of Ruskin College and the adult education movement, who was James's opponent for the presidency of the college, which became a 'Clerical v. Radical' election. In the event, Conservatism prevailed over Progressivism; James was elected, with Ball carrying on as senior tutor and continuing to promote the teaching of social science while running study groups composed of students and industrial workers.

As president, James was expected to carry on the tradition of preparing men to serve Church and State, but it was a mission that was increasingly under challenge from the growing influence of Liberalism, the fast-changing domestic, social and economic conditions and, finally, the onset of international crisis and war. A powerful orator whose sermons on the purpose of school education had been published in book form, he needed to draw on his 'moderate and reasonable Conservative'[2] outlook in order to adapt to the more intellectually curious and liberal-minded student cohorts.

Brought up on Cadoxton's own brand of moderate Conservatism from an early age, and inculcated with the Reverend Longdon's brand of High Anglicanism, Lakin's curiosity had been aroused by Edgar Jones's literary interventions and stimulating history, English and Classics lessons. This had prepared him well and assured that he had the confidence to

contribute as a well-informed observer of politics in discussions
with friends and fellow students. He entered Oxford with a
considerable energy for the classical tradition of Greco-Ro-
man history and philosophy that was still the bedrock of St
John's teaching and scholarship, combined with traces of the
Welsh Liberalism with which Headmaster Jones had drilled
his charges in preparation for the wider world. Unsurprisingly,
therefore, on his arrival at St John's, one of the first people
he befriended was a Nonconformist Welsh Liberal. William
Watkin Davies had grown up in Barmouth where his father
Gwynoro was a Calvinist Methodist minister and long-standing chairman of Barmouth Urban District Council, and one of
David Lloyd George's oldest friends. Prior to Oxford, Watkin
Davies had studied history at Aberystwyth and through his
father had already got to know Lloyd George (by now the
Chancellor of the Exchequer): in the month before going
up to Oxford he had played (and beaten) the proponent of
the 'People's Budget' in a golf foursome, which also included
Arthur Hooper, the recently defeated Liberal MP for Dudley.[3]

Unsurprisingly Watkin Davies arrived at Oxford imbued
with a self-confidence and impatience to get stuck into student
life that was unknown to Lakin and some of the other freshers
as they sat down apprehensively to their first dinner in hall. 'At
last I have begun my course at Oxford,' Watkin Davies noted
in his diary the following day. 'From my earliest years I had
set a career at Oxford as an object always to be arrived at.'[4]

Despite his determination to get to the university, and
the strong support of his parents who had always backed
his studies, Lakin, like many others, would have found the
early days more of an ordeal. Thomas David, the son of a
coal tipper, who like Lakin had won a scholarship to the

county school, was the only other student from Barry who went up to Oxford at the same time. David, a brilliant maths student, had been admitted to Jesus College with the benefit of a Welsh Mathematical Scholarship awarded through the Central Welsh Board exam.[5] At St John's, Lakin must have felt a little trepidation as well as excitement at his surroundings as he walked through the Canterbury Quadrangle, built on the benevolence of Archbishop Laud, in the 1630s, or on his first visits to the chapel for choral services. His own college lodgings offered sparse but cosy furnished rooms where he was waited upon by a scout. Shortly after arrival, his postcard home – 'Safely installed at St John's'[6] – reassured his proud parents that he was settling into unfamiliar surroundings. His easy-going nature and ability to mix well with people from different backgrounds would have helped him acclimatize quickly to college life, while his openness to ideas and thirst for discussion made it natural to gravitate to like-minded people.

On meeting Watkin Davies (who thought Lakin 'extremely agreeable' from their first acquaintance) he found that they had not only a Welsh background in common but were studying history under the same tutor. Others in their circle included Ernest Willmore, the son of a general labourer from Hertfordshire, whose journey to Oxford to study science had been made possible after winning a scholarship to Berkhamsted School; William Conrad (W. C.) Costin, a former captain of Reading School, brilliant history student and future president of the college; and John Sever, the son of a printer and bookbinder, who had come up to Oxford from Manchester Grammar School to study history. Two other friends taking history were Philip Gibbons, the son of a provision merchant, and educated at Wycliffe College, Gloucestershire, and James Laycock, son of a Home Office clerk, who had been at Monkton Combe School in Bath.

All were studious and able undergraduates and would regularly debate the prospects of the Liberal government (which following the hung parliaments of 1910 had remained in power with the support of the Irish Nationalists and the fledgling Labour Party) and the books they were reading over tea and cocoa, sometimes late into the night. Their backgrounds did not reflect those of the typical English public-school student, and the absence (or avoidance) of some of the rituals associated with those boisterous cohorts at a college known for its Conservatism must to some degree have set them apart. The practice of 'debagging', with its damage to person and property, was particularly objectionable for this cluster of seriously minded students. College rituals apart, politically they must have appeared as a distinctive group: some, like Costin, were advocating socialism, while all had varying sympathies for the reform-minded government and the cause of women's suffrage.

Within this group it seems to have been William Watkin Davies, the Welsh Nonconformist Liberal, who assumed the mantle of unofficial head: his Lloyd George connections at the time of Liberal Party dominance together with his keen observance of the changing political situation drew respect from peers, who often sought him out on the burning political questions. Both Watkin Davies and Willmore kept contemporaneous diaries of their time at Oxford and it is clear from these that the friendship between the two grew to one of intimacy, with Willmore hardly believing his luck to be in such company and fully expecting Watkin Davies to be a future Liberal politician. Already of a similar political persuasion, Willmore would be won over by his friend to a whole range of new causes that began to shake British politics, from Welsh disestablishment to Irish Home Rule, as they sought to introduce liberal values to the college's conservative environment. The intensity of their discussions, cultivated on long afternoon walks over Christ Church Meadow or to the outskirts of Oxford, brought them closer together and often provided the basis for topical debate over tea with Lakin, Costin, Sever and other friends.

For Watkin Davies and Willmore, their shared Nonconformist backgrounds meant chapel every morning, regular bible classes and temperance; their curiosity in religious practices extended to visiting other ceremonies, including those delivered by President James, though both were dismayed at the continued refusal of Oxford's Convocation (with James's backing) to allow those who were not Church of England to study for theology degrees. In their first weeks they joined the Oxford Liberal Club and the Oxford Union, which Watkin Davies, impressed by the quality of the speeches, preferred to 'the indecorous levity and rowdyism of the Litt and Deb at Aber'. Over the next couple of years, they would participate in the political debates of the Junior Common Room.[7]

Though neither a nonconformist liberal nor a temperance advocate, Lakin shared their interest in current politics and took part in many of the discussions, though he did not follow them – or other Oxford contemporaries like Harold Macmillan – in joining the Oxford Union. He seemed to have little interest in a career in politics at this stage and, in any case, his first few weeks at Oxford gave him little time for activities other than studying. Though he had the relative advantage of having taken his Responsions in Latin, Greek and algebra at Ystrad Meurig prior to going up, he had a busy time meeting tutors and appraising himself of the lectures he needed to attend at different university and college buildings. His moral (or personal) tutor, responsible for his general well-being and adviser on academic matters, was John Powell, a fellow and lecturer in Classics who, according to one of his colleagues, 'married classical scholarship and the study of new chapters in Greek literature with a genial whimsicality'.[8] His expertise in Greek verse was admired by Rudyard Kipling, who later requested a Greek translation of his poem 'Justice'.

Lakin was required to take a further Responsions in logic in the second (Hilary) term, for which he had the services of John Stocks, lecturer in philosophy and a noted translator of Aristotle. It was quite a demanding schedule and he had to accommodate the pressure of studying for examinations while preparing for his weekly supervisions; at the same time, he was keen to explore the attractions of Oxford. There was added excitement in his first weeks at the university following the matriculation (as an ordinary commoner) of the Prince of Wales (Edward VIII), who had arrived at Magdalen College with his equerry, Major The Hon. William Cadogan of the 10th Royal Hussars. The prince enjoyed more informal relations than his ancestors, taking part in sporting events and mixing more freely with fellow undergraduates. Magdalen was one route to the River Cherwell for walks along the bank, while St John's, located at St Giles – then a quiet tree-lined boulevard disturbed only by the occasional motor car and horse-drawn tram – offered a diversion north into the main Banbury and Woodstock Roads; a short way in the other direction was the centre of town.

For his preliminary examination in jurisprudence he needed to study 'The Outlines of English and Constitutional History after 1066', 'The Institutes of Gaius', and translations of Latin prose and logic. His law tutor at St John's was William Holdsworth, who was then in the early stages of compiling *A History of English Law*, his epic study that would be published in seventeen volumes over sixty years. Holdsworth was an 'exceedingly genial' tutor who invited Lakin, Watkin Davies and Sever for tea in his rooms for supervisions and to go over past prelim papers. This learned and popular tutor enlivened his lectures with examples drawn from literature: Charles Dickens's *Bleak House*, he believed, offered valuable insight on the peculiarities of the English legal system.

For English constitutional history, Lakin was taught by Ernest Barker during the latter's last year at St John's before he moved on to New College. A miner's son and the eldest of seven children from rural Cheshire, Barker had won a scholarship to Manchester Grammar School before going up to Balliol College, initially to study classical moderations and Greats, and then reading history under A. L. Smith. Barker's history lectures were a tour de force, ranging from the Norman conquest (which he described, to the amusement of his students, as neither 'Norman' nor a 'conquest') to key moments in European history. Finally, he turned his attention to the fortunes of British Liberalism after 1848, as it moved away from laissez-faire individualism and a suspicion of the state towards a more optimistic interpretation of how freedom could be enhanced through collectivist interventions by the state. This last topic formed the basis of his book, *Political Thought in England from Herbert Spencer to the Present Day* (published two years later), with its conclusion that an increased role for the state was an inevitable part of British politics in the era of the rise of socialism, the party system and representative government. The fault lines between Conservatism and Liberalism had altered and both now contained aspects of state intervention in their domestic policies, while the demands for Home Rule and Welsh disestablishment pushed at the boundaries of a unitary state, though both claims could be resolved, he believed, within a multinational single nation. Barker was destined for an outstanding career as a political theorist and historian (he would later become Cambridge University's first professor of political science), and even by the time of his late thirties his impressive range of sources was evident in his work. Always keen to illustrate how the writings of Plato and Aristotle could illuminate current dilemmas, his influences extended to social psychology and economics, while he maintained that literary sources, notably Carlyle, Ruskin and Matthew Arnold, could help inform the wider critique of laissez-faire. This 'tall, lanky ... gifted lecturer', who maintained his Manchester accent, was a popular and inspirational figure capable of arousing his audience to outbreaks of applause. Lakin's tutorial partner Watkin Davies could only wonder at the 'huge influence a man like Barker has on the intellectual development of those he teaches'.[9]

Lakin would have felt a strong affinity for him given his own humble journey to Oxford. But it was Barker's politics that were likely to have made the lasting impression. Barker's moderate liberal philosophy was evident in his belief that democracy could be augmented through discussion and the promotion of civic education through a range of voluntary organizations, churches, trade unions, the Workers' Educational Association and even the gentlemen's clubs of St James's. He rejected doctrinaire ideologies and argued for social mixing in opposition to both class struggle and privileged elitism. He eschewed nationalism in favour of a patriotism that retained a loyalty to English institutions and was clearly driven by a strong sense of civic duty: in later years he would advocate community centres as vital places of local democracy and encourage the widest discussion of the rights and duties of citizens among a broad variety of organizations. If his belief that democracy and pluralism, when embedded in voluntary organizations, could enable people to govern themselves was optimistic, he picked up earlier than many others the threat that could be posed to individual freedom by the abuse of state power.[10]

A. L. Smith, Barker's old tutor, was another of Lakin's history lecturers. 'A little man, somewhat advanced in life, with a round head, high forehead and a good shock of curly brown hair [he had] a good voice and very pleasing delivery.'[11] Smith was a committed teacher and administrator (a future master of Balliol) and the father of nine children, who had succeeded in building up the history school. Whatever he lacked in published research he seemed to make up for in his teaching, with his lectures on Hobbes, Locke and Mill 'brilliant and illuminating'.[12] His dedication to his students extended on occasion to providing lodging for those who needed it and taking on classes beyond his remit. His teaching won him awards as well as the admiration of his students, while his pastoral support and time taken over his lectures proved popular with first years like Lakin as they adapted to university life.

Lakin and his peers, who were stimulated by political ideas and took a close interest in current events, found much to discuss at afternoon tea in their rooms, at the Cadena coffee house in Cornmarket or, weather permitting, on long walks on Port Meadow. He found time for some activities outside his studies and did not neglect his sporting interests, which, as he recalled to his daughter, also won him respect among some of the less academically inclined public-school 'toughs'. His footballing ability got him into the St John's 2nd XI and he featured in regular matches against other colleges, including a match against Magdalen College 2nd XI where he recalled the Prince of Wales, playing for the opposing side, getting 'quite a roughing up'.[13]

During 1913 Lakin and his circle became absorbed by developments in domestic politics. The Welsh Church Act, nearing the end of a long campaign by Nonconformists, passed its third reading at the beginning of the year before a predictable battle with the House of Lords. However, the Parliament Act of 1911, a consequence of the constitutional crisis that followed the House of Lords rejection of David Lloyd George's Finance Bill of 1909, now ensured that the opposition of the Lords could not ultimately stand in the way of reform. It was a cause Watkin Davies had long promoted even before he got to Oxford and he followed the debates in Parliament and the Oxford Union with intense interest, scrutinizing the various positions and machinations as the bill went through different stages. Likewise, the Home Rule Bill, introduced by Prime Minister Herbert Asquith the previous year and the basis for a bicameral parliament in Dublin while maintaining representation in the House of Commons, was also held up by House of Lords opposition, and was only guaranteed eventual passage by the same legislation. The militancy of the women's suffrage movement, notably the direct-action tactics used by members of the Women's Social and Political Union (WSPU), was another main talking point for the liberals and socialists at St John's as well as being taken up in the many gatherings within the Oxford women's colleges. The suffragette campaign had brought significant clashes with Liberal politicians who had refused to allow a vote. Asquith had remained opposed, while Lloyd George was sympathetic. Lloyd George's protégés in Oxford were supporters of women's suffrage, even going along with the milder acts of civil disobedience. 'It was my first experience of this madness of suffragette interruption,' Willmore recorded in his diary after an Oxford Union debate, 'and my uppermost feeling was one of delight'.[14]

For his second year, Lakin took lodgings with his friend Philip Gibbons at 130 Walton Street (the former site of Bedford House School), on the edge of the working-class quarter of Jericho – less than a ten-minute walk from their college. Gibbons was an outstanding history student and another with a keen interest in politics, and the two would have much to discuss during what turned out to be their last full year. While Lloyd George received most plaudits among the St John's Liberals, much hope was invested in Charles Masterman, a prominent Liberal MP for an East London constituency who had played a significant role in helping to draw up the 1911 National Insurance Act that provided health insurance for workers and the unemployed. Masterson would have a chequered career as a parliamentarian, frequently losing seats and seeking re-election, but it was his contribution as an intellectual that (according to contemporaneous diary accounts) most stimulated Lakin's cohort. His *Condition of England*, published in 1909, was a robust analysis of 'an arid time of transition, when in politics the Conservative Party had been rejected by the people, and their successors had not really been approved'[15]. His bold interrogation of the current predicament considered the speed of technological change; the restructuring of the class system into 'conquerors', 'suburbans' and the 'multitude' at times of unprecedented opulence; and the implications for a social order less dependent on religion. He predicted a 'dark', uncertain future. For the last student generation before the onset of war, filled both with hopes and concerns, his conclusion offered much food for thought.

> We know little of the forces fermenting in that strange laboratory which is the birthplace of the coming time. We are uncertain whether civilization is about to blossom into flower, or wither in a tangle of dead leaves and faded gold. We can find no answer to the inquiry, whether we are about to plunge into a new period of tumult and upheaval, whether we are destined to an indefinite prolongation of the present half-lights and shadows, whether, as we sometimes try to anticipate, a door is suddenly to be opened, revealing unimaginable glories.[16]

Discussions in Lakin's circle intensified as they sought intellectual inspiration for the changing world. Towards the end of November 1913, they founded the 'Anonyms', an informal debating club that met on Friday evenings after dinner in the rooms of one or the other of the group. The club was limited to twenty-five members, with John Sever as the secretary, and was aided by the appearance of several St John's tutors as guest speakers. Over the ensuing months members would hear papers on a variety of topics: on positivism, the uses of a classical education, and 'the rise of romanticism in

English poetry'. In February 1914 Gibbons and Lakin hosted a discussion led by John Sever on 'The Faust Legend Before Marlowe'. The talks were wide-ranging across literature, history and politics, with a talk from an idealistic Indian student on public opinion in his country, and a typically thoughtful contribution from Sidney Ball – that 'busy bee-hive of ideas'[17] – on socialism and syndicalism. The Anonyms did not have the experimental dynamism or significance of the 'Mutual Admiration Society', founded the previous year by Dorothy L. Sayers – one of Lakin's future book reviewers – and five of her friends at Somerville College, on the other side of St Giles. Women students at Oxford at this time could attend lectures, use the libraries and sit exams but still could not take degrees at the end of it, and had to be chaperoned and were frequently patronized by male counterparts, but this group, a pioneering cohort at Oxford, read each other poems, satirized religion, wore outlandish costumes, toasted Molière on the anniversary of his death, produced a mock *Hamlet* and generally introduced a modern and challenging portrayal of women as intellectuals.[18] Their range of topics, with less focus on current politics, was broader and more heretical in nature than the Anonyms. Nevertheless, the Anonyms of St John's, according to Watkin Davies, was a 'very intellectual and highly agreeable circle'.[19]

As he returned to Barry for the summer holidays, Lakin must have felt some pride and satisfaction at his progress. Over the previous year he had done well in his studies, passed another Responsions examination in logic together with a compulsory divinity exam in the spring, and completed an examination in jurisprudence. He felt he was well prepared for his chosen career, which he still expected to be in the Church. At the same time, he had found himself part of an interesting, intellectually curious and scholarly circle where he was able to indulge his newly acquired taste for prolonged discourse on human affairs in civilized surroundings. There is no indication he presented any significant piece of original research to these gatherings or any publication while at Oxford; rather his interests seemed to be confined to sharing thoughts on politics and literature while deriving pleasure from stimulating company. Occasionally, Watkin Davies and Willmore (who had founded the college's Temperance Society in the same period) were put out by the extent of his conviviality and that of some of the other non-teetotal Anonyms. 'It is a great shame,' Willmore noted in his diary following an evening in Sever's room devoted to a paper on English superstitions, 'that people like Laycock, Lakin and Vincent should be so fond of drink. It is particularly annoying since they are all becoming parsons.'[20]

Despite the political uncertainties, by the end of 1913 there was little sense among them of the turmoil that would shake the world in 1914. Indeed, earlier in the year, over tea and rock cakes with Watkin Davies, Costin and Sever, Lakin and his friends had discussed the 'economic impossibilities of European war. We are all agreed that such a war is unlikely.'[21] Nor was there much concern back in Barry when he returned for Christmas, where his parents, having just recovered from a minor domestic crisis after their nephew and former apprentice Bernard Tolley, in his own search for freedom, had eloped with the niece of the Barry postmistress,[22] must have been reassured that they had made another wise investment in helping him get to Oxford. Lakin had his own stories from Oxford to tell his older cousin and younger brothers and was fully expecting to add more during the final year of his degree.

On his return to Oxford at the beginning of 1914, his daily life continued as before. There were regular meetings of the Anonyms, more critical discussions of the Liberal government as it battled with the House of Lords, the suffragettes and the Conservative opposition, and more anticipation of what the world after Oxford might mean for them. In May, the Welsh Church Bill passed its third reading. 'At last we have won the battle,' Watkin Davies noted in his diary.[23] It also marked the end of an earlier passage of Lakin's life, in which High Church had been so prominent. Since his time as a choirboy and loyal disciple of the Reverend and Zoe Longdon, his horizons had been lifted by the liberal education of Edgar Jones and his staff and further illuminated through the intellectual inclinations of his Oxford friends.

All this changed, however, as the international crisis intensified from June 1914 and throughout that summer once war was declared in July. On his return in October, he found that two-thirds of his fellow students were absent. Oxford itself was different, with several colleges being used as hospitals and army uniforms a common sight on the streets. His first week back saw a major setback in the war effort when the Germans ended their long campaign against neutral Belgium by taking Antwerp and forcing the British and their allies back to West Flanders.

Therefore, what proved to be Lakin's last term at Oxford began in unusual conditions under the shadow of war. In the month before he arrived back, his history tutor Ernest Barker, along with other members of Oxford University's history faculty, published their explanation for the conflict in a slim volume – *Why We Are at War* – composed of extracts from government documents, the historical background (including a chronology of events) and a comparison of the underlying differences between political systems. Above all, however, it was written as the justification for the action taken by the government and allies:

> We are not politicians, and we belong to different schools of political thought. We have written this book to set forth the causes of the present war, and the principles which we believe to be at stake. We have some experience in the handling of historic evidence and we have endeavoured to treat this subject historically.[24]

'Treating the subject historically' took them back to the 1648 Peace of Westphalia, to the German victory in the Franco-German War of 1870–71 and the formation in 1882 of the Triple Alliance between Germany, Austria–Hungary and Italy. According to the authors, the Triple Alliance 'has been the grand cause of the present situation; because ... they have traded upon the prestige of their league to press their claims East and West with an intolerable disregard for the law of nations'. Most to blame was the 'threatening attitude of Germany towards her Western neighbours ... provocations and threats it was impossible to overlook'.[25]

The German position, they argued, was driven by 'a doctrine of the super-nation', 'ardent nationalism' and 'the glorification of war'.[26] The present conflict was a result of two clashing principles, namely a *raison d'etat* (inspired by Machiavelli and Nietzsche) pursued by the Germans, and the rule of law that had guided the British since the Peace of Westphalia and was 'deeply engrained in 'Anglo-Saxon blood'.[27] It was this belief in 'the law of nations' that took Britain to the aid of the Belgians, 'for the peace of all nations, and for the right of the weakest to exist'.[28] 'This is the case of England,' the authors concluded. 'England stands for the idea of a public law of Europe and for the small nations which it protects. It stands for her own preservation, which is menaced when public law is broken.'[29]

His tutor's public intervention no doubt added a new significance to the relevance of Lakin's studies, as well as bringing home to him the seriousness of the escalating situation. Despite attempts to carry on with their studies as normal, it was impossible to get away from the impending crisis – a lecture by Gilbert Slater, principal of Ruskin College, on 'Religion and War' stimulated some further interest among Lakin's circle – but the implications of the war now took precedent over everything else. There was strong support for Belgium in Oxford, and a 'Belgium Day' was held in November when St John's and the town itself were decorated in yellow, red and black in solidarity with that country's refugees. Apart from Watkin Davies, who remained sceptical of the case for war throughout the conflict, all Lakin's group joined the Officer Training Corps (OTC) soon after their return. Lakin, Willmore, Gibbons, Sever and Laycock were up early for regular morning drills with rifle and bayonet, took part in firing practice, were inspected at afternoon parades and measured for their army uniforms.[30]

At the parade on 24 November, there was an announcement calling for volunteers willing to accept commissions, with the strong likelihood they would be favourably received.[31] This presented the dilemma of if, and when, to join up. Lakin was the first in the group to do so, applying for a commission that would come into effect at the end of December. Ernest

Willmore, together with Gibbons and Laycock, followed him shortly after, while Watkin Davies continued with his studies along with Sever and Costin.

One of the last Oxford gatherings Lakin attended was breakfast with Sidney Ball, Ernest Willmore and ten or so others to meet the head of Toynbee Hall, the settlement in East London that provided a centre for social reformers working to reduce the gap between affluent and poorer communities. In June, Ball had co-founded Barnett House (the forerunner to Oxford University's social policy department) in memory of Canon Barnett, the social reformer and Anglican clergyman, and Lakin and his circle had followed this initiative as well as some of his other numerous projects, which included the Social Science Club (hosted in his rooms), the University's Political Economy Club, and the gatherings he arranged between Oxford students and the Oxford working classes who had shown interest in higher education. The onset of war added significant weight to Ball's concern over the 'condition of England' question. For Lakin, who would always hold happy recollections of his time at Oxford, it would mean a dramatic upheaval in which he was thrown together with others of his class and beyond.

Chapter 4

Lieutenant Lakin

Lakin's decision to join up was one born of duty and patriotism and did not seem to require an inordinate amount of circumspection or angst as it did for Watkin Davies, Willmore and others. Like many of his generation his upbringing at school and in the Church had cemented the belief that moments of national crisis should be met by an unquestioning obedience and unshakeable loyalty – a value system that would change during the First World War and its aftermath. Nor did there seem to be much political thought behind his decision. His studies had been enhanced by different viewpoints: his High Anglican Conservatism had no doubt been mollified by listening to university friends and, like Oxford contemporary Harold Macmillan, he was receptive to 'Tory-Democrat, Liberal-Radical and Fabian Socialist' ideas, though unlike Macmillan he was not active in the various university societies.[1] If he required any persuading, then he need only turn to Ernest Barker's justification for the war on the grounds that 'England stands for the idea of a public law of Europe and for the small nations which it protects. It stands for her own preservation, which is menaced when public law is broken.'[2] The principle of the rule of law, the law of nations and the rights of weaker countries had been drilled into him at Barry County School, and it would have been no surprise to hear that the Glamorgan Fortress Engineers would be under the command of former headmaster, Major Edgar Jones.

Lakin was formally given notice of his appointment as temporary second lieutenant in the 8th Battalion of the South Wales Borderers (SWB), effective from 28 December, the day before his twenty-first birthday. The 8th Battalion of the SWB had been formed in September 1914 at Brecon and for the duration of the war came under the orders of the 67th Brigade, assigned to the 22nd Division. As a junior officer with little experience of leading anything, he was being prepared for a difficult assignment with an uncertain future; ahead of officer training, the only indication of his new responsibilities was the receipt of a cheque book and authorization to draw up to fifty pounds for his outfit allowance. After a last Christmas with his family in Cadoxton, in January he was sent to camp at Seaford, on the south coast, for his induction into army life. At the same camp in the weeks before Christmas, the SWB along with others in the Welsh Regiment had been on strike over poor living and sleeping conditions after being housed in temporary huts susceptible to the rain. Some of the soldiers were Welsh miners and had experience of industrial battles, and the threat of mutiny was sufficiently serious for their superiors to cede to their demands for full leave on full pay. As the war progressed the Seaford camps would give rise to tensions between conscientious objectors and conscripted soldiers. At Seaford during the winter and spring of 1915, and then at Aldershot from the end of May, Lakin was trained in the basic skills of map-reading and combat: he learnt to use a compass and set a map in harsh conditions, and how to build trenches under different time restrictions while remaining concealed from the full range of enemy attack. As a junior officer he was also required to avail himself of knowledge of military law and disciplinary procedures.[3] The rest of the time was idled away playing football or reading. It was a waiting game, in the period before being sent into action. At least there was one familiar face: Charles Campbell Woolley, the son of a bootmaker from Barry, who had earlier been appointed second lieutenant in the same battalion.

As summer began he received news from some of his Oxford contemporaries. Philip Gibbons, who along with Sever had been awarded a first-class degree in history, was now stationed at the Felixstowe School of Instruction, together with Laycock and Costin. 'Life is not great + somewhat dull,' Laycock wrote to Lakin in July. 'One month has gone – two weeks are to follow and then-?'[4] Ernest Willmore, having joined the OTC with Lakin before leaving Oxford, was also unsure of his immediate future. He had initially intended to remain in the Home Service, but following the rising death toll among school and university contemporaries he 'came to the decision to apply for a commission in Kitchener's Army'. 'It is from a strong feeling of duty,' he wrote to his close friend Watkin Davies, 'that I am going. I realise very fully and vividly what are the things I may have to go through & as you know I am none the bravest.'[5] Watkin Davies himself had continued with his studies while holding grave doubts about the justification for the war, which he expected to be over in a few months. His opposition to the war grew into a

wider distaste for militarism and a scepticism over the choices
made by his former school and university friends. This meant
that his close friendship with Willmore ran into difficulties,
with growing tensions between them. Willmore, by now at
Dover Castle on Zeppelin watch, began to question the basis
of Watkin Davies's pacifism and his analysis of the war. Their
exchange reflected wider arguments among students of their
generation over the validity of the war. In June, while wishing
him the best for his finals, Willmore was still able to praise
Watkin Davies as his 'brilliant Welsh friend who is such a
Lloyd George genius'. However, a month later, irritated by
what he regarded by Watkin Davies's downplaying of the
seriousness of the war, his attitude to his friend had changed
significantly:

> Do you remember your confident statement only 3 months ago
> that it was to be over in August? Can't you see what a big affair
> it really is ... You are a queer mixture of excellent qualities with
> total lack of courage & self-control to put them to good use.
> You do lack character.[6]

By August, after Willmore had had his first experience of
shooting at Zeppelins, he was still asking his friend to explain
the reasons for not enlisting.

The uncertainty over the war was felt in Cadoxton, where
Lakin's parents and siblings were growing anxious as they
awaited news of his imminent call to action in France. They
valued his home visits and his regular reassuring letters but,
with the rising number of daily casualties, knew that he would
soon be embarking on a dangerous mission. His mother
Annie was now suffering from regular ill health and her

concern increased once news of his departure was confirmed at the beginning of August, despite Lakin's further attempts to placate them. His brother Stan, aged fourteen, was also concerned and, as the eldest sibling in the absence of Lakin, was conscious of the new responsibilities he had to the family, as well as his loyalty to a brother he greatly admired. He wrote to Lakin on 5 August,

If you don't know whether you're to come through it or no somebody else does. Don't think perhaps I shan't see dad and mama anymore. I know it's hard not to think so but never mind Cyril, I have took this letter you sent me serious and I never think it rotten that my elder brother gets everything. I am proud to have a brother who has been to Oxford gained a commission and willing to fight for his country, not like some boy's brothers. But Cyril if you don't come back I will try my very hardest to repay them for what they have done for you although I don't think you have much faith in me, but I will but let's hope for the best. Poor mama was upset Sunday write her a nice letter and don't forget me for I shan't you.

Your ever loving brother Stan

PS Please write me strictly private letters so as you can tell me what you think.[7]

Presumably Lakin's earlier letter to his brother (now lost) had explained to him the seriousness of war, the obligations they had to their parents and the possibility of him not returning. These were the dilemmas that faced him and his fellow soldiers in the 67th Brigade as they took the train from

Aldershot to Folkestone and then, on 5 September in fine, warm weather, embarked on SS *Seriol* bound for Boulogne for service on the Western Front. After arriving in Boulogne just after 2 a.m. the following morning, they marched to Ostrohove Great Rest Camp where they settled for the rest of the night under canvas.

The next two days were spent on route marches before leaving Boulogne by train for Flesselles, where the battalion received orders to march in hot weather to La Neuville on the banks of the River Somme. They had their first experience of trench warfare at Chipilly on 15 September before moving on to Chuignes three days later to take over from French troops who had faced heavy attack following an explosion of a seventeen-ton German mine. In addition to the forty-five French casualties, the first two men from the SWB lost their lives here. Two further SWB men were killed at Fontaine-lès-Cappy – one from a sniper's bullet and the other from an accidental bomb explosion.[8]

The most eventful episode of their relatively brief time on the Western Front occurred on the afternoon of 21 September when movements in enemy trenches in Chuignes were picked up, with further troops seen marching into the trenches in the early evening. At 7 p.m. a captain in the French mining section reported that, per intelligence obtained from their tunnellers, the enemy had finished 'tamping' a mine, i.e. placing the explosive underground, where it could be detonated at any moment. Lakin's battalion, along with the 7th Battalion of the SWB worked with French engineers to produce camouflets (counter mines), which they exploded at 9 p.m., driving the enemy out of their trenches to face an onslaught of rapid fire from the French 10th Battery, with significant German casualties. British casualties were mainly caused by shrapnel. During the next two nights they faced occasional sniper fire.[9]

The following three weeks were spent marching in wet weather between Framerville and Herleville to take up further trench positions, before being relieved by other battalions. After billeting at Proyart, their next assignment was to relieve the Royal Scots near Dompierre (after the latter had passed on instructions on trench operations), where a corporal was killed and another soldier wounded by *minenwerfer*, the short-range mortars used by the German army. On 21 October, after being relieved by the 1st Royal Scots they marched to huts on the bank of the Canal sur Somme close to Froissy, only to receive orders to march for another two hours to Morcourt where the battalion was billeted and rested for two days. It was here on 23 October that Lakin heard the first rumours that his battalion would be leaving France for Serbia. In the afternoon they marched on to Gentelles, where they rested and checked their equipment. Rumours were now 'prevalent' that they would soon be leaving France. On 25 October they were ordered to move to Longeau, from where they would board a train for Marseilles.

The conquering of Serbia by Austria–Hungary, Germany and Bulgaria, which saw the eventual loss of 200,000 Serbian soldiers and the retreat of their army through the Montenegro mountains to Albania, had brought multinational forces to their aid. Serbian forces were exhausted and depleted while also suffering from a typhus epidemic. By the middle of September, 'it appeared that the only way to prevent Bulgarian intervention against Serbia would be a show of force, namely the landing of Anglo-French forces in the Balkans'.[10] This was also intended to divert German troops from the Western Front. The SWB received instructions that they were to be part of this mission, where they would fight alongside Greek and Serbian allies to prevent Greece from being invaded and to free Serbia from enemy domination. On the evening of 26 October, 31 officers and 859 other ranks embarked on the long 350-mile train journey from Longeau in North East France to the South of France. Travelling was difficult: the men were accommodated in cattle trucks with only straw for bedding, and Lakin and the officers in carriages. They all lived off rations of bully beef and biscuits and exercise was limited to stretching their legs at infrequent halts. Eventually arriving in Marseilles at 12.30 p.m. on 28 October, they joined the other battalions on board SS *Huntsend* – a former German passenger ship that had been seized by the British in 1914 (and which a month later would aid the evacuation of Allied troops from Gallipoli). On 30 October, SS *Huntsend* departed from Marseilles, and was originally bound for Alexandria until the orders were received to reroute to Salonika. The voyage was calm, according to the war diary, with machine guns mounted and prepared. They arrived in Salonika on 5 November but were not allowed to disembark until the following day.

Spirits among the men were high on arrival in Salonika – the accompanying SWB's ambulance unit that docked at the port sang Welsh hymns[11] – but once the mountainous terrain was visible in the distance and they had completed an awkward embarkation at the port, excitement mixed with the uncertainty of landing in unknown territory. Salonika's history of wars and crises meant that it was used to its status as a contested territory, inhabited by invaders or liberators. This had been reinforced in more recent times with the Italo-Turkish War, the First Balkan War and the Second Balkan

War, while the city had also been plagued by two cholera epidemics. The Greek rulers were also divided: Venizelos, the prime minister, welcomed Allied support, while King Constantine I disapproved (prompting Venizelos's resignation). However, as American war correspondent Richard Harding Davis discovered, the local people themselves welcomed Allied soldiers:

> The inhabitants received them calmly. The Greek officials, the colonel commanding the Greek troops, the Greek captain of the port and the Greek collector of customs may have been upset; but the people of Salonika remained calm. They were used to it. Foreign troops were always landing at Salonika.[12]

As they trundled up from the waterfront to the citadel overlooking the sea, negotiating a way through the cars, trolley cars and stationary fishing boats, they encountered an abundance of cafes and restaurants, and were gently accosted by locals, some chattering in different languages and carrying bags on shoulders while offering their wares; head-covered women carrying baskets, children scampering under their feet. Tired after their long journey, they put up for the night in the centre of the city. The next day they congregated in Café Floca and other amenable pavement cafes, which helped them acclimatize to unfamiliar surroundings. The day after their arrival at Salonika, Lakin and his troops marched to Samli where they were accommodated in bivouac shelters. The weather was now cold and wet and the next few days were spent pitching tents and route training. Their role, as part of the 67th Brigade, would be to support the Allied troops in defending the area east of the River Vardar, building trenches west of Doiran Lake and patrolling the villages along the River Struma, defending the front from any attack from the 'Bulgars'. The defensive line along this sixty-mile battlefront became known as the 'Birdcage', while some likened it to an internment camp once they became hemmed in and dependent on what seemed to be a long-drawn-out waiting game.

For the SWB, it would mean travelling on difficult roads and moving between hill villages, often at night, sleeping in makeshift camps and living off very limited rations of bully beef and biscuits. They would have to survive one of the coldest winters in recent years, which as usual would be followed by the boiling heat of the summer, in which sickness and disease were common. On 19 November they received orders to move on to camp on the west of Salonika, south of Dudular village, where they carried out further training on waterlogged grounds in cold conditions. From there they moved on to a new camp at Arapli. Here 'the role of the battalion was to hold an outpost line along the Galiko riverbank half a mile east of the bridge to about a mile west of the bridge' in preparation for any attack.[13]

Although they were not engaged in conflict during this time, travel was difficult and moving from camp to camp along muddy and uneven roads slowed them down, making it difficult for wagons to transport goods. Leather jerkins were issued to protect against the weather – some men and officers had already been sent to hospital on sickness grounds – and one bivouac was issued for each two men for shelter; Lakin shared a bivouac with his captain (and, by now, good friend), Herbert Down, the son of a farmer from Herefordshire's cider-making country, who had been working as a bank clerk before the war. In December they travelled through Akbunar and on to Pirnar, where they rejoined the 67th Brigade. Together with the 7th SWB and East Lancs 9th they dug trenches on one side and moved their bivouacs to the reverse slopes of the hills. At Pirnar work continued on the trenches despite the shortage of essential equipment – empty ration cans were used instead of barbed wire in some cases. This work continued up until Christmas Eve when four wagons were sent to Salonika to buy fresh vegetables and ingredients for a meal for the following day, bringing a temporary halt to the bully beef and biscuits that had served as basic rations for the previous three weeks.

On Boxing Day, Lakin, just short of his twenty-second birthday, still in the early months of his first time abroad and still loyal to his religious convictions, wrote to his parents to give them his latest news, to tell them he was thinking of home and to reassure them – perhaps with some exaggeration – about his welfare:

I am sure you are all wondering how I spent my Christmas and I am more sure that you will be glad when I tell you that it was one of the happiest of my life. For one day at least, God was good enough to dispel all the thoughts of war from our minds. True we were away from home – and home seems more to one at Christmas tide, doesn't it? But still, the enemy were too far off to touch us in any shape or form. There was good food to eat and plenty of it, and the day was so gloriously fine that it made one feel glad to be alive. A huge parcel post had arrived late on Christmas Eve, and on that night we went to bed with the determination of waking up to a real good old, Christmas.

I woke, strangely enough, just on the stroke of midnight, and could not help lifting the flap of the bivouac which Down and I share together, for the night was so perfect. The tumult of the shooting dies. Peace!! Peace!! Peace!! It was all around you: you could feel it in the very stillness of the air. The moon was so bright that it outshone all the stars except one – perhaps the very one which led the three wise men to Bethlehem some 1915 years ago. Can you realise what it means to be on the East tempting you to Bethlehem: the stillness broken except for the friendly yelp of a dog on a different hill, as if to comfort the shepherds while they 'watched their flocks by night, all seated on the ground'.

And to sleep again – to be awakened at dawn by the tinkle of the church bell of the village just behind us. Only a rudely-fashioned cracked old bell but it sounded like the sweetest melody on earth to me as it rang out the message to the poor villagers, 'Come and Worship'. Do you think for a moment I realised that I was thousands of miles away from home in a land which only a few years ago was under heathen Turkish domination? I tell you I was nearer to you all in spirit than I have ever been in flesh and body.

It had been arranged that we were only to work on our defences from 9 till 11 a.m. It had, unfortunately been impossible to arrange an early celebration owing to the padre being so far away from us. But we had arranged for one upon the slope just near at 11.30 a.m. Two biscuit boxes served as an altar and at the appointed time we had our hearts desire. Have you ever felt the sun come streaming through the chancel windows as you are 'meekly kneeling upon your knees'.

Perhaps you have, but I wish you could realise the beautiful feeling one gets when out in the open, the Eastern sun breaking through the protesting clouds, and strikes you full in the face just as you partake of the Feast.[14]

But my Christmas also had its practical side. Practical, you know, out here means either eating or working, generally both.

I told you that we were determined to have a good day, so we had sent several wagons back to Salonica to get extra food some days before. Though the journey is not a long one, the road is terribly bad, and speculation was rife as to whether the food really would turn up. But it did and early on Christmas morning I was sorting among the fresh meat, bread (what a luxury after biscuits), vegetables, flour and currants. Happily, there were also cigarettes, and plenty of rum, with which we were to make rum punch. Then I went to look after our own little goodie goodies. What a feast! From macaroni to Johnnie Walker and from almonds to a real live turkey! You would not believe what it meant to us after living for three weeks on half-rations of bully-beef and biscuits. Can you imagine how willingly we did that two hours work? We were all laughing and joking and hard at work, each one of us. You would have smiled to see Down with a pick and myself with a shovel, as good a pair of navvies as ever rolled up shirt-sleeves! After our work, and our holy communion, came the preparation for the bumper. It was truly a grand feast for both officers and men. A seven-course dinner at the Savoy is good but our bumper was far better. Not that we overdid it. Oh no! If you had been three weeks on short rations, I'll bet you would put a little bit away for the rainy days which will probably follow.

In the evening we had a concert, a splendid one, with the usual votes of thanks to artistes and to the officers. But though they are usual, I'm glad to say they are also genuine, and I'm sure there is not a better company in the Army than ours as regards the confidence placed by officers in their men, and vice-versa. We had our Christmas carols, and a splendid message from the King to finish up the night and we all went to bed as happy as could be. So you see we had a real good time.

To-day is Sunday, but that makes no difference to our work:
we are hard at it. I do hope your day was as happy as mine.[15]

From Boxing Day the work on trenches recommenced,
and through January 1916 their time was spent building and
manning trenches (twice a week by day and twice a week at
night) at Pirnar in increasingly difficult conditions of snow,
cold and damp. An outbreak of lice and having to use mules
to bring depleted food rations added to their difficulties, but
apart from the sighting of two German or Austro–Hungarian
planes they were not troubled by the enemy until 7 February,
when in the early hours all ranks of the brigade were instructed
to stand 'in a state of constant readiness'. Not for the first or
last time, it came to nothing. Trench-building, arms drills
and practice attacks took up the bulk of their energies and
the biggest battle in these months was against the weather
and disease. Unlike other battalions, the 8th did not suffer
great numbers of casualties but their work was tough and
relentless, with disease a constant threat. From the beginning
of April, the 8th SWB remained in battle reserve and finally
instructed to report for guard duties at Salonika, which they
reached after another five-hour march. Back at Salonika they
were given permission to use the Turkish baths and provided
with anti-cholera inoculation by the medical officer. More
maintenance work, field training, fire-watching, parades and
practice attacks consumed their time at the beginning of the
summer months. In June the SWB lost two men and had seven
wounded due to an accident during a bomb-training exercise,
but malaria was now the main enemy. By the beginning of
July, having marched between Salonika and Pirnar and then
on to the village of Akbunar, sickness had become prevalent

among officers and on 23 July, after Captain W. V. Franklin was admitted to hospital, Lakin was required to take on the role of acting adjutant. This role necessitated that he keep the war diary, as well as assisting commanding officer Lieutenant Colonel Sword (who had only just rejoined the battalion after a spell in hospital).

Weather and living conditions were proving to be more challenging than the threat from the enemy, with the evacuation of sick men and officers a daily occurrence. Another twenty-five mules were needed to transport belongings and goods, but a thunderstorm flooded the River Galiko, making progress difficult to Kukus, (where a revived Captain Franklin relieved Lakin from adjutant duty). From there they carried on to Jenikoj along the River Struma in time to witness French bombardment of enemy trenches, and then on to their eventual destination of Klindir, where battle was being engaged. Since being relieved of his adjutant role Lakin had been part of a reconnaissance trip to locate enemy lines behind the mountains, and from his observation post on 21 August he wrote to his parents,

My dearest mother and dad,

Four days ago I resumed my important job – but in a different & far more healthy spot. It is really very nice up here – perched on a mountain & just watching their 'little goings on'. Of course we never know when they may take it into their dear little heads to plonk a few over – but we are hoping that they will take no notice of us. In any case it would be difficult for them to hit us – & they have their work cut out in front of them.

It is a curious life this – on one side of the hill you are

watching carefully a titanic struggle; on the other side you walk calmly about picking blackberries! By jove! Nothing has reminded me so much of home as some stewed blackberries we had for dinner yesterday. So you see I'm getting along very happily despite all the strafing. Of course I'm away from my regiment most of the time, but I'm meeting some good fellows – and I'm seeing a lot which makes all the difference.

But we may get landed in the soup any moment. I've had a good introduction anyhow [and] until we do get it in the neck I'm quite content.

There is no news to give you really. I expect the papers will tell you more than I dare. How are you all getting on? I hope there are a few letters waiting for me at my battalion. Sending for the present my fondest love to you all, your loving son Cyril.[16]

At Klindir they received orders to act as the 'Corps Reserve . . . owing to a strong attack by the Germano-Bulgars on the front occupied by the 26th Division' and given further instructions to stand by and be prepared to move at forty-five minutes' notice. In the event, they were not called to action and on 27 August the battalion received orders to relieve part of the Doiran line held by the 122nd French Division and bivouacked under the hills near Kalinova. The next morning they were met with 'about 15' high-explosive shells, one of which hit the parapet on the reverse slope, killing one man and wounding thirty others.

More worrying by the beginning of September was the outbreak of malaria and sandfly fever from infected dugouts, with around fifty cases needing evacuation to hospital. Sickness continued to be the bigger threat to the forces than the Bulgars and on 11 September Lakin was called to relieve Second

Lieutenant Booth, another malaria victim, on the observation post on Hill 350. From this position he had a good view of the Doiran front, from the 'Pip Ridge' to the River Vardar on the west, flanked by the British.

On the night of 13–14 September heavy Allied artillery and an attack launched by two other battalions of the 67th Brigade brought heavy enemy losses, including many wounded and captured, while the SWB remained on divisional reserve helping to collect the casualties, though there were few losses on the Allied side. The division tried to hold position but 'enemy fire made this untenable' and in the retreat there were heavy Allied losses. The following day Lakin, still at his observation post, was relieved on grounds of sickness and eventually evacuated to hospital in Malta.

Letters from home (including a humorous postcard from his cousin Lily Tolley) were forwarded to his hospital bedside, where his sickness was severe. His war was over and his future uncertain.

Chapter 5

Recuperation: New Horizons

Lakin was one of many soldiers invalided out with malaria, an illness often neglected in accounts of First World War casualties. In all, 1.5 million soldiers were infected by a disease that extended to all armies 'as the Malarian parasite had no alignment and could be transmitted unseen across theatres of war. The activities of soldiers aided its progress by increasing mosquito numbers through operational activities following transmission, especially as soldiers tended to burrow underground which is conducive to water-logging and favourable to malaria.'[1]

The total number of malaria cases among Allied troops was 617,150, with 3,865 fatalities. On the Macedonian front, the malaria epidemic was particularly serious in the period between July and September 1916 when Lakin contracted the disease, with 'ten allied casualties for every one inflicted by the axis powers'.[2] The 'hardships, exposure and unpreparedness under war conditions' in 1916 exacerbated the higher than average mortality rate in Macedonia (1.01%) in comparison with 1917 and 1918.[3]

Lakin caught malaria at its peak epidemic before more concerted efforts to prevent the spread of the disease. He was very ill and after a period in hospital in Malta, 'came home to die', as his parents feared at the time.[4] His eventual recovery, a slow rehabilitation after long periods of convalescence, was never complete, and he would suffer from ill health and fatigue (including two later bouts of tuberculosis) for the rest of his life: 'It really did mess him up. After that he was always delicate and often needed to sleep in the afternoon.'[5] On his return he spent most of his convalescence cared for by his mother at the house of his grandmother, Eliza Lakin, in the village of Sully, three miles along the coast from Barry. Eliza had died in April 1916 and 'Velindra', a red-brick, red-tiled, five-bedroom house overlooking the sea, was in an ideal location in which to recuperate.

It was a long haul back to health. The war had changed everything. In all, 127 members of St John's College – fellows, undergraduates and students – died in the First World War. While convalescing, he heard news of James Laycock's death, killed in action in Ypres in July 1917. Ernest Willmore, whose criticism of what he saw as Watkin Davies's 'cowardly attitude' sharpened further once he was under attack from enemy shells in France, did not expect to return from the war. In fact, after he was wounded in the head while coming to the aid of his men, he spent the remaining days of the conflict at home, resuming a more muted correspondence with Watkin Davies that was interrupted by his frequent headaches. They were never able to revive their earlier friendship before Willmore died in London following a brain operation in 1920. Just before the end of the war Barney Janner, serving as a private with the Royal Garrison Artillery in France, nearly died from a mustard-gas attack.

Frank Webber, another of Lakin's school friends, was twice wounded while serving with the 2nd Battalion of the SWB in France and returned with a deformed arm.

In Oxford there was now a very different atmosphere, as some students resumed their studies at a subdued and sparsely populated university. As the war progressed, the pacifism earlier espoused by William Watkin Davies had become much more prominent in the city and opposition to conscription among students grew significantly from mid-1915. At St John's, Sidney Ball, senior tutor, was asked to support several cases of exemption from conscription. Some were unhappy at being exempted from combatant service only. These included Raymond Postgate, later a notable socialist thinker, historian and food writer who, on losing his appeal, refused to pay a fine and was sentenced to a month in prison. His friend John Langdon-Davies, another St John's student, was also imprisoned and had one of his scholarships removed as a result.[6] Some of the socialist conscientious objectors, like Postgate and Langdon-Davies, were emboldened by the ideas behind the Russian Revolution, while for others, including several Christian groups, it was the sheer horror of the casualties that evoked their moral opposition. Once the Oxford Military Service Tribunal had been established in March 1916, the public scrutiny of conscientious objectors increased, causing some tensions with the Oxford public as well as divisions between the Trades Council (which supported the war) and local socialist organizations.[7]

Oxford must now have felt like a different world to Lakin. His sickness did not amount to the kind of mental trauma that others had experienced following shell shock or similar injuries that were reported and subsequently depicted in literature, such as Captain Baldry in Rebecca West's novel *The Return of the Soldier*, but he had to reassess his prospects. In his period of recuperation, he was nursed by the Voluntary Aid Detachment (VAD) units, which provided civilian support for war casualties. The local press estimated that 10,000 men from Barry enlisted for the war effort, and the 270 who died in the conflict were commemorated widely across the town in churches and other memorials; in 1919, approximately 20,000 people packed King Square to celebrate 'Peace Day'. J. C. Meggitt wrote, produced and funded a short book, *World Tyranny or World Freedom: The True Meaning of the Great War*, which was distributed to 7,000 schoolchildren.[8] Resources were stretched in the wake of a serious outbreak of Spanish flu, with many returning soldiers falling victim to the disease as well as spreading it on to others; casualties included Ivor Hiley, the son of another Cadoxton butcher, and two other members of his family, though Barry itself was not as badly affected as the Rhondda or parts of Cardiff.[9]

Lakin received some good support beyond his family. The Reverend Longdon and Zoe Longdon had always favoured him from his days as their loyal disciple with a bright future ahead of him and they helped get him back on his feet. He was also keen to do his bit in support of others who had suffered injuries and, together with Zoe Longdon, took part in a theatre production of *Beauchamp and Beecham* in aid of the local VAD hospitals, held at the Theatre Royal, Barry shortly before Christmas 1917. This 'comedy in khaki', which had recently been performed at London's Lyric Theatre, played to a packed house and enabled Lakin to practise his chivalrous manners in the lead role as 'Private The Hon. Robert Belchambers Beauchamp'. All the actors were from Barry and, according to the local press report, 'from every point of view the production was a success, and the artistic fashion in which all acquitted themselves was a feature of the performance and that was greatly appreciated and enjoyed'.[10]

The popularity of the play extended to a repeat performance early the following year with another big turnout, this time overflowing, with 'large crowds' waiting for the doors to open. Lakin was again in the lead role as the 'appealing young gentleman . . . who successfully cast aside his rifle in order to win, by his personal attraction only, the heart of Constance, a sweet little "modern girl" who put merit before position'. Mr Maddox, the theatre manager, played Major Hubbard, Constance's father, while Zoe Longdon 'rendered perfectly Lady Castlevain'. The performance was enhanced by the orchestra's 'delightful programme of music', while the chairman of the Barry War Charities Committee explained the purpose of their work.[11]

These two performances helped Lakin to rebuild his life, recover some self-esteem and begin to think about applying for jobs. He had the expectation of a war pension and disability allowance and received the news that he had been awarded Victory and 1914–15 Star medals for his service in the two campaigns, to add to his Silver War Badge ('For King and Empire; Services Rendered'), granted after his discharge on grounds of sickness.[12] But he was still isolated, without a clear sense of what he was to do in the future. The war seemed to have tested his faith and ended his previous aspirations to pursue a career in the Church. In his own way, he shared some of the disillusion of the youth of his generation, evident in the work of the war poets and later depicted in the memoirs or novels by Vera Brittain and Alec Waugh (both of whom, as a literary editor in the 1930s, he would commission for review). In any case, he never returned to Oxford University, and reconsidered his career plans. As he had not completed his degree prior to his call-up he was given special dispensation – like many others – to be exempt from further examinations under provisions made by Oxford University (decree 7, June 1917). Therefore, in October 1917, he had been able to take his BA (on the payment of a fee) despite not completing his degree studies. He was still interested in the law and used the later part of his convalescence to study for his bar exams. Making the right connections was important, and he followed his father into the Freemasons, being admitted to the Prince Llewellyn Lodge in Cardiff.

However, he needed a job. In 1918 he received a letter from the Ministry of Food that confirmed his appointment as secretary to the Area Meat Distribution Committee at its divisional headquarters in Angel Buildings, Cardiff, at a salary of £350 p.a. The Ministry of Food had been set up by Lloyd George once he succeeded Asquith as prime minister in December 1916. D. A. Thomas (Lord Rhondda), the owner of Cambrian collieries, industrialist and Liberal politician, was appointed as its second Food Controller in June 1917. In this role he established twelve regional food commissioners, prohibited food imports and in 1918 imposed strong rationing measures, with serious implications for the mining communities of the South Wales Valleys and other distressed areas. One consequence of the rationing regime was the revival of the Independent Labour Party (which had opposed the war), with new branches in Merthyr and the Rhondda contesting the restrictions.[13]

Lakin's background as the son of a butcher, together

with his father's contacts in the local meat industry, no doubt came in useful in this role where he had the task of ensuring families received essential deliveries. If it was a controversial, difficult area of work, then he would have felt he was making an important contribution to the post-war effort, while it may have reminded him of his earlier days delivering meat to Cadoxton residents on his cycle rounds. He impressed in this work and from the beginning of April 1920 was promoted to sub-commissioner on an increased salary of £450 p.a.[14]

Now on the road to recovery and relieved that his correspondence with the Ministry of Pensions had brought the news that he was to be awarded an additional backdated disability grant, he looked for employment opportunities away from the meat industry. In July 1920 he applied for the position of secretary to the Glamorgan Territorial Association, enhanced by a reference from Lieutenant Colonel Sword, his former commanding officer in France and Salonika, who recommended him as 'one of the very best in the subalterns, capable and zealous and devoted to duty'.[15]

He did not get that position, but by now his ambitions lay further afield. He was studying hard for his bar exams and was helped by Austin Poole, one of his former law tutors at St John's, who provided a testimonial so that he could be exempted from the constitutional law and legal history component. He now believed a career in law was a possibility and saw his future lying beyond Barry. In any case the town was changing. He and his family had seen it grow to be the biggest coal-exporting town in the world by the beginning of the First World War – a remarkable expansion from a trio of barely connected villages:

By 1914 Barry was a place of nearly two hundred streets, mostly well paved and well lit: it had good gas and water supplies and all the facilities of early 20th century town life. It was filled with a sense of destiny and with hope for the future. Its ambitions knew no bounds: there were plans for a third dock, a transatlantic passenger service, an iron and steelworks and a zinc works: on a cultural and academic level some inhabitants dreamed of an opera house and even a university.[16]

Many of these hopes were dashed by the economic and social costs of the First World War. In addition, its cosmopolitan population, which had helped drive its economic prosperity, was showing signs of division with recently demobilized seamen resenting the lack of jobs and what to them appeared as unwarranted competition from black workers. The Seamen's Union had called for a ban on foreign labour while several white seamen resented the apparent affluence of black seamen, some of whom they found in better housing conditions, and in mixed-race relationships with white women. Tensions had intensified during the war and now, in its aftermath, they were succeeded by a 'pattern of racial violence which the problems of demobilisation imposed on many British ports'.[17] On the back of disturbances in Liverpool and other ports, in June 1919 the streets of Cadoxton were engulfed in serious race riots. The trigger for the riots occurred after Frederick ('Skanny') Longman, a dock labourer who had recently been discharged from the Royal Field Artillery, was stabbed to death by Charles Emmanuel, a black seaman of French West Indian origin who had served in the merchant navy. In the days before the attack Emmanuel, who lived near to Longman in an area that housed several black families, had been verbally abused and physically assaulted by him and others. Longman, who had twenty previous convictions for assault, and other accomplices had resented the growth of the black community in Cadoxton during the war and directed their antipathy on their near neighbours. The Barry riots were at their peak when a series of similar riots broke out in the UK in the same period, including those in Newport and Cardiff. These were attributed to 'post-war dislocation and white male sexual jealousy' in the midst of economic insecurity.[18] The night before Longman was killed by Emmanuel there had been a major disturbance in a house in Foster Street, where the body of Peter Johnson, who had earlier died of heart failure, was awaiting burial, with local residents from the black community gathered for the funeral. Rioting ensued and there were reports that the dead body was manhandled.

After the killing of Longman, Emmanuel (who would later receive a five-year imprisonment for manslaughter) was followed home and attacked, as large crowds of rioters descended on Tredegar Street and Beverley Street and the other areas where black families were concentrated, while fighting continued on Weston Square at the bottom of Vere Street. Various incitements were given to the crowd and several black men were chased in the surrounding streets and assaulted, as were police offers attempting to halt the conflict. The rioting was only brought to a halt after heavier policing and the imposition of 300 soldiers from the Duke of Westminster Regiment. The black community in Cadoxton was grateful for this response and one of its representatives wrote to the head of police praising them for the 'protection' and their 'admirable tact and foresight', while 'thankful for the sympathy shown us by other societies in the district'. However, the letter ended by acknowledging the help of the police in putting pressure on the government 'to adopt a plan as soon as possible to send us home for we know we are not wanted here'. James Gillespie, a Jamaican seaman living in Barry Dock, applied for repatriation and wrote to Prime Minister Lloyd George after his house had been destroyed by rioters.[19]

Lakin, now living in Sully, was sheltered from the disturbances, though his father and family would have experienced them at close hand. By 1919 Harry Lakin had retired from running his butcher's shop and was planning to hand over the business to his nephew, Bernard Tolley. Mindful perhaps of the change in fortunes in Barry and seeking to invest in a long-term future for his children, in late 1921 Harry Lakin sold both his butchery business and Velindra and bought Highlight Farm, a property comprising twelve rooms and outbuildings and with over 130 acres of land in the parish of Wenvoe, on the outskirts of Barry. Initially, Cyril Lakin joined his family, though it was younger brother Stan who would eventually take over the running of the farm (which was still in the Lakin family a hundred years later), and while over the years Lakin would remain in close contact with his family, it is clear that he wanted to get away and pursue other ambitions. He did not want to be constrained by family pressures or allow previous loyalties to dictate his life.

Some insight into his thoughts can be gleaned from a commonplace diary he kept at that time. In it, he entered jottings and verbatim extracts from favourite poems, which reveal his desire to escape both earlier trappings and the effects of his debilitating illness. Unlike his brothers he was not preparing for a life on the farm. He took heart from an adolescent J. R. Ackerley, whose poem 'The Prodigal Son' objected to 'living like a weed' and sought to 'leave the farm and fields of sows' to 'take the road without the cows'.[20]

His musings contained anecdotes and prophesies, scraps of advice and memorable phrases from chosen authors like Alexander Pope ('Worth makes the man, and want of it the fellow'). His interest in verse extended to the *Oxford Poetry* edition of 1920, which included the works of two Somerville near-contemporaries: Vera Brittain's 'The Lament of the Demobilized' and Hilda Reid's 'The Magnanimity of Beasts'. Suggestions on how to become a writer came from Sir Arthur Quiller-Couch: 'Almost always prefer the concrete word to the abstract (and) almost always prefer the direct word to the circumlocution.' From John Ruskin's *The Ethics of the Dust*, an early Socratic dialogue with the young women of Winnington Hall, a girls' finishing school in Cheshire (where he taught in the 1860s), there was stark counsel on values to live by, to think not of faults, but to 'look for what is good and strong':

> If on looking back your whole life should seem rugged as a palm
> tree stem, still, never mind. So long as it has been growing: and
> has its grand green shade of leaves and weight of honeyed fruit
> at the top. And even if you cannot find much good in yourself …
> think that it does not much matter to the universe either what
> you were or are: think how many people are noble, if you cannot
> be: and rejoice in their nobleness.[21]

His diary also contained a newspaper cutting that summarized the career to date of William Berry, a former newsboy on the *Merthyr Tydfil Times* who had become the unlikely owner of the *Sunday Times*.

In June 1922 he received the welcome news that he had passed his final examination for the Bar. The *Western Mail*, which reported the news in its social and personal column, hinted that he was likely to establish a practice in South Wales.[22] However, his lack of private finance was always a drawback in his legal ambitions, and it was at the *Western Mail* itself where he gained his first major career breakthrough. Not for the last time, this came about through connections and recommendations. After recovering from his war wound, Frank Webber, Lakin's old schoolfriend, was making his way at the paper where his elder brother Robert had established himself as an influential voice within the Welsh newspaper industry. Frank Webber, like his brother (whom he would succeed as the *Western Mail*'s general manager) was a good contact – a 'Mr Fix-it'[23] – and it was through him that Lakin gained his early experience on a newspaper, writing his first articles and taking on some editorial duties.

He was becoming adept at making the right connections and impressing those with influence, while success in his bar exams and upgrading his Oxford degree to an MA brought him more confidence to match his improved prospects. A bigger break for him emerged when, presumably through the Webbers, he secured a role as assistant to David Davies, a former acting editor of the *Western Mail* and proprietor of the *Swansea Evening Post*. Davies was not only a veteran journalist and newspaper man but also a well-known public figure in South Wales. He had been mayor of Swansea in the war, then stood as Conservative Unionist candidate for Swansea West at the 1918 general election, where he lost by 1,200 votes to Lord Melchett, the Liberal Party industrialist standing with Lloyd George's backing in the 'coupon' campaign. Well travelled, outspoken and a noted orator, he had been a long-standing opponent of Sunday trading laws, while praised for his philanthropy and support for a variety of local causes in Swansea, from prisoners' relief, arts and crafts societies to the presidency of Swansea Cricket and Football Club. He was a dedicated Conservative, which was reflected in the outlook of his newspapers.

Lakin's move to Swansea (lodging in King Edward's Road) was evidently a productive, if brief, period in his life. As an assistant to David Davies, he had the opportunity to learn more about the newspaper world, while becoming a trusted and capable lieutenant again. His admittance into the Davies family circle resulted in his first serious love affair, with Davies's daughter Marjorie ('Topsy'). That year – 1923 – his thirtieth, brought major developments in his life and a rapid change in his prospects. He was made aware by Davies that there was an opportunity to work in London for William and Gomer Berry, the press barons from Merthyr Tydfil, who owned the *Sunday Times* and the *Financial Times* and held a controlling interest in the *Western Mail* among a range of newspapers (and would soon expand their growing empire further as part of the Allied Newspaper Group). Lakin left Swansea for London in May, the same month that a native of his mother's hometown of Bewdley, Stanley Baldwin, took over as prime minister.

It was an exciting opportunity, one which he had been craving for several years, and he arrived at the *Sunday Times* offices with the right recommendations, though on the wrong day. It was a Saturday; the paper had already gone to press, few people were in the office, and he was told to return on Monday. What was intended to be an initial day trip turned out to be a long weekend, which, as he was short of funds, necessitated taking his watch to the pawnbrokers in order to subsidize suitable accommodation at short notice. He lodged at Toc H, the international Christian hostel that had been founded by the army chaplain Philip (Tubby) Clayton, Neville Talbot and the Reverend Dick Sheppard as a rest home for soldiers. He would stay at the house for several weeks as he settled in and got to know London. If his Christianity had waned since the war, the redemptive and spiritual side of his new lodgings must have resonated with his own recent rehabilitation.

His friendship with David Davies and the Webbers meant he was already connected to influential South Wales newspaper circles by the time he met Sir William Berry, who had started the Berrys' press empire and had recently been knighted by David Lloyd George in his notorious 1921 honours list. As well as its owner, William Berry was the *Sunday Times*'s editor-in-chief – he always took a hands-on role with his newspapers – and it is clear that Lakin made an early and lasting impact on the older man, who was seemingly impressed with his capacity for work and his flair for generating new ideas. Lakin's first role was an unusual one by later standards: effectively he was a wide-ranging personal assistant to both William and Gomer Berry, responsible for organizing meetings, liaising between them and editorial staff and carrying out various instructions on their behalf. Ensconced at the bachelor flat the brothers shared in Arundel Street, off the Strand, he worked initially with W. T. Slatcher, the Berrys' confidential secretary. Gradually, he would incorporate much of Slatcher's work as the brothers extended their trust in him; he was given more roles and it was not long before he himself was suggesting ideas for editorial change and alterations on the production side.

Lakin became part of William Berry's entourage, and was viewed by the press barons as one of a new generation who would enact important changes on their instructions. The increased responsibilities took him to the heart of the running of a national newspaper, which must have been exhilarating in comparison with his earlier years. His excitement with his job and where it was taking him is evident in his letters home to his parents, as was his pride in the trust afforded to him by 'Bill Berry': 'I'm doing awfully well at Slatcher's job while he's away. It's swelling work.' At a garden party hosted by the Berrys, 'one lady said I'm sure you're a relation of Sir Wms. I nearly said I wish to God I was, but Bill was standing too close.'[24]

His personal news was equally promising. After what had been an impulsive courtship, he became engaged to Topsy shortly after arriving in London; his parents had still to meet her by the time the engagement had been announced in the *Western Mail* at the beginning of July. 'It's been congratulations all the week! I think you will like her, because she's got plenty of sense and doesn't mind work. Mr and Mrs Davies like me, so you might return the compliment.'[25] He had kept in close touch with his family, writing regularly to 'Dearest Mother and all', worrying about Annie's health ('do be careful because it's easy to do enough damage to last for years') and reminiscing about haymaking on Highlight Farm in the hot weather. He also wrote separately to his father to share his concern over the running of the farm, which was struggling to make its way financially and would remain a concern for some years. His fear that his younger brothers had not been able to make a milk delivery service sustainable reflected more general worries about their prospects: 'Those boys ought to see that it's the only thing to give them a chance of making a decent income & getting enough capital to open out on a bigger scale with perhaps two farms. If they don't do something *extra* to farming, they are going to be stuck in the rut for ever. They ought to have the sense to see that.' For his part, he told his parents that he was working 'as hard as I can', that he 'hadn't *quite* given up smoking' and was 'trying hard – real hard' to save money. [26]

If his private life was prospering, his work was more than satisfying. 'I've been arranging for Gomer's and Bill Berry's holidays – writing and telegraphing in French, rearranging their houses in Scotland,' he told them in late July. In the autumn he was arranging a trip to America for Gomer Berry (he is 'taking nobody except his missus – otherwise might have been a chance for me'), and as winter approached he was sorting out holidays in the sun for William Berry, his elder brother Seymour Berry, a coal owner and businessman (whose sixty directorships were borne from a fruitful friendship with D. A. Thomas) and Sir David Richard (D. R.) Llewellyn, another coal owner and Liberal Party industrialist:

> I've had a great week of it fixing up a trip to Madeira immediately after Christmas, first for Sir Wm and his tribe, then Seymour and now D. R. Llewellyn.
>
> Fitting three families' nurses + maid on one boat after nearly all the cabins had been booked – & getting the best accommodation money can buy, is no small job. But if they set their mind on anything, nothing on earth can stop them ... but they leave it to me! Well I have grown more 'cheek' this week than ever before – & the funny thing is people come eat out of your hand if you bluff enough and swank enough.

Meeting with Welsh friends helped him settle in the capital and he still saw Frank Webber regularly when the latter was down for business meetings. The Webbers continued to offer him hospitality. At dinner one night at the Aldwych Club, he heard a talk by George Riddell, chairman of the company that owned the *Western Mail* and a close confidante of Lloyd George. Robert Webber, seated next to him, 'paid for all I could eat and as much champagne as I thought I could carry!' After dinner they went to the Constitutional Club for more drinks and entered into a prolonged conversation with Major William Cope, who was then the MP for Llandaff and Barry, and James Childs Gould, Conservative MP for Cardiff Central, about the forthcoming general election that, controversially, had been called by Stanley Baldwin:

> It was funny to get those two together on that night, because Gould wouldn't say where he stood politically. It was very interesting, and I think old Cope looked at me hard and kept on thinking where he had seen or heard my name before. They are all very pally. Bob Webber tells somebody how I stood in the same relation to Sir Wm as he did to Riddell. They are all very useful friends, anyhow.[27]

His parents were always eager to hear his news (Harry Lakin knew Cope through his own political involvement in Barry) and they looked forward to welcoming him home for Christmas, when they could also celebrate his thirtieth birthday on 29 December. 'Tell father Lakin to call in a good stock for Christmas – I want one good feed this side of 30. Everybody says I look 23 though.' In appearance he was younger than his years, but he had still not shaken off the effects of malaria and

before Christmas found himself in the Central London Ear,
Nose and Throat Hospital for a mastoidectomy – an operation
for an infection under the bone of the ear. It was serious enough
for Slatcher to be in touch with his family and a worried
Topsy to hurry to London. She had been urging him to see
a doctor about his nose and was convinced his condition was
related to that. The Berry brothers sent sympathetic messages
and he had regular visitors from Toc H, but in the end the
operation was successful and he relayed an optimistic account
to his parents, who, though unable to travel to see him, had
sent on a woodcock, eggs and butter to the hospital. 'It was
great fun. I wasn't the least bit sick after it & about two hours
later I was sitting up smoking a cigarette.' Dressing the wound
was more difficult and painful and it remained on for some
weeks afterwards, but he was out of hospital in time to return
to Barry where his family were eagerly awaiting all his news.
He also had a surprise visitor: his parents had invited Topsy
over for Boxing Day. They had got to know each other in the
preceding months, and on her visits to London she had written
more than once to reassure them that Lakin 'was looking very
fit and seemed bucked up with life and his work'.[28]

Chapter 6

The Berry Brothers

Lakin had moved quickly from recuperation and the feeling of lost hopes and an uncertain future to relief and readjustment to civilian life. He had now reached the moment of renewed ambition. Along with others of his Barry generation, he retained the determination to go out and make a difference in the wider world. He was enjoying his new status, while the rapid change in his circumstances and the ease with which he was making his way may have brought with them the naivety of one who was flattered by powerful patrons. His personal charm, amiability and obliging disposition had endeared him to friends, mentors and fellow soldiers, and he evidently realized that this could also be beneficial in winning important allies.

He could not have timed his arrival at the *Sunday Times* any better or chosen more influential sponsors. The Berry brothers were moving into their prime, consolidating their influence among politicians and in the process of building a press empire that would match those of Beaverbrook (*Daily Express*) and Rothermere (*Daily Mail*). The three Berry brothers, Seymour,

William and Gomer, would all become millionaire lords,
which was some way from their relatively humble origins in
Merthyr Tydfil. Their father, John Mathias Berry, was born
in Haverfordwest, Pembrokeshire, and after school took a job
as a railway clerk, before moving to Merthyr as stationmaster
at Taff Vale Railway Station, which connected the town's
major iron and coal industries with Cardiff. Merthyr had
become 'the largest, most industrialised and technologically
advanced town in Wales', and its capitalist enterprise and
industries were driving the transformation of the towns, ports
and infrastructure of South Wales.[1] Berry senior augmented
his income on the side by selling tea, and this entrepreneurial
endeavour later enabled him to open an estate agents as well
as acquire an auctioneer business in the town. His status
within Merthyr Tydfil increased substantially and he became
a JP, mayor, and political agent to D. A. Thomas, the coal
owner and Liberal MP for the town from 1888 to 1910. His
influence was such that 'It was said that no political event of
any importance could occur in South Wales, without J. M.
Berry hearing about it.'[2]

His three sons and daughter were brought up in a strict
nonconformist household with money and care provided for
their education. (Henry) Seymour Berry, the eldest, trained as
a teacher before taking over his father's businesses, which he
built up to be prominent concerns in Merthyr and throughout
Wales while at the same time making substantial investments
in real estate. In 1914 he became a director of the Britannic
Merthyr Coal Company (the first of his many directorships),
and the following year he joined his father's old friend and
influential patron D. A. Thomas to look after his extensive
business interests in the coal industry while the latter was Food

Controller in Lloyd George's Cabinet. Seymour Berry's work, regarded as a significant contribution to the war effort, won him commendation in high places including among South Wales businessmen. He helped to enlarge D. A. Thomas's coal empire by acquiring David Davis and Sons and North's Navigation Collieries, enabling the Cambrian Combine to produce more than 8 million tons of coal annually.

In addition to his directorships in the coal industry, Seymour Berry expanded his interests in the publishing world, becoming chairman of the *Merthyr Express* in 1917 to add to his chairmanship of Tarian Printing and Publishing in Aberdare and deputy chairman of the *Cambrian News* in Aberystwyth and Messrs Gee and Co in Denbigh. His major financial interests in the coal and steel industry included John Lysaght Ltd, the iron and steel manufacturers, which he bought in 1919 with William Berry, Lady Rhondda (who took over her father's interests and inherited his title after his death in 1918) and D. R. Llewellyn in what was dubbed the 'biggest industrial transaction in the history of South Wales', amounting to £5 million. The company employed around 15,000 workers, with interests in Australia and the shipping industry. They sold the company the following year for £6 million. In 1919 Seymour Berry and D. R. Llewellyn acquired for £2 million Graigola Merthyr of Swansea, which produced 600,000 tons of anthracite annually, and the two were now estimated to control about 25% of the total output of the South Wales coalfields. In the first seven months of 1920 Seymour Berry, D. R. Llewellyn and their various companies purchased Celtic Collieries, Cynon Colliery, Blaenclydach Colliery and the Crown Patent Fuel Company for £2 million, and for £4 million the Aberpergwm mineral estate, an area covering twenty miles of coalmines that they estimated had reserves of 1,200 million tons of unworked coal.

Seymour Berry's business dealings won him recognition beyond Wales. On being invited to share his views on the 'Methods That Make Millions' for a magazine series, he listed his 'Seven Essentials to Success'. These ranged from management acumen, close attention to detail and having a clear purpose, to the 'systematic study of markets and general trade tendencies', a scrupulous observance of conditions of contracts as between buyers and sellers and between employers and work people', 'the encouragement of talent among employees', and collective bargaining on wages. His motto, 'Labour is worthy of its hire, but so is capital', was in tune with the entrepreneurial spirit of the age, even if in practice it brought him into conflict with trade unions.[3] His standing in Merthyr made him a popular choice among its influential circles as a potential parliamentary candidate, but he always declined the invitation, preferring to concentrate on his businesses while regularly giving his public support to the Conservative candidate from his home at Buckland Hall in Brecon. From here he continued to use his wealth as a philanthropist for various local causes, which ranged from Merthyr Hospital and the museum, to the male voice choir and sheepdog trials.

In Merthyr he was given freedom of the town in 1923 (one of the first Berry family events Lakin attended), but as the more politically outspoken of the three brothers and the one at the heart of ongoing battles between the interests of capital and labour, he was embroiled in frequent clashes with the Independent Labour Party – which was intent in exposing the extent of his wealth and interests in the coalfields – as well as disputes generated by strikes over wages and conditions. The culmination of these conflicts took place during the General Strike of 1926 (the year he was ennobled as Lord Buckland).

Apart from holding a directorship in the *Sunday Times* and providing early financial help to his brothers, he was not directly involved in the newspaper business. It was William Ewert, the middle brother (apparently named after the former Liberal prime minister, despite the erroneous spelling), who was responsible for their rise in the newspaper world. At the age of fourteen, after winning an essay competition organized by his local paper, the *Merthyr Times*, he was talent-spotted by William Waite (W. W.) Hadley, its editor, and given a job as an apprentice reporter and office boy. (Forty years later he would reciprocate by making Hadley editor of the *Sunday Times*.) In his late teens William Berry left Merthyr for London and spent five years as a journalist on the *Investors' Guardian* and *Country Gentleman*, and for the Commercial Press Association, as well as experiencing periods of unemployment. His big break came when he launched his own periodical, *Advertising World*, helped by an advance of £100 from Seymour. After long hours writing most of the material himself, he made a success of it and brought his younger brother Gomer – then working as a floor walker in a Merthyr department store – to London to help him. An ideal partnership followed, with William Berry looking after the journalism and editorial side and Gomer assuming responsibility for business matters, while Seymour remained a supportive financial backer. After selling *Advertising World*, the brothers set up a publishing company, Ewart, Seymour and Co, before purchasing a series of smaller magazines including, in 1909, *Boxing*. It was a shrewd move as that sport had increased in popularity following Jack

Johnson's defeat of Tommy Burns at the end of the previous year, enabling him to become the first black world heavyweight champion. The Berrys increased the circulation of *Boxing* from 100,000 to 250,000, which as well as increasing profits strengthened their connections in the financial world.

It was through one of these links that they made their first major purchase. James White, 'a jovial red-faced villain with a bowler hat, a clipped moustache and a strong north country accent',[4] was a financier and former boxing promoter whom William Berry had once lent £500 so the former could avoid possible bankruptcy. Over lunch at the National Liberal Club in 1915, White was able to repay Berry's generosity by providing funds so that the brothers could carry off the unlikely acquisition of the *Sunday Times* for £80,000. West de Wend-Fenton, owner of the *Sporting Times* ('The Pink 'Un'), was sitting at a nearby table and informed them the paper was up for sale, partly as a consequence of its main shareholder, Hermann Schmidt, a German businessman, being interned on the Isle of Man during the war.

The Berrys' takeover was accomplished with the support of White, now running the Beecham Trust on behalf of Sir Joseph Beecham (who had inherited his father's medicinal business), and other benefactors, including continuing ones such as the disreputable arms dealer Sir Basil Zaharoff, Sir Arthur Steel-Maitland, then chairman of the Conservative Party (and future minister and MP for Erdington, Harry Lakin's old patch), and Sir Leander Starr Jameson, a former prime minister of Cape Colony, who led the ill-fated raid over the Transvaal border in 1895 and was an inspiration for Rudyard Kipling's 'If—'.[5] The *Sunday Times* had been in severe financial straits in a market that had still not entirely overcome the country's religious reservations on taking the paper on the sabbath, and it was a unique opportunity for the Berrys even allowing for the dubious interests of some of their early backers. James White soon relinquished his directorship of the *Sunday Times*, before further financial difficulties over the next decade led to his eventual suicide from prussic acid.

William Berry immediately took on the role of editor-in-chief, a position he would hold permanently and reflected his insistence on maintaining a personal interest in the day-to-day process of publishing a newspaper. One of his innovations at the *Sunday Times* – which he later expanded at the *Daily Telegraph* – was to broaden its content by including more articles on literary and political matters to add to the material on financial affairs, so that it could provide better competition with *The Observer*. He continued to write for the paper; his notable contributions included a despatch from the Somme in 1917. In 1919 the brothers purchased the *Financial Times* and the St Clements Press and within two years had expanded again to incorporate Kelly's Directories, the *Daily Graphic*, *The Bystander* and the *Weekly Graphic*, while assuming controlling interests in various Welsh newspapers, notably the *Western Mail*, but also the *Cardiff Weekly*, the *Merthyr Express* and the *Pontypridd Observer*. In early 1924, together with Sir Edward Iliffe, a Midlands newspaper proprietor who had been elected as Conservative MP for Tamworth the previous year, the brothers set up a new company – Allied Newspapers Ltd. This enabled them to extend their interests into regional papers, including the Manchester-based *Daily Despatch*, *Evening Chronicle*, *Sporting Chronicle*, *Sunday Chronicle*, *Empire News* and *Athletic News*.

Overall, these acquisitions set them on the way to rivalling the other major press barons. Sir William was the driving force behind the 'House of Berry' as it became known (or 'Beri-Beri' as some of the old-guard critics of the Welsh upstarts sometimes described them in private[6]). In 1924 William Berry was in his mid-forties, married to Mary Agnes ('Molly') Corns, the daughter of a wealthy family who had been educated by governesses and in America, and with whom he had four sons (all of whom went to Eton College) and four daughters. Molly was an independent character but someone William Berry always sought for advice on his various projects. With a prosperous marriage and a successful business behind him, Sir William (Lloyd George had made him a baronet in 1921) had also accumulated several properties, notably a place in Curzon Street, Mayfair and a huge Elizabethan mansion near Chertsey in Surrey. At other times in the 1920s, as well as the bachelor flat he shared with Gomer Berry in Arundel Street, off the Strand, he co-occupied a larger apartment in Whitehall Court, Westminster with Seymour and D. R. Llewellyn. Having largely discarded his Merthyr accent, 'his voice was that of an English gentleman' until 'in moments of excitement a slight Welsh lilt crept back into it'.[7] According to Lady Rhondda, who had known the Berry brothers since childhood, William Berry was 'dignified, well-groomed always, popular, shrewd, very tactful, a first-rate after-dinner speaker, a man of marked social gifts, extremely likeable, genial, smiling, kindly, enjoying life very much'.[8]

Although a Conservative, he normally kept politics at a safe distance, which did not prevent him developing close friendships with politicians, and he was a regular at the London clubs. As editor-in-chief of the *Sunday Times* he was actively involved in the paper, which he insisted should keep its focus on news and factual details and not be diverted by sensationalist content. He continued to write leader articles and would often stay at the office until the early hours to see through the production. His keen involvement in the newspaper extended to its format and layout and he was constantly thinking about improving circulation and widening the appeal of the readership, which he perceived to be informed and educated: Lakin would be a pivotal ally in his endeavours to modernize the production and broaden the range of contributors.

Gomer Berry's contribution to the brothers' press empire was largely on the business side and, particularly in the early years, the division of responsibilities between the two was regarded as the basis for their success. His passage through the newspaper industry was along the advertising and sales route. He never had the same energy for news or the aptitude for journalism as his brother and did not take as close an interest on the editorial side, though in later years, once they had gone separate ways, he did assume a stronger a role on the *Sunday Times* and a more stringent political line as a firm supporter of Neville Chamberlain's appeasement policy. Less of a convivial, charismatic personality than William Berry, he was more 'aloof', even 'shy', with a more 'impetuous' side than his brother.[9] Like his brother he had a large family of six children with his first wife (who died in 1928) and divided his time between different properties: from 1920 he was at Farnham Chase in Surrey, before moving to Wyfold Court, an Elizabethan mansion of 1,190 acres near Henley-on-Thames, and then Chandos House, Queen Anne Street in Marylebone, an eighteenth-century townhouse built by the Adam brothers.

Lady Rhondda, a prominent suffragette and editor of the groundbreaking feminist journal *Time and Tide*, wrote

very warmly about the Berrys. In her gushing account of
the brothers she had known since growing up in Merthyr,
they were 'scarcely individuals. They are a family organism.
They think alike, act alike, never argue . . . If you are dealing
with the Berrys you are never dealing with one of them, but
with all'.[10] As press magnates and business owners they were
already a powerful concern by the mid-1920s. In the future,
as their press empire expanded, the unity between William
and Gomer Berry would not last, leaving Lakin, their protégé,
with dilemmas and – at the worst point – a divided loyalty
between the two.

Lakin was relishing the opportunity the Berrys had given
him. They had introduced him to a new world and through
them he had made other important contacts. He was also
enjoying London life and was mixing in interesting social
circles, if at this time these were mainly confined to the Welsh
side. His work for the Berrys was wide-ranging and he was
able to adapt his knowledge of the law to be of some practical
use in legal actions, while he accompanied the Berrys on
business trips to Manchester and Newcastle where they held
controlling interests in regional newspapers. At one point,
William Berry suggested that Lakin might move to Newcastle
for a few months to sort out their papers, which were in a
'terrible state'. He was flattered but reluctant to relocate. 'I
didn't want to leave him – for good. I'm afraid I might get
stuck there,' he wrote to his parents.[11] In the end William's
nephew went instead.

'Being stuck' in Newcastle, even for a short period, would
have been an unwelcome distraction from his London life. He
was now living in St George's Square, Pimlico (though kept
in touch with Toc H friends) and work often extended into

congenial evening engagements. He was having 'a peak time', he told Harry and Annie, who were always eager to hear his news. To celebrate the new year of 1925 Frances Stevenson (Lloyd George's secretary and mistress) and her sister invited him and the son of Thomas Macnamara (Minister of Labour in Lloyd George's government of 1920–1922) to dinner at Bodenino's, followed by a cabaret and dance, from which he did not return home until 2.30 a.m. The following night (New Year's Eve) he was at the Chelsea Arts Ball and 'Bystander Party' at the Royal Albert Hall. 'It was the greatest show I've ever seen,' he reported back to Highlight. 'The colours were marvellous. I borrowed a costume from a Toc H lad. I don't suppose I'd get asked if I were married!'[12]

There were now strong overlaps between his social life and his work routines – Frances Stevenson's sister Muriel later became his secretary at the *Daily Telegraph* – and this brought him new connections, enticing opportunities and a full diary. His assimilation into this world also put severe strains on his relationship with Topsy and by late 1924 the engagement had been called off. Perhaps the burden of long journeys from South Wales to London was proving too difficult, or the feeling that they had grown apart once he had become immersed in his new set-up, but in any case the decision seemed to have come from his side, leaving the daughter of the Swansea press magnate upset and resentful. There were only 'hard looks' and 'bitter words', Robert Webber conveyed to him after seeing Topsy at a wedding.[13]

His work for the Berrys took him to Westminster to liaise, consult and advise on various aspects of their business interests. In March 1925 he was at the House of Commons to discuss a libel action against the *Daily Graphic* and found himself in

conversation with Mabel Russell, then only the third woman
to take a seat in the Commons. She had won a by-election at
Berwick-upon-Tweed two years earlier that had been caused
by corruption allegations against her husband's agent, who
had overspent election funds. Her husband Hilton Philipson
had been a National Liberal candidate, but following the
petition initiated by other independent Liberals she decided
to stand as a Conservative, winning the seat with a majority
greater than that won by her husband and breaking the long
period of Liberal Party dominance over the constituency.
The daughter of a travelling salesman and dressmaker from
Birmingham, she was a well-known actress and former Gaiety
Girl known for her charm and wit, and Lakin was excited
to tell his parents about her invitation for him to join her in
the Lady Members' Room for tea and the chance to listen
to the news on her 'non-aerial' set. This was his first visit to a
place he would get to know well in later years, and a time to
take in the political atmosphere a year after the first Labour
government was defeated by Stanley Baldwin's Conservatives:
'It was wonderfully good. There were two Labour members
there as tight as lords. They are blighters to go talking about
the idle rich.'[14] Shortly after, he made his first visit to 10
Downing Street to see Sir Ronald Waterhouse, Prime Minister
Stanley Baldwin's secretary, and was suitably impressed by
the surroundings.

His new opportunities at this point were facilitated entirely
through his Welsh connections. The Berrys kept him occupied
with a range of tasks. 'I suppose you didn't hear Gomer on
the wireless giving *my* speech?' he asked his parents after the
announcement of the younger Berry's plan for a new maternity
ward for the Infants Hospital in Vincent Square, Westminster,

which would be a memorial to his first wife. 'He paid me a great compliment by using every word! And there have been 14 sacks of replies to the appeal in one day!'[15] The new ward, eventually constructed at a cost of £50,000, would double the number of available cots in the hospital. In addition to drafting speeches – a skill he would later nurture and adapt through editing, journalism and broadcasting – he was now trusted sufficiently to deal with some of their business and financial interests. This included travelling to Southampton to purchase a yacht for William Berry, with the enquiries and transactions carried out in Lakin's name as various vessels were offered for prices ranging from £30,000 to £60,000. They repaid faith in him, someone they regarded as not only a young and enthusiastic aide but a protégé with real flair and ability, with tickets to the Boat Race or to see a fight at the Albert Hall (he shared William Berry's interest in boxing). More significantly, they enabled informal forms of political patronage through their Welsh entourage. His membership of the Constitutional Club in London, effectively a gentlemen's club for supporters of the Conservative Party housed in a red-and-yellow terracotta building near Trafalgar Square, was backed by two grandees of the *Western Mail*: Robert Webber and Sir William Davies, the paper's editor-in-chief and a man of sharp political insight 'who enjoyed the confidence and friendship of leaders of Welsh life'.[16] D. R. Llewellyn, the South Wales coal owner and close associate of Seymour Berry, was another industrialist with influence in those circles who offered Lakin advice on occasion.

Back in Barry, his parents were always pleased to hear his news and proud of the life he was making for himself in London. He still wrote home regularly, reassuring them that he was 'A1', and constantly reminding them that keeping in touch would be easier if they had a telephone put in. Annie was still active in the Conservative Association and would sometimes combine visits to London with those commitments. At other times his parents would come for a long weekend, with Harry sometimes escaping to Sandown Park for a day's racing. In 1925 Lakin had to have another operation on his nose, and his parents stayed in London while this was successfully concluded. His mother still held concerns about his general health and warned him about overwork.

Some weekends Lakin would take the Friday night train to South Wales and his brothers would meet him at the station and drive back to Highlight. Things were not going well at the farm, however, and they had difficulty making it into a sustainable concern, leaving them short of ready cash. He did his best to help but by early 1925, while hoping the lambs would bring in some useful income, he concluded that it might be time for them to sell: 'I think it is a rotten business not having any money handy. Chuck it if you can get a decent price for the farm.' He thought it would be 'fairly easy' to get a farm 'somewhere near London', but was aware that they would be 'coming away from everybody you know'. By early summer they had the farm on the market for £9,000, with discounted advertisements in the *Sunday Times* and *Western Mail*. 'We'll soon find a topping little place for you + will all live happily ever after,' he cheerily ended his weekly message.[17]

His own circumstances were prospering as usual. He was popular at work and among women friends, hinting to his parents that now he was over thirty it might be time to get married. During the summer of 1925 he had been 'going strong' with 'Jenny' but things had changed after a holiday in

France. Travelling with his old schoolfriend Frank Webber, they were about to join the train in Paris on their return to London when they noticed a minor kerfuffle among a group of distinguished-looking dignitaries who were boarding the train further down. It transpired that it was the exiled King George II of Greece, surrounded by his entourage and porters. Their attempts to hoist their luggage into the carriages had been temporarily disrupted by two young women who had pushed in front. After Lakin and Webber had finally got on the train they found themselves in the same carriage as one of the women. 'Do you know who they were?' Lakin asked her, before revealing the news of their fellow passengers. As his daughter later recalled: 'My mother was saying goodbye to all her girlfriends when she finally sat down opposite him and started talking. They got friendly on the train . . . she must have got my father's address and after hearing no more she got hold of theatre tickets and invited him.'[18] Vera Savill 'was the best and last of "25"', Webber told his friend.[19]

By the mid-1920s all the Berry brothers were enormously wealthy, with large families and grand houses in the country as well as their central London bases, but they still had serious ambitions to expand their newspaper empire. In 1926 they bought Amalgamated Press, the largest publisher of periodicals in the world – their titles ranging from women's magazines to children's comics – from the estate of Lord Northcliffe. In doing so, they prevented his brother Lord Rothermere from acquiring it, and in December 1927 it was announced that William Berry, Gomer Berry and Sir Edward Iliffe had bought the *Daily Telegraph* from Lord Burnham. William Berry, who with his thirty-year background in the press was the prime mover behind this purchase, was committed to keeping it as a 'serious' newspaper, but at the time of the takeover it 'was thoroughly run-down. Its premises were decrepit, its presses out-of-date, its staff old and eccentric, its readers both elderly and dwindling in numbers'.[20] More capital was urgently needed.

The remaining editorial staff were worried about their jobs but change in staffing was gradual. Its editor, Arthur Watson, a solid journalist and 'punctilious teetotaller' with a liking for gardening and fast cars, was kept on, though his influence diminished once William Berry's role as editor-in-chief was made clear. Other staff were retained but the decisive change in direction was confirmed when the Berrys introduced their own people, including the printer Edward Hunter (another Welshman), W. T. Slatcher and Lakin, who was quickly perceived by his new colleagues as a flamboyant, 'good-looking young Welshman' who was 'being groomed for the editorship of the *Sunday Times*'.[21]

Lakin continued to work for the Berrys on both their main papers; in time he would occupy the unusual dual roles of being literary editor and assistant editor of both. He was the Berry's right-hand man and through him they were able to enact some of their most significant reforms, particularly on the ailing *Daily Telegraph*. Shortly after the takeover he visited the *Daily Telegraph*'s library and got chatting to its young assistant, Leonard Russell. Russell, who looked after the books sent in for review, was used to being visited by W. L. Courtney, the paper's long-standing literary editor who was well into his seventies by the time the Berrys took over. To Russell, Courtney was emblematic of the archaic environment. To him 'the place seemed to be dying', and before the Berrys assumed control he had been looking to move on. The arrival of

Lakin, a much younger man, suggested to Russell that change was in the air: 'We knew that he came from upstairs: that he was one of [William Berry's] entourage, had been called to the bar and had learnt a little journalism on the *Western Mail* of Cardiff.'[22] On his first visit, Lakin borrowed a batch of Edgar Wallace and Sydney Horler thrillers, a departure from the old tradition of selling on review copies of literary tomes to Foyles, and another sign to Russell that the old order was coming to an end.

Chapter 7

Vera: An English Marriage

Vera Savill was born in Chislehurst and brought up in nearby Elmstead, Mottingham in what was then a rural part of Kent. Her own background was quite different from the rest of the villagers and indeed from that of her future husband. Her father Frank Bertram Savill had made his wealth through a family line of Essex merchants that extended back to the mid-nineteenth century, when his father and uncle (Ebenezer and Alfred) founded the Savill Brothers Ltd brewery in Stratford, East London. This was the high tide of the Victorian breweries, which thrived on the rise of public houses, transformations in transport and the acquisition of new tastes. At the time of Vera's birth on 4 August 1900 (the same day as the future Queen Elizabeth, the Queen Mother) the brewery owned pubs throughout East London and Essex, from Bethnal Green to Chigwell, while her father also had interests in the shipping company Shaw, Savill and Albion, of which his brother Walter was a director. Her grandfather owned properties in Belgravia and occasional trips to London were cherished by Vera as she grew up in mainly rural settings; after Kent her family moved to Three Bridges, Sussex while she was still a young child.

As customary among wealthy families – including those of the nouveau riche – she was educated at home by governesses. Surrounded by three or four servants must have made for a lonely existence, particularly after Mervyn, her older brother and only sibling, was sent away to Wellington School. Her house, a large nondescript red-brick building, did not offer much in the way of diversions, and any aspirations to pursue artistic or intellectual interests were constrained by the lack of support from parents together with the limited expectations placed upon young women of that class. Her aspirations went beyond finding a good marriage; like her brother she was 'bookish' and interested in literature, though without anybody available to nurture those passions. The main leisure pursuits of her father outside business were mainly confined to sport, which meant he and his family were frequent spectators during the flat-racing season at Ascot and Windsor, sometimes taking their daughter along.

At sixteen Vera moved to London, living initially at the plush family residence in Belgravia. This transfer from country to town was a blessing in many ways, though the opportunity to enjoy many of its freedoms and benefits arrived earlier than she could have anticipated. The passion for racing had brought its costs for the Savills, and her father, along with Mervyn and Vera herself, lost a significant amount of money betting on horses, which left them in debt to the bookmakers for some years after. This necessitated a change in plans for their daughter, and instead of being prepared for a debutante's ball Vera found herself looking for work in order to help pay off outstanding monies. Initially, she helped out at Margaret

Usmar's antique shop in St James's before being taken on as an assistant at the Mary Manners hat shop in Bruton Street, off Bond Street, in Mayfair.

Mary Manners was owned by Judy Watts, who would become a firm friend, part-mentor and confidante of the younger woman. She was in the process of extricating herself from an unhappy marriage to Colonel Humphrey Watts, a rich Manchester industrialist whose textile firm, S. and J. Watts, had been founded in 1798 by his great grandfather, a former farmer and weaver. After his father moved the firm to Portland Street, in the centre of Manchester, he entertained royalty and other distinguished guests at Abney Hall, a Victorian Gothic mansion that would later be used in several TV dramas. When Judy Watts first married him, they resided in Cheadle Hulme, then a tiny Cheshire village, where she had two children, before Humphrey Watts bought Haslington Hall, an Elizabethan mansion built on the construction of a former medieval manor house, after the First World War. Used by the Wattses as a country home, it was an imposing residence distinguished by its timber-framed design decorated with herringbone, a brick exterior and a slate roof, and extended over two storeys and across six bays. However, it was a long way from the social life of London's West End that Judy Watts had got to know in the First World War.

Born in Edgbaston, Birmingham, Gladys Mary Parkes ('Judy' came later) was the daughter of Sir Edward Ebenezer Parkes, a Conservative MP. The son of an ironmaster from the Black Country who had made his way up from the workshop, Ebenezer Parkes was another businessman-turned-politician who had followed Joseph Chamberlain on his route to Liberal Unionism and opposition to Home Rule. Rising through

Birmingham municipal politics and a close confidante of Chamberlain, he was elected Liberal MP for Birmingham Central in 1895, taking the Conservative whip in 1912. Knighted in 1916, he did not seek re-election in 1918, the year before his death. By this time, his daughter had had two daughters with Humphrey Watts, whom she married in her early twenties. Both daughters had distinguished lives ahead of them: Eleanor Watts, later a friend of Evelyn Waugh, was an artist, patron and socialite; her second daughter, as Felicity Peake, would be air commandant, founding director of the Women's Royal Airforce and the last director of the Women's Auxiliary Air Force. Her nephew James Watts would briefly become a Conservative MP, while the novelist Agatha Christie was a relative on her husband's side.

Once the First World War was under way, Humphrey Watts joined up and went to France with the Cheshire Regiment while his wife, accompanied by her young daughters and their nursemaid, moved to London to help with the war effort. She took up a role as an official driver and enjoyed what was stimulating, if demanding, work transporting senior military men, while 'her beauty and attractiveness fluttered the heart of many a Staff Officer', as her daughter recalled.[1] During this period, she and her daughters moved several times, from Blackheath to Victoria and finally settling in Chelsea. After the war finished, Judy Watts could not face returning to Cheshire and a life of domesticity. She and her husband had 'drifted apart', while she had found many new friends and more independence in London. Anxious to 'do something' with her eye for fashion and design, she learnt millinery and set up her own hat-making business, initially in the Piccadilly Arcade, then another bigger site in nearby

St James's Street, and finally the larger premises at 25 Bruton Street. As well as the hat shop, she also established a millinery business, Chenarre Soeurs, which quickly prospered.[2]

Leaving the family home to start up a business was a radical step at the time, though her choice to lead a more independent life illustrated the predicaments as well as new opportunities facing women in the years after the First World War. Judy Watts, a 'very elegant, enterprising woman',[3] did not have a rebellious urge to shake up the system or experiment in a new kind of living. She was not a modernist poet or a Bloomsbury aesthete, did not hold forceful political opinions or aspire to literary success. But her mild bohemianism and desire to live off her initiative and enterprise in its own way matched those ambitions – to 'have a shop of one's own' – and reflected a wider change within middle-class women at that time, particularly in London. For Vera Savill, her friend and assistant, she was the ideal mentor: an older woman who had seen more of life and was determined to live freely and to follow her passion for creating elegance and style. In the shop, Vera learnt from Judy Watts more about the fashion world and effective sales techniques, and met some influential customers – Mary Manners provided hats for Buckingham Palace among other clients. She picked up practical tips and technical skills for how to cut and fit a felt hat on the heads of rich ladies while not making any slip with the scissors. One thing she did not take from Judy Watts was the latter's adherence to Christian Science beliefs, which were popular among upper middle-class women of that generation. Vera remained sceptical of religion – as she would be about politics – and her independence of thought was not influenced by the convictions that individuals left alone with God are responsible for their well-being.

By then Vera was living in Earls Court Square, Kensington with her brother Mervyn. Despite Mervyn being away at school for much of her childhood they had remained close, with Vera often coming to the aid of her difficult and demanding sibling. Mervyn Savill wished he had gone to university (the change in family finances had prohibited it) to study modern languages and literature, for which he displayed an evident talent. His reluctance to work did not diminish his lifestyle, which he maintained by constantly securing loans from friends and family, and as a result he attained a growing reputation for being a spendthrift: 'Mervyn was brilliant at languages and brilliant at spending other people's money.'⁴ With homosexuality banned (though prevalent within bohemian circles), his private desires also came at a price. Vera, however, invariably came to his defence and, valuing their independence from relatives, they cohabited happily enough, enjoying games of Scrabble, with Vera bailing him out of difficulties when necessary.

This changed after Vera's chance meeting with Cyril Lakin in that summer of 1925. After their introduction on the train in France they met shortly after in London and the relationship soon blossomed. By January 1926 *Western Mail* readers were informed of Lakin's second engagement, to 'Miss Vera Savill, only daughter of Mr and Mrs F. B. Savill of 11 King Street, St James's, London.'⁵ Following their engagement Vera moved to Lakin's new flat in Pimlico (he had recently taken a bigger residence within the same square) in preparation for their wedding. She was aware that he had had several girlfriends (some of whom continued to pursue him after his engagement), and that he was a young man 'on the up' and in a hurry to get somewhere. The stark difference in their backgrounds – Vera, the privileged daughter of a rich merchant, Lakin the son of a butcher – was never an issue between them. Her own family situation had changed – in 1925 the Savills sold the brewery to Charrington – and she valued her own freedoms that had been partly necessitated by circumstances. From a wealthy background where she wanted for nothing, she now set out to recast herself as a modern, independent middle-class woman capable of making her own choices in life. After all, Judy Watts, who became a close friend, had shown the way. Vera knew that Lakin's good looks and charm made him attractive to other women but also realized that he was looking to settle down and that she could bring more order to his life.

The effect of the relationship on Lakin was profound. Until this point, and even allowing for Oxford and service in the war, most of his friends and acquaintances were Welsh. His rapid rise was made possible through his connections with a list of influential and wealthy Welsh newspapermen and public figures who had propelled him towards what looked to be a prosperous career path. But Vera gave him something different. She widened his circles and added lifestyle changes she thought would enhance his growing status as an editor and influential representative of Fleet Street. As a couple they dined in the West End and attended other parties with Judy Watts and her new boyfriend Stephen Phillips, while she introduced him to parts of London – Belgravia, Chelsea and Mayfair – he knew only casually. She threw out the Freemason's apron he had acquired from the Prince Llewellyn Lodge in Cardiff and encouraged him to bring guests home for cocktails; she would get the chance to extend this love of entertaining once he became a literary editor. It was not as if he needed to smarten up. Unusually for a man of that generation, he was always aware of his appearance and intent on finding the right camera angles for photographers. His good looks were enhanced by appearing much younger than his age. His engagement photographs produced by the Lafayette studios – presumably arranged with the help of Vera's family contacts – show a man ten years younger than his actual age of thirty-two. He normally wore double-breasted suits, never left the house without a hat and even took to wearing plus fours on the golf course.

Their wedding at St Michael's Church, Chester Square, Belgravia was a quiet affair ('you can bring six guests', Vera told Lakin[6]) mainly attended by family and close friends. Harry and Annie made the trip from Barry, leaving their other sons in charge of the farm. Guests included Vera's close friend Judy Watts and Stephen Phillips (who served as best man), while Frank Webber, who might have expected to be given that role, attended along with others from the Welsh newspaper world; Leonard Rees, editor of the *Sunday Times*, represented Lakin's own workplace. They held a reception at Vera's parents' house nearby, before a short honeymoon.

On their return, they started to look for larger accommodation, which became more imperative once Vera became pregnant. Their decision to rent an old farmhouse in West Wickham, Bromley, built on a Romano-British site, provided them with more space, a relatively easy journey into London and, for him, a reminder of his former home. It was an ugly building, but at least spacious enough to start a family (their daughter Bridget was born in 1927) and to entertain at weekends. For him there was golf nearby, while for Vera, who had given up her job in Mayfair after her marriage, there was the chance to pursue her passion for gardening.

Lakin's letters home, which continued to provide updates on his propitious and expanding connections, now extended to his social life. He regaled his parents with stories of new friendships, Vera's expensive taste in stockings and his performance on the golf course. Despite their different class backgrounds, Vera made an immediate impression on the Lakins. Always decked out in the latest London fashions, her smart appearance and 'drawly' voice may have cut an unusual figure around the farm, but they took to her 'terrific sense of humour' and independence of spirit. Annie, who had always kept a close eye on her son's activities, friendships and love affairs, was won over by Vera's obvious affection and care for her son. For years afterwards, Vera's rare visits to the farm would be regarded as 'high days' by the Lakins.[7] Security in his position had helped reduce uncertainty in the financial situation of his parents and brothers. Although they had not found a buyer for Highlight Farm and had by now taken it off the market, their finances had improved slightly – helped by generous loans from Lakin.

The year of their marriage had been a difficult one coming soon after the General Strike and the continuing miners' dispute had brought tensions between Welsh industrialists and trade unions, with continuing hardship for working-class families. The coal strike had wide impact. It was decisive in the intensification of the struggle between a more militant SWMF and 'the most powerful capitalist combination in the South Wales coalfield ... the Berry-Llewellyn-Rhondda group ... [whose interests] extend like red threads through the mesh of capitalism in South Wales'.[8] The SWMF was from this point on the most radical and politically advanced section of the British miners, with strong communist influence and a growing internationalist outlook fuelled by their allegiances with Russian unions (who provided support during the strike), which would be revived in the 1930s in opposition to fascism. The coal owners found an ally in the South Wales Miners' Industrial Union, a 'company union' that was opposed to the political stances and the strike tactics taken by the SWMF; their positions were represented in the *Western Mail* and other Conservative papers owned by the Berrys.

Lakin viewed these developments and the hardships in Wales from a distance, as he travelled back for the odd weekend. He now had more contacts with coal owners than coal tippers in Barry, and occasionally would bump into them in the first-class carriages of the Cardiff–London train. On one occasion shortly after the strike he was surprised to find D. R. Llewellyn in the dining carriage, who relayed to him the inconveniences the strike had brought for his proposed summer holiday to France. The general economic uncertainty would continue for years. Lakin's own finances were hardly stable; he often found himself overdrawn at the bank and had not yet found a way of sustaining his more affluent living, even with Vera's advice on making wise investments. This had no effect on his rapidly rising career prospects, however. His situation became more secure once the Berrys had taken over the *Daily Telegraph* and he now divided his work for them between both newspapers. This extended role and the state of his personal finances effectively ended any remaining ambitions he had to practise as a barrister, though his new job did at least enable him and Vera to take a late summer holiday to Madeira, while the Berrys occasionally invited him to accompany them on foreign trips.

The pride and enjoyment the two Berry brothers felt at the

peak of their power and influence faced a temporary setback with news of the sudden death of Seymour, Lord Buckland (after he fell off a horse on his estate). His two younger brothers were the chief mourners at the funeral procession from Brecon to Merthyr where

> The streets were so choked with mourners that the cortege could scarcely force its way through to the English congregational church in Market Square. In the chapel, only three women of special distinction were allowed to join the congregation of six hundred men and bells tolled for half an hour before the coffin was carried in by six police officers under the command of the Chief Constable.[9]

Lakin travelled back to Wales to join the mourners. Outside the Berrys' nearest family, he was now regarded as one of their closest associates in their various business ventures. By 1929 it was increasingly evident that the Berry brothers saw him as pivotal in their big plans to modernize the *Daily Telegraph*. In addition to the initial editorial changes led by William Berry in his hands-on role, they now sought to transform the building itself at 135 Fleet Street (which the paper had occupied since 1882). Designed by Charles Ernest Elcock, the new building, which opened in June 1930, had an art deco design with Egyptian decorations and a majestic colonnade façade, enhanced by the work of sculptor Samuel Rabinovitch. Inside the building, journalists and visitors were transported between floors by high-speed American-style lifts that could ascend the six floors in eight seconds. Original blue rubber floors and white Italian marble staircases greeted guests once they vacated the elevator. The imposing building was a statement of the power and influence of the Berrys as Fleet Street barons. It was, the *Daily Telegraph* declared, 'the most modern up-to-date newspaper office in the British empire'.[10] It was a symbol of the prestige the Berry brothers now exercised in Fleet Street. The canteen (where staff were served by waitresses dressed in black-and-white aprons), editorial dining room and bar were on the sixth floor, but the two owners had their own 'sumptuous' suite on the fifth floor that was complete with smoking room and dining room.

William Berry, the older of the two remaining brothers, had been the driving force of these changes and in Stanley Baldwin's honours list of 1929 was made Lord Camrose (after the village in Pembrokeshire). Back at the *Daily Telegraph*, he made his emerging protégé Cyril Lakin assistant editor and literary editor. Despite his lack of journalistic experience, in his role as assistant editor Lakin was made responsible for changing the layout of the paper, which still had its first page devoted to advertising. The need now was for extended editorial space with more leader page articles. Camrose's faith in Lakin's willingness and ability to carry out his directions was because he knew that 'he had flair, though not as a writer, and that he knew the way that he [Camrose] wanted things done'.[11] Lakin was given his own office on the eastern end of the first floor next to Arthur Watson, the editor. Making his way along the corridors 'decked out with oak panelling, antique bronze, wall lights', he now considered the best ways of modernizing the style of the paper itself. The range of content and balance given to news and opinion needed reviewing, while another pressing concern was to alter the typeset and format of the newspaper. More news was needed, as was a breadth and depth of material that would meet Camrose's ambition of producing news content that surpassed all his rivals. Lakin introduced a magazine-style design for the leader pages in a similar layout to the one then used by the *Daily Mail*, though the content differed in subject and tone. Lakin agreed with Camrose and Watson that readers did not want 'propaganda' but serious content backed up with moderate politics based on sound principles. These were the ideals on which he later launched his political career.

The aim was to be a smaller paper, modern and attractive in style, cheaper in price but richer in content. To modernize the design of the newspaper he needed to know more about different typefaces. To this end he and Leonard Russell, the young library clerk whom Lakin had taken on as his new assistant, spent two weekends reading up on the different type and type sizes from a manual that had just been produced for the *Daily Telegraph* by the son of the editor of the *Daily Express*. As a result of his and others' endeavours, fifty-two Linotype machines and five new presses were brought in, which would soon be able to print the *Sunday Times* as well as the *Daily Telegraph*. By February 1930 the *Daily Telegraph* was a broadsheet paper (comprising a twenty-four-page newspaper and a thirty-two-page supplement) with the machinery capable of printing 40,000 copies every hour, and was technically well ahead of its rivals. These changes were all part of a concerted drive by Camrose to increase circulation and appeal to a broader and well-informed readership. Initially a newspaper with circulation figures of under 100,000 upon takeover, the results of these modernization measures would exceed even the ambitions of its owners, with figures of 300,000 in 1932 and 750,000 by the end of the decade.

Leonard Russell, who would later succeed Lakin as literary

editor of the *Sunday Times*, had a warm affection for his boss and, along with other colleagues, saw him as 'very much the crown prince'. He 'had winning ways, and was handsome, like a milder version of Basil Rathbone as Sherlock Holmes'. Even at that early stage, in the opinion of Russell and others, Lakin was 'the unspoken editor-elect' – the only question seemed to be, for which of the two newspapers. Camrose, who had taken him on as his assistant knowing full well that he held only limited experience on a newspaper, 'was impressed and doubtless more than ever convinced, without finally making up his mind, that the young man whom he had promoted from his private office was going places, either at *The Telegraph* or (more likely) *The Sunday Times*'.[12]

Russell, as a young aspirant journalist himself, was in awe of his new boss; he admired his style and panache, and once the Lakins rented a weekend cottage in Edenbridge in Sussex (conveniently situated next to Holtye Golf Course) he would occasionally join them. He enjoyed Vera's hospitality, where he was served cocktails, foie gras on toast and good champagne. He recognized Lakin's journalistic ambition and the adrenalin that came from being a busy, sought-after person of importance in the Berrys' new empire, but this had not 'precluded him having a life of his own . . . He wouldn't for a moment have thought of giving up his cherished family life for a great social success.'[13] Vera was crucial to his life and work. She understood that he would never fully recover from his near-fatal bout of malaria during the war and that he often needed to sleep in the afternoon. Lakin being made literary editor was a pleasing development for her too; she had a keen interest in literature, while her capacity for entertaining was encouraged through an allowance provided by the newspaper so that writers and editors could mingle. That would have to be done back in London, however, as Lakin had not listened to Vera's advice to sell shares and they lost investments in the Wall Street Crash of 1929. This necessitated a move to Garden Court in Middle Temple where, as a barrister in name, he was entitled to live at a moderate cost. At least it was a short walk to Fleet Street.

Chapter 8

Fleet Street Editor

Cyril Lakin was now able to enjoy the main advantage handed to him as the protégé of the Berry brothers: the relatively free reign he had in introducing ideas and innovations to two different national newspapers. He had first made his mark modernizing the *Daily Telegraph*'s layout and by rebalancing its content. Now, in his role as literary editor, he took this a stage further by bringing in a host of new writers, including younger contributors, and more women to review for the expanding book pages; this was his skill. On his own admission he was not a writer; his attributes were as talent-spotter, catalyst of new projects and a sympathetic editor able to get the best out of his authors and reviewers. In the past he had been successful in cultivating contacts with people of influence and he now brought this to his editing work, emboldened by the freedom and resources at his disposal. He could not have picked a more exciting time to be a literary editor, arriving on the cusp of a new era that would be defined by an influential generation of writers who questioned orthodoxies and literary conventions. At the same time, as the literary editor of two leading national newspapers, he had to balance the very different challenges brought by the 'middlebrow' book clubs, the rise of the 'star reviewer' and the emergence of a left-wing cohort more outspoken and less observant of existing rules. Lakin's ability was to spot and encourage new talent while retaining good relations with those from older and more conservative traditions. It put him at the centre of the literary world, with access to writers, book presentations and dinners, while as an influential editor he was targeted by publishers and prospective authors.

His first significant recruit to the *Daily Telegraph* was Howard Marshall, then a twenty-nine-year-old trainee BBC announcer. In June 1929 Marshall had been employed on a temporary contract in the BBC's news section at its first base in Savoy Hill, before moving to its Talks department later that year where part of his role was to produce material for the new BBC publications *The Listener* and the *Radio Times*.[1] It was probably in these circles that Lakin first met Marshall and it is not difficult to see the younger man's appeal: he was fluent, energetic, scholarly and full of ideas and suggestions, which, as a keen sportsman, included offering himself as an 'eyewitness' reporter at rugby matches. In the future Marshall would be one of the BBC's most sought-after voices, presenting a range of programmes on sport, current affairs and politics. His 'liquid, gravelly voice' made him a natural on the airwaves and he was the first recognisable BBC cricket commentator. Later, he would be its Director of War Reporting and a regular host of state and royal broadcasts. At the *Daily Telegraph* he became its main cricket and rugby correspondent, though to begin with Lakin (utilizing his dual role as assistant and literary editor) gave him a wider portfolio that included regular contributions to the 'Books of the Day' column.

Marshall's first effort in September 1930 did not reach the heights of later columns, though its subject, Lord Askwith's biography of the Anglo-Welsh Liberal Unionist, Lord James of Hereford, may have struck a chord with his editor. By December, Marshall was reviewing books of his own interest, among them a Christmas selection of 'Books for Boys' that included adventure stories, pantomimes and storybooks. Reviewing the 'Novels of the Year' at the end of that month, he warned readers against authors who had become 'absorbed by intellectual theories and experiments which have no contact with the natural flow of ordinary life'. Admiring the large number of talented writers who had come to prominence, Marshall noted the move away from 'false sentimentality' to 'barren reason', and looked forward to a 'mean where we shall find less arrogant pessimism and more humility, less cold thought and more genuine feeling; less cleverness and more experience of life'.[2] This emphasis on the 'experience of life' was a feature of Marshall's writing beyond the reviews and the rugby reporting, and resulted in his book *Slum*, an account of rising poverty and inequality during the depression that reflected his mild socialist views and strong social conscience.

Marshall was convivial company and remained a close friend of Lakin long after he had moved on to bigger things as the BBC's cricket commentator. One of their joint initiatives was to launch the Junior Book Club at the end of 1932. This was a cause close to the heart of Marshall, while Vera took a strong personal interest in the scheme, acting as its literary secretary. Lakin and Marshall brought in the Reverend

Dick Sheppard, C. A. Alington (headmaster of Eton), A. E. Henshall (president of the National Union of Teachers) and Lady Baden-Powell to front the project, with prominent advertisements appearing in the *Daily Telegraph* and the *Sunday Times*. By comparison with some of the other book clubs that had grown in recent years, the sponsors took a more cautious and paternalistic approach in hoping that the Junior Book Club

> will be welcomed by all thoughtful parents. It is unnecessary to stress the influence books may have for good or evil upon the youthful mind, and in these days of rapidly changing values it is particularly important that children should be wisely guarded in their reading ... The Junior Book Club lifts this task of selection from the shoulders of the perplexed parent. It will select, out of all the new books published each month, the 'book of the month' for boys and girls between the ages of 7 and 15.

Marshall's moderate tone was one that Lakin sought to balance with more radical recruitment to the book pages. Throughout his time as literary editor, his selection of writing talent incorporated traditional essayists, several women writers, left-wing poets and intellectuals, as well as 'middlebrow' authors. Marshall's Tuesday 'New Fiction' reviews co-existed for a while alongside the likes of S. P. B. Mais, an author of travel books and guides, but more exciting contributors were on the way. Lakin's biggest scoop was in 1931 when he enlisted Rebecca West, proudly described ahead of her first contribution 'as the most brilliant woman literary critic of our day'.[3] It is not clear when he first met West – who would be another good friend – but it is quite possible that they had been introduced through Lady Rhondda, who had published

West (as well as Winifred Holtby, another Lakin reviewer) in her feminist magazine *Time and Tide*.

West made a big impact at the *Daily Telegraph*. Already established as a journalist, critic and writer as well as a leading proponent of feminist causes, her regular Friday reviews spanned a vast range of topics and genres, from biography and history to fiction and travel writing. Her eloquent, assertive, uncompromising style was admired for its depth of knowledge and lucid expression while at the same she did not suffer fools or avoid contentious or controversial subjects. (Her antipathy towards the 'pretentious' Bloomsbury Group was reciprocated in Virginia Woolf's snobbish disdain for what she saw as West's search for middle-class respectability.[4]) Her trenchant criticism was apparent in her very first column when, in reviewing another French novel, she dismissed André Gide, then the most prominent French author and future Nobel Prize winner, as 'obsessed by horrid little boys and by the mentally afflicted to such a degree that he has taken to issuing books which consist simply of paragraphs of criminal children and lunatics'.[5]

In early 1932 her attention switched to the threat posed by the spectre of totalitarianism, notably in the Soviet Union. Aldous Huxley's *Brave New World* – a dystopian satire that anticipated aspects of state domination later portrayed in George Orwell's *Nineteen Eighty-Four* – resonated with what West perceived was the kind of society Bolsheviks and others sought to establish. A society where 'emotional and intellectual life is entirely flattened out, so that the state which supplies the material needs of the citizens shall run with a triumphant smoothness, as it is intended by Bolshevist Russia. If the individual is drowned, at least he is drowned in a bath of communist happiness'. She compared Huxley's book with Dostoevsky's poem 'The Grand Inquisitor' in his novel *The Brothers Karamazov*, describing it as 'almost certainly one of the half-dozen most important books that have been published since the war'.[6]

The following month, in 'What Can Mrs Sidney Webb Mean by This?', she took issue with *Nine Women*, a history of women in the era of the French Revolution whose author was Galina Serebryakova, wife of the Soviet ambassador Grigori Sokolnikov. Noting its lack of historical knowledge, West denounced the book as 'propagandist literature' and questioned the wisdom of Beatrice Webb, Fabian social reformer and late convert to Soviet communism, in agreeing to provide the preface. Serebryakova wrote a long, indignant reply to West in the *Daily Telegraph*, refuting the charges of historical inaccuracy, prompting a further riposte from West. Later, after the Soviet purges, Serebryakova would spend years in the Gulag while her husband, forced under interrogation to denounce Nikolai Bukharin and admit to conspiring against Stalin, was murdered by the NKVD (forerunner to the KGB) in 1939.[7]

West's range of subjects was vast – sometimes reviewing six or seven books in a column – and her criticism unrestrained by allegiances, orthodoxies or personal loyalties. T. S. Eliot was a 'sham classicist' who had had a 'pernicious' effect on English literature;[8] J. B. Priestley's novel *Faraway* was 'simple . . . even dull [and] extraordinarily predictable'.[9] Her passions were evident too, not only among her Christmas recommendations (which included arts and crafts, original reflections on the genres of travel and biography, together with Dickens, Freud and Blake) but also in the space she gave for new writing and, particularly, women writers. These were mainly novelists but also included Vera Brittain's memoir of the First World War and Lady Rhondda's account of her early upbringing in Merthyr. With encouragement from her editor, West's feminism extended beyond her review page into a feature article ('Why need wives be denied the right to earn?') in which she denounced the attempts by governments, employers and unions to stop married women from working during the Depression.

Rebecca West had a profound influence on Lakin and was crucial to his objective of broadening the appeal of the *Daily Telegraph*, which was still conservative in much of its outlook. A radical writer and by now an authoritative voice in prominent literary circles, she relished the freedom ascribed to her in the pages of the newspaper. 'God knows you need me, you little bunch of simpletons,' she teased Lakin, 'not only to teach you about literature but about life.' No doubt Lakin was partly in awe of her, but at the same time understood the importance of nurturing the talent he now had at his disposal. And she recognized this quality in him: he was 'the wisest boss I've ever had except you,' she told Irita Van Doren, her editor at the *Herald Tribune*.[10] She was also attracted to him. The former lover of H. G. Wells and Lord Beaverbrook, she had recently married Henry Andrews, a banker, apparently out of a need for some security, though she had retained her independence and the confidence in her own sexuality. A regular at Vera's informal literary dinners and get-togethers for reviewers, she gently chided Lakin for the conventionality of his family life. 'She was in hot pursuit and was obviously in love with him,' his daughter recalled.[11]

After his pivotal role in the relaunch of the *Daily Telegraph*

Lakin was called on to do a similar job at the *Sunday Times*, where the books pages had been in decline for some years. This was in 1933, shortly after the death of Leonard Rees, the *Sunday Times*'s long-standing editor. It meant that Lakin, as a direct consequence of the power and patronage of the Welsh press barons, was in the unique position of being assistant editor and literary editor of both newspapers. He took with him Leonard Russell, his assistant, leaving the latter with the clear impression that Lakin expected to be named as long-term successor to Rees as *Sunday Times* editor, while Russell would become its literary editor. W. W. Hadley, the former editor of the *Merthyr Times* who had given Lord Camrose his first journalistic job, was handed editorial duties in the aftermath of Rees's death. He was sixty-six, of short stature and – complete with trilby and umbrella – had the manner and appearance of a civil servant. A man of limited journalistic experience whose horizons were mainly confined to close observance of day-to-day politics, he contrasted unfavourably with the much younger, flamboyant protégé of Camrose.

As the *Sunday Times* had now moved from the Strand to occupy the fourth floor of the same Fleet Street building as the *Daily Telegraph* (with access to its vast resources), switching between roles was not as challenging as it could have been for Lakin and Russell. Russell held a lot of affection for Lakin, who had taken him from a nondescript role in the basement library to a literary milieu of authors and reviewers – a journey that would eventually culminate in him realising his own literary ambitions. His loyalty to his boss extended to tolerating the latter's 'disdain' for administration (who often left his assistant to do the 'donkey work'); Lakin had a particular reluctance to reply to letters, preferring to stuff unanswered correspondence into the drawers of his desk. 'His complete disregard for pettifogging office rules as long as it was done was a revelation to me,' Russell would later note.[12]

To Russell's relief, Lakin ended the 'big bow-wow mannerisms' that had plagued the old *Daily Telegraph* offices, and this ability to identify priorities, take decisions and smooth over difficulties, as much as harnessing new talent, was now required at the *Sunday Times*. Desmond MacCarthy and J. C. Squire, vastly experienced writers from another vintage, were the lead reviewers and were used to getting their own way. MacCarthy, Cambridge Apostle, member of the Bloomsbury Group and former literary editor of the *New Statesman*, had exasperated Leonard Rees for delivering late copy, championing Asquith against Lloyd George and expecting privileges as a result of the status he enjoyed in literary circles. Now, aware that Lakin had been appointed to make necessary changes, MacCarthy wrote to him, setting out what he expected from his editor and how he saw his role as reviewer. He asked Lakin to 'state conditions to which you wish me to conform as a contributor and I will let you know if I can adapt to this without losing interest in my work'. MacCarthy reminded Lakin that he had himself been a literary editor for six years 'so I know the difficulty of an editor's job: he has to get the best out of his contributors & maintain the balance of the paper. It is not easy. I suppose my name is of some value to the paper,' he added. On the more practical question of keeping to deadlines and word length, MacCarthy did not envisage any significant changes on his part, for

'as you know often a writer's best thoughts occur to him while writing & he cannot tell in how many sentences he will be able to pin them down. The alternative is to abandon the pursuit of them. I don't want to do that; I am getting too near the end of my life'.[13]

In the event, Lakin smoothed his ego, reassured him of his value to the paper and was soon welcoming him for drinks at Vera's literary gatherings.

J. C. Squire was another former literary editor of the *New Statesman*, though his reputation – for good and ill – had been forged on the *London Mercury* where, as editor throughout the 1920s, he managed to suppress his own disdain for modernism while publishing some of its leading exponents. His widespread influence on the literary scene riled his many critics; for them his conservatism was supplanted by 'his capacity as editorial sponsor and reputation-broker' of a generation of upcoming writers. The Bloomsbury Group nicknamed his coterie the 'Squirearchy', Virginia Woolf found him 'more repulsive than words can express, and malignant into the bargain', Lytton Strachey called him a 'little worm' and Leavis thought him a 'philistine'.[14] He was often caricatured for his eccentricity, and was satirized by Evelyn Waugh in *Decline and Fall* as 'Jack Spire of the *London Hercules*'.[15]

Despite his recent knighthood, by the time Lakin knew him at the *Sunday Times* Squire's influence had waned, and his status as literary critic was in sharp decline. He had a growing drink problem, no longer enjoyed the same respect within literary London and had dumped any traces of earlier idealism to join the January Club, a discussion group founded by Oswald Mosley and other members of his new British Union of Fascists (BUF) to cultivate support among the rich and powerful. At the *Sunday Times*, he had been marginalized by Rees to an obscure column: 'J. C. Squire's Corner'. Lakin therefore had another task of smoothing ruffled feathers while trying to coax more from his ageing colleague.

In fact, Squire was probably more important to his editor. It was through Squire that Lakin was elected to the Athenaeum, providing him with more useful contacts, a leisurely base and convivial company for the remaining years of his life. He became a regular clubman among the clergymen, diplomats, scholars, surgeons, civil servants and authors, serving at different times on its Library, General and Executive committees.[16] Lakin's ability to deal with the awkward Squire was probably helped after he had got to know Robert Lynd, by then a veteran essayist for leading weekly magazines – an ideal type of the 'successful middlebrow journalist of his day'[17] – and an old friend of Squire. The Lakins and the Lynds had met en route to Canada for an overseas press convention and started to meet socially once the Lakins had moved to Chelsea. In the mid-1930s they took on two adjoining houses in Hasker Street (living in one and letting the other) that had previously hosted an upper-class commune. They purchased the houses at a cheap price from two rich widows they had met on another journey, while at the same time agreeing to rent a holiday cottage in Kent, which brought an end to the Sussex farmhouse. These changes enabled Vera to host more literary evenings for their expanding milieu. Lynd, an Irish writer, Protestant nationalist and Sinn Fein sympathizer – as well as former literary editor of the *News Chronicle* – and his wife Sylvia, an Irish poet and novelist, were at the centre of a literary coterie in Hampstead, where they had hosted James Joyce's wedding reception.

More conciliation was required at the *Sunday Times*

after Rebecca West – 'all of a flutter' on being given another newspaper column by Lakin[18] – upset Jimmy Agate, the paper's drama critic whose first volume of *Ego*, his prolific diary series, had come under her scrutiny in the review section. Comparing the dandy-like theatre-critic-about-town with Mr Pickwick, West had referred to the apparent disjuncture between his 'facts' and the 'real world' they were supposed to inhabit. Her comments on his complicated financial affairs, in which imminent insolvency frequently co-existed with extravagant living on a nightly basis at the Café Royal and The Ivy, had to be moderated by Lakin after Camrose's intervention. As always, however, West got her way in the end.[19,20]

More careful negotiation was needed when Pelham ('Plum') Warner, the former cricketer who had spent the preceding winter in Australia as tour manager of the England team during its infamous 'bodyline' tour, objected when his review of Bruce Harris's book *Jardine Justified* failed to appear.[21] Sorting out difficulties with experienced and sometimes awkward contributors could be time-consuming but he was still able to invest time in seeking out new talent. These included bringing in several promising women writers, including Eiluned Lewis, who became a member of its editorial staff following the success of her first novel *Dew on the Grass*, a semi-autobiographical work derived from her upbringing in rural Montgomeryshire, which provided a contrast with the spurt of writing that was then emanating from the industrial heart of the Welsh mining districts. Other women writers who featured in the *Sunday Times* review pages or at the book exhibitions included two former Oxford contemporaries: Vera Brittain, whose *Testament of Youth* was one of several First World War memoirs reviewed at this time, and Dorothy L.

Sayers, the author of the Lord Peter Wimsey books, who was one of Lakin's regular *Sunday Times* writers, reviewing three or four detective stories and mysteries every week.

Beyond the reviews, Lakin was occupied with raising the profile of the newspaper to the wider public. Now working across the two main newspapers and deeply immersed in literary life, he had become more than an editor: he was a kind of literary impresario,[22] promoting authors, publicizing their work and hosting events. The *Sunday Times* book exhibitions were the original brainchild of Sir Herbert Morgan, a long-time Welsh business associate of Camrose and Gomer Berry who frequently offered them advice on advertising. Lakin took up the challenge and hosted the large gatherings for several years, inviting leading writers of the day and liaising with publishers and editors. The event became an important annual showcase and meeting point for all those involved in the book trade. After he had convinced Desmond MacCarthy to remain a reviewer, he persuaded him to open the first exhibition in 1933, held at Sutherland House, Curzon Street in Mayfair (the palatial residence of the Duke and Duchess of Marlborough). This was the first of many large audiences – 'book lovers in a queue' the paper reported – who attended for talks and to meet writers. Subsequent exhibitions were held at equally grandiose venues, including Grosvenor House on Park Lane and Dorland House, Lower Regent Street in St James's. Leading authors were invited to talk on a broad range of topics from the ubiquitous detective fiction and biography, to a session on literature and wine, to sporting subjects; Howard Marshall chaired a talk by Douglas Jardine, England's former cricket captain of its 'bodyline' tour to Australia. *Sunday Times* journalists and writer friends of Lakin (like Sylvia Lynd) took the chair for the likes of Aldous Huxley, J. B. Priestley, Dorothy L. Sayers and Stephen Spender. Away from the packed halls that greeted famous authors and visiting royalty, ambassadors, politicians and other dignitaries – 13,000 attended the 1936 exhibition – there were displays of typesetting, printing, binding and centuries-old illustrations of handwriting and illuminated manuscripts. It was an ambitious undertaking on Lakin's part with the intention of putting the *Sunday Times* at the centre of the literary world, and as such it grew in prestige, with senior politicians as well as authors opening and chairing sessions.

Notwithstanding the public attention generated by the exhibitions, it was Lakin's reviewers at the *Daily Telegraph* who continued to absorb his time as editor. By the mid-1930s Harold Nicolson, diarist and (National) Labour MP, was one of its lead reviewers, earning an annual £1,000 for turning out his Friday 'Books of the Day' appraisal of five books for three weeks a month, which he usually delivered to its offices by hand while collecting the next batch.[23] His subjects combined an assessment of leading authors with studies of the changing nature of world politics (illuminated by his visits to America) and reflections on the British government's attitude to events in Hitler's Germany.

In late 1935 Lakin made a double swoop for two writers close to their prime to review works of new fiction. In the Tuesday slot he recruited Cyril Connolly to replace James Hilton (whose *Goodbye, Mr Chips* had been published the previous year), and on Fridays Cecil Day-Lewis, one of the leading poets of the new generation, took over from the English crime writer Francis Iles. The founder of the Detection Club, Iles's 1932 novel *Before the Fact* had been adopted by

Alfred Hitchcock for his film *Suspicion*, while his earlier *Malice Aforethought* was regarded as a classic crime novel. It was the high point of detective fiction (Lakin himself was a devoted follower) and Connolly's selections of crime thrillers with a twist were particularly noticeable. The detective story had become not only a popular genre, but one through which relations between classes, the fragility of familial bonds, burning social questions and international conflicts could be examined as much as the description of character and the construction of plots. Connolly's columns, along with other *Daily Telegraph* fiction reviews of 1936, became the backdrop to *The Face on the Cutting-Room Floor*, an intricate novel published by Gollancz the following year under the pseudonym of Cameron McCabe (also the name of its leading character). The book was originally thought by some to be the work of Connolly himself, but was later found to have been written by twenty-two-year-old Ernst Bornemann, a German communist refugee from Nazism and a follower of Bertolt Brecht. Bornemann's unusual approach involved writing alternatively in the first and third person and by imposing, through an appendix, its own form of literary criticism. Bornemann played off reviews by Connolly, Iles, John Brophy and others in an interrogation of the accepted unwritten rules of detective fiction, along the way displaying a knowledge of literature, Marxist social criticism and fascist mentality that was regarded as 'boring repetition'[24] or 'too clever'[25] by contemporary reviewers (though later considered as ahead of its time).

Cecil Day-Lewis, who was himself writing detective stories under the pseudonym Nicholas Blake while reviewing new fiction for the *Daily Telegraph*, was another one cited by Bornemann. He was Lakin's best reviewer. Intriguingly,

Day-Lewis was then in his communist phase, during which time he spoke occasionally at Communist Party of Great Britain (CPGB) public gatherings, attended international writers' congresses and hosted branch meetings at his cottage in Cheltenham (where he was a schoolteacher). From late 1935 he had his post opened and his activities reported on by the police constabulary in memos to MI5, Britain's security service.[26] Their interest in him was in his status as an 'intellectual communist', though unlike his fellow left-wing poets and friends such as Stephen Spender and W. H. Auden, he was seen by MI5 as the 'most convinced and practical Party man'.[27] Yet any dogmatism that prevailed in his edited collection *Mind in Chains* – published the following year – and in his stated intention to Tom Wintringham, editor of *Left Review,* that he would produce a 'communist guide to literature', was singularly absent from his *Daily Telegraph* contributions. Here he surveyed a whole range of new writing in lucid prose and perceptive criticism, with appreciative notices for Ignazio Silone's satirical *Bread and Wine,* E. M. Delafield's *Faster! Faster!,* John Buchan's adventure *The Island of Sheep* and Graham Greene's *A Gun for Sale.* The predictability of Richmal Crompton came in for harsher treatment, while his belief that 'there can be few more striking indications of the vulgarity of our age than the cleavage between serious fiction and "entertainment" writing' also distinguished some of his less favourable reviews. His reviews of Klaus Mann's *Journey into Freedom* and Storm Jameson's *None Turn Back*, in addition to praise for the odd 'sociological' or 'realist' novel, were the occasional reminders of his left-wing beliefs.

'I think that Day Lewis is easily the best reviewer of novels

I have come across in the last few years,' Lakin wrote to Arthur Watson, editor of the *Daily Telegraph*.

> 'On the other hand, I do not know how far his communist views are going to land him. Up to the present there has been no sign of propaganda in his reviews, and I do not think there will be any as long as he writes for the *Daily Telegraph*. I have only seen one letter from a reader asking whether he and the communist writer are the same. Obviously, his communism is not of the kind which precludes him from asking or receiving more money: to us he is either worth six guineas or nothing.'[28]

At the *Sunday Times* in late 1936, Lakin had a hand in promoting the work of another talented poet of the emerging generation – and one of his fellow countrymen. After publishing his first verse in literary magazines in his late teens, by the age of twenty-two Dylan Thomas was beginning to win the admiration of notable critics. Two years earlier his first collection of poetry, *18 Poems*, had alerted the poet and literary hostess Edith Sitwell to his promise and she had recommended him to Lakin, who was initially unconvinced and 'had somehow failed to take up her imperious request to review'.[29] Now, she 'pestered' him again and this time convinced her editor that Thomas's new *Twenty-Five Poems* demonstrated more of his outstanding potential. Her review, which finally appeared on 15 November, reads as an announcement of a new talent. Praising the 'huge scale' of his 'magnificent' work and its 'superb' form, theme and structure, she described the eighth poem as the work of 'one who could produce sonnets worthy of our great heritage'. She ended her review by heaping more praise on the young Welshman: 'I could not name one poet of this, the younger generation, who shows so great a promise, and even so great an achievement.'[30]

Over subsequent weeks the review produced one of Lakin's biggest postbags and controversies in the *Sunday Times*, with indignant correspondents brought up on Victorian poetry denouncing its 'obscurantist' modernism, and even whether it should be considered serious verse at all. 'Is this poetry?' asked 'WP' of Matlock. 'If it be poetry what in the name of the muses does it mean?' Writing from the Athenaeum, Edward Vandermere Fleming, contributor to the *Poetry Review*, warned against what he saw as the growing tendency to 'worship' the 'unintelligible in poetry'. 'Miss Sitwell's poet,' he added with some condescension, 'has something to say but he has not yet learned how to say it'.[31]

The following week's letters pages ('In Defence of a New Poet') provided space for supportive comment. The poet and critic Pamela Hansford Johnson accused Thomas's critics of 'tak[ing] instant fright' and preferring to 'pounce gaily on [Sitwell] before bothering to read the poetry itself'. She pronounced Dylan Thomas, 'with the possible exception of Mr James Joyce, the greatest living master of words'. Mr Morgan of Llanelli also defended Thomas and modern poetry, which 'like modern painting, music and architecture frees itself from ornamental redundancies and "gets down to it"'. From Paris, Edith Sitwell responded to her critics with a staunch defence of Thomas: he '*is* a poet and a very fine one'. 'As for Mr Edward Vandermere Fleming,' she continued, rising to the challenge, 'I will confine myself to telling him that when Mr Thomas and I want to be taught our job by somebody who writes in the "Poetry Review" we will make the request. I would as soon ask a writer in the "Poultry Gazette" to teach me to train eagles to fly.'[32]

The correspondence in the *Sunday Times* offered more insight on Lakin's ecumenical editorial approach, in which he was keen to support writers of a new generation while at the same time keeping on board more sceptical critics steeped in earlier traditions who were attracting criticism elsewhere. In November 1936, in two articles for the *New English Weekly*, George Orwell felt the need to defend the genre of novel-writing, which he believed was in a period of rapid 'deterioration'. Orwell, who had just published his first two novels (*A Clergyman's Daughter* and *Keep the Aspidistra Flying*) picked up on a dilemma that faced Lakin in his daily work, denouncing the 'disgusting tripe that is written by the blurb reviewers' who, under pressure from big publishers, attempted to seduce readers:[33] 'Five thousand novels are published every year and Ralph Straus implores you to read all of them or would if he had all of them to review.'[34] Straus was one of Lakin's long-standing staple reviewers at the *Sunday Times* (and a fellow clubman) and his outpourings made for a contrast with Lakin's *Daily Telegraph* reviewers of that time. The latter might have partly realized Orwell's hope for 'a paper that would keep abreast of current fiction and yet refuse to sink its standards'.[35]

Lakin continued to thrive in the literary scene of the mid-1930s. There were dinners and parties at The Dorchester and Grosvenor House, book launches at Quaglino's restaurant and the Savoy, while he occasionally mixed with the BBC's *In Town Tonight* crowd. If petty rivalries characterized the diaries and letters of that time, then political partisanship was often less apparent in the relations between literary personalities. This was particularly true of Lakin, whose ability to empathize with all shades of opinion and earn respect among difficult reviewers comprised his main assets. He and Vera had become good friends of Viola Garvin, literary editor of *The Observer*, at the time when the *Sunday Times*'s circulation overtook that of its main rival. A further example of Lakin's open-minded outlook is evident in his meetings with Victor Gollancz. Encouraged by Dorothy L. Sayers (whose Lord Peter Wimsey novels were published by Gollancz from the early 1930s), Lakin struck up an acquaintance with the left-wing publisher. He lunched with Gollancz at the time when the latter was keen to promote his newly formed Left Book Club to satisfy the large numbers of socialists (so Gollancz told Lakin) who read the *Daily Telegraph*.[36]

In the mid-1930s Lakin was still the 'crown prince' in the editorial offices of the Berry newspapers and he had justifiable ambitions to eventually succeed W. W. Hadley, who had temporarily – or so it was believed – replaced Leonard Rees, the long-standing editor of the *Sunday Times*. It seemed inconceivable to Lakin that Hadley, Camrose's former boss in Merthyr and by now in his late sixties, would stay in post. Indeed, an excited Rebecca West rang to tell him that Gomer Berry had let slip at a dinner party that his own appointment as editor was imminent. Lakin was exultant at the news and that evening took Leonard Russell out to dinner at the Trocadero on Shaftesbury Avenue in the West End, where he told his assistant he would make him the new literary editor in what he imagined to be a new enlightened era for the newspaper under his editorship.[37]

Lakin never received the call from Gomer Berry and, 'looking dreadfully dejected and quoting from some source which Russell couldn't identify, muttered despairingly that it was a "six-barred, barbed-wired, spike-topped mess-up"'.[38] He feared that his big chance had gone in the prime of his life. It was not clear why Hadley continued in the role other than some enduring loyalty – one of Lord Camrose's traits – from the owners. At the end of 1936 Lakin, who up until this point had enjoyed a rapid series of promotions, was confronted with a further dilemma over his future at the newspapers. The Berry brothers – Camrose and Gomer (made Lord Kemsley from 1936) – had decided to go separate ways, partly to secure the inheritance of their respective children, with Lady Kemsley (Gomer Berry's second wife) being particularly forceful in pushing for the separation. It meant that Camrose would have full control of the *Daily Telegraph* and the *Financial Times* with Kemsley owning outright the *Sunday Times* (Sir Edward Iliffe took over Kelly's Directory). The problem for Lakin was that he was very much 'Lord Camrose's man', a protégé of the journalist-turned-press baron and the elder of the brothers. Camrose reciprocated the affection of the younger man, later describing their friendship as 'of a most intimate character' and telling Vera that 'among all the assistants I have had I never felt happier than I did with Cyril'.[39]

In the event he chose to go with Kemsley's *Sunday Times*, perhaps partly because he had not given up entirely the hope of becoming its editor, though his decision was mainly to do with the different work patterns. He still suffered from bouts of illness and tiredness and he felt that working on a weekly carried fewer demands than the stress of a daily newspaper. He continued as assistant editor and literary editor (taking Leonard Russell as his assistant) at a salary of £2,000 p.a. plus £500 expenses. It was a fateful decision with significant consequences for his future.

The end of 1936 also brought sad news from Barry. In the

years since leaving home he had remained very close to his mother, visiting regularly, offering advice and remonstrating with her to take things easy on the farm, while she was always eager to learn more about his latest accomplishments. After suffering from ill health for several years, Annie had a sudden seizure on Christmas Eve and remained ill over the festive period before suffering a final relapse on 4 January. She was sixty-four and her illnesses in recent years had been a source of worry for her eldest son. The *Western Mail* paid tribute to her work in the church and among the women's organizations of Llandaff and Barry Conservative Association.[40] The funeral at Merthyr Dyfan Cemetery on 8 January heard tributes from Lakin, Vera and Harry, with the Webbers and other local press and politicians in attendance.

Vere Street, Cadoxton. Harry Lakin's butcher's shop was
towards the top on the left.

*Credit: Photograph by H. Shirvington, courtesy of the Vale of
Glamorgan Libraries collection. Further information may be
found at https://www.peoplescollection.wales/items/1318576.*

Badges worn by family and friends of Harry Lakin during the Barry Urban District Council election in Cadoxton in 1906.
Credit: Chris Lakin.

Buttrills Hill leading to Barry County School.
Credit: Photographer unknown; image courtesy of the Vale of Glamorgan Libraries collection. Further information may be found at https://www.peoplescollection.wales/items/1620421.

Barry County School Rugby XV. Lakin is on the far end of the front row next to Frank Webber.

Credit: Chris Lakin.

Edgar Jones, Headmaster of Barry County School.
Credit: Courtesy of the Estate of Margaret Siriol Colley/
garethjones.org.

Cyril Lakin at the time of his engagement to Vera.
Credit: Cyril Henry Alfred Lakin by Lafayette
half-plate film negative, 13 February 1926
© National Portrait Gallery, London.

Fleet Street editor.
Credit: Bridget Lakin.

Cyril, Vera and Bridget Lakin in 1942.
Credit: Bridget Lakin.

**In the BBC studios presenting *Westminster and Beyond*
with Maurice Webb.**
Credit: BBC Photo Library.

Chapter 9

Appeasement: Divided Loyalties

In February 1933 Gareth Jones became one of the first foreign journalists to accompany Germany's new chancellor when he joined him on a flight from Berlin to Frankfurt, where the latter was to address a large rally during a rancid and turbulent election campaign. 'If this aeroplane should crash then the whole history of Europe would be changed,' Jones recorded in his article for the *Western Mail*, for 'a few feet away sits Adolf Hitler . . . the leader of the most volcanic nationalist awakening the world has ever seen.' Hitler, travelling with his propaganda chief Dr Joseph Goebbels – whose features reminded Jones of the 'dark, small narrow-headed, sharp Welsh type which is so often found in the Glamorgan valleys' – was still an enigma for many observers. 'How had this ordinary-looking man succeeded in becoming deified by fourteen million people?' he wondered.[1] Over the next six years, Hitler would remain an enigma for some who admired his labour camps, while others in influential positions in politics, business and the press saw his regime as a necessary bulwark against communism. For much of the British public throughout the 1930s, with the still fresh memory of the First World War, there was a belief that his regime could at least be placated or 'appeased'; that war could be avoided 'by making "reasonable" concessions to German and Italian fascists'.[2]

Gareth Jones, son of Lakin's old headmaster Edgar Jones and educated at Aberystwyth University and Trinity College, Cambridge, was a brilliant scholar and linguist whose facility for German, Russian and French, coupled with an insatiable curiosity and a righteous determination to go after the truth, brought him into the company of some of the most influential figures in international politics. Eschewing the academic career for which his scholarship had prepared him, his nose for a good story and ability to find himself in the right place at the right time during tumultuous events made him an ideal foreign correspondent. He had previously interviewed Lenin's widow and, from the vantage point of the Empire State Building, Al Smith, the governor of New York – 'one of the most vulgar, rudest, cheapest men I have ever seen'[3] – during his unsuccessful campaign to be the Democrat candidate for the 1932 presidential election. In 1934, at a flying gala he attended with Idris Morgan, a contemporary from Barry County School who was then working for Barclays Bank in Berlin, he heard Hermann Goering, Hitler's second in command, give a rallying call to thousands of supporters. Goering's core message – that Germany was a 'Nation of Aviators' and that 10,000 German bombers were on hand to deter foreign invaders – left a deep impression on Jones.

Jones was helped in his work by David Lloyd George, for whom he was employed as a foreign affairs adviser in two separate spells. Jones knew Germany well – he had visited it

every year for a decade prior to his flight with Hitler – and
he quickly saw the dangers posed by Hitler's ambitions. He
had also been aware at a very early stage of the twin threat to
Europe's peace posed by the dispute between Nazi Germany
and Stalin's Russia over the Polish corridor – a dilemma that
later resulted in the Molotov–Ribbentrop (Nazi–Soviet) Pact.
Jones's awareness of the full consequences of Stalinism – a
perceptive insight he shared with only a select few at that time,
including Rebecca West – absorbed more of his attention
from March 1933 after his first visit to Russia. His clear-
sighted attitude and persistent objection to being discouraged
from following the evidence before his eyes led him to the
Ukrainian famine. His description of it for Western readers, in
a series of groundbreaking articles under his byline, appeared
in the *Manchester Guardian* and the *Evening Standard*, helping
establish his name as a rising foreign correspondent. When his
work for Lloyd George came to an end Jones sought advice
on securing a full-time journalistic post, and after turning
down the BBC, which struck him as a 'prison' and where he
feared he might be put in charge of its Cardiff office – its poor
coverage of Wales made it 'a job I wouldn't like for the whole
world' – he took up a position on the *Western Mail*, to which
he had previously contributed as a freelancer. Among those
advising him on his journalistic career were the editorial staff
at the *Sunday Times,* and it may well have been Lakin, with
his connections, who recommended him to the Webbers in
Cardiff.

His first series of articles for the *Western Mail* in April 1933
continued to state the reality of famine while adding incisive
wider critiques of Stalinism. However, these revelations and
subsequent controversy proved too much for his editors as

well as for some left-wing intellectuals; Walter Duranty, the *New York Times* Moscow correspondent favoured by the Soviet regime, rejected his findings. At the *Western Mail*, Robert Webber now commissioned a series of articles from Jones on Wales and aspects of Welsh culture, which produced interesting and original results – on the dying artisan crafts of rural Wales and the cultural significance of the eisteddfod – while temporarily removing him from the burning international questions of the day on which he thrived.

Jones's investigations may have caused some embarrassment to Lloyd George, who enjoyed a good relationship with Maxim Litvinov, the Soviet Union's foreign affairs minister. Lloyd George had learnt much from Jones's first-hand experience of Germany and Russia and in the course of his work had introduced his young assistant – who was always following the path of a new story – to important contacts within the world of international politics. One thing Lloyd George picked up from Jones's reports from Germany was a positive view of the labour camps, which he compared to his own schemes for tackling unemployment in Britain. While Jones had some sympathy for a country he knew well and where he had many friends, he retained a realistic assessment of Germany's prospects under Hitler and its long-term implications for Europe. Lloyd George, on the other hand, seemed to swallow some of the more questionable rhetoric, while he was always open to being courted by international leaders. His visit to Germany in the autumn of 1936 – the year after Jones had been murdered by bandits in Manchukuo, which some suspected had been ordered by Stalin following his exposure of the famine – was a source of rich propaganda for the Nazi regime.

Lloyd George's guide for his meeting with Hitler was

his friend Philip Conwell-Evans, a Welsh academic close to Joachim von Ribbentrop, the German ambassador in London. Conwell-Evans was secretary of the Anglo-German Fellowship, an organization established to enable closer links with Germany and a better understanding of their objectives, but which soon began hosting exclusive parties for members of the Nazi and British political hierarchies in staunch opposition to Hitler's critics. As secretary, Conwell-Evans became the 'go-between for the regime and leading members of the British elite'.[4] A few months after his visit to Germany in autumn 1936 (by which time Hitler had defied the Treaty of Versailles and Locarno Treaties by re-occupying the Rhineland), Lloyd George wrote to one of his protégés and future biographer, William Watkin Davies – Lakin's old Oxford friend – who was himself planning a forthcoming trip:

> I am writing to Professor Conwell Evans who accompanied me to Germany and who is in close touch with the German Embassy, informing him of your desire for facilities to investigate the German achievements under Nazi rule . . . The works of reclamation and drainage of land, the housing of industrial populations outside the towns and the great national roads are certainly all well worth seeing. But I would not miss a visit to some of the great factories where new welfare conditions have been introduced.[5]

The Anglo-German Fellowship was the mildest of several pro-German organizations that veered continually towards extreme positions before, during and after the period of appeasement. Others, such as the Nordic League and the Right Club, were more explicitly – and, at times, virulently

– anti-Semitic, while their support was largely contained within elite groups of parliamentarians and businessmen. Fascism on British streets was largely the product of Oswald Mosley's BUF, though its support had waned by 1936; the strength of its appeal was at its height at the large Olympia rally in 1934, which had ended in violence amid clashes with counter protesters. During his last months at the *Daily Telegraph* Lakin experienced the venom of the BUF when he and other editorial staff had to prepare a response to the accusation that their boss and editor-in-chief, Lord Camrose, was a 'Jewish international financier' disloyal to the crown whose newspaper conspired against the patriotic interests of the country. This claim was made in April 1936 in an article for the BUF's *Action* newspaper by John Beckett, its editor and head of publicity. Camrose was enraged by the accusation together with its erroneous assertion of a Jewish heritage and was particularly indignant at the claims that he was unpatriotic and that his newspaper, which he had transformed and nurtured into what he believed to be a balanced, curious, quality broadsheet, was publishing anti-British material. Lakin shared Camrose's values and his patriotism, and during the long-drawn-out eighteen-month saga of the legal dispute had accompanied him to Buckingham Palace for private meetings with the King and his people to reach an agreement on the press handling of the new royal family following the abdication crisis. (Ironically, one of Beckett's other legal cases had followed his arrest outside Buckingham Palace for disorderly behaviour when protesting the forced abdication of Edward VIII, a pro-German advocate.)

By the time the case came to trial in October 1937 Beckett, a former Labour MP and one-time election agent to Clement

Attlee, had left the BUF along with William Joyce, another of its leading members (and the future Lord Haw-Haw), after they had fallen out with Mosley. Earlier that year the two had founded the National Socialist League as a rival to the BUF. In court, Camrose set out his objection to the article:

> It conveys to the ordinary man, any ordinary reasonable man reading it, first that I am a Jewish international financier with no loyalty to the state, no sense of patriotism, and that in my conduct of the *Daily Telegraph* I was prepared to allow, and did allow, my duty to the public and the country to be subordinated to my personal financial interests and the interests of business associates who, like me, paid no regard to the interests of the country – paid no regard to interests other than our own selfish interests.
>
> Then he says that it also means that I will allow the policy of the *Daily Telegraph* to be dictated by persons who were indifferent to the interests of the country and consider their own financial advantage only and if it means that I am one of the class of such persons and that in the conduct of the *Daily Telegraph*, I pay no regard at all to truth, and that I have deliberately published lies.[6]

Representing himself, Beckett, who, it transpired later, had Jewish ancestry,[7] accepted that he had been misinformed that Camrose was Jewish – 'if I may say so he is an obvious Welshman'[8] as he put it – but continued to insist that the *Daily Telegraph* was part of an organized campaign by the press lords to target those of the fascist persuasion. His defence was unconvincing and he was subsequently found by the jury to have defamed Camrose; he, his former paper and its publisher were ordered to pay damages of £20,000, made up of £12,500 to Camrose and £7,500 to the *Daily Telegraph*, plus costs. Apart from the libel involved, there was no evidence that the *Daily Telegraph* held specific grievances or a grudge against the BUF. As Camrose suggested in his evidence, their view was that the BUF no longer commanded much public support and its events were therefore less newsworthy (though it had previously reported on another Beckett libel case).

By this time the *Daily Mail*, which in 1934 had welcomed the BUF in its 'Hurrah for the Blackshirts' headline, had relinquished its overt support for Mosley, but Lord Rothermere and others continued to hold sympathy for the regimes in Germany and Italy. Others like *The Times* were, in 1937, already moving towards the position of appeasement. 'I do my utmost, night after night, to keep out of the paper anything that might hurt their [the Germans'] sensibilities [and include] little things which are intended to soothe them,' editor Geoffrey Dawson confided to Lord Halifax (who would become Foreign Secretary the following year).[9] Camrose's *Daily Telegraph*, while cautiously welcoming the arrival of Neville Chamberlain – the son of Harry Lakin's hero – when he replaced Stanley Baldwin that year, remained sceptical of German ambitions after it had re-occupied the Rhineland in defiance of the Treaty of Versailles and the Locarno Treaties.

Lakin was still scarred by the First World War, while the need to avert another remained utmost in his mind, as it did for many of his generation. Nevertheless, he was now, as assistant editor at Kemsley's *Sunday Times*, in the difficult situation of having to adhere to a position that seemed increasingly implausible to his better judgement as the events of 1938 unfolded. Kemsley, from the time he assumed sole ownership of the *Sunday Times*, had been clear that Britain's main enemy was communism and that an arrangement with Hitler was acceptable if it halted the ambitions of the Soviet Union. From the outset he established a strong relationship with Chamberlain that was sustained through weekly meetings between W. W. Hadley and the British prime minister at 10 Downing Street. Hadley, his reliable servant of limited talent, independent outlook and strength for the political battles of the newsroom, remained impeccably loyal to both Chamberlain and Kemsley and dutifully related back to his boss the latest concerns of the prime minister. These reports were often misplaced, overly deferential and naively optimistic. In early February 1938 Hadley told Kemsley that relations between Chamberlain and Foreign Secretary Anthony Eden remained good despite widespread press reports of a rift between them. Dissident voices in the *Sunday Times* offices raised objection and over the following days newspapers continued to carry stories of the disagreement over foreign policy between the two senior members of the government. After another exchange of notes between Hadley and Chamberlain, on 13 February the *Sunday Times* published a full denial of any friction in a leading article 'by our political correspondent'. Entitled 'Political Canard. Premier and Mr Eden in Complete Agreement', it claimed the paper had been informed by 'the highest authority [i.e. Chamberlain himself]' that 'there was not a word of truth in all this'.[10]

Within a week, Anthony Eden had resigned as Foreign Secretary citing irreconcilable differences on the international situation, most notably Chamberlain's attempts to reach an agreement with Italy (by then already in support of Germany) after it had left the League of Nations. It had meant that it was impossible for them to continue working together. In Cabinet, Eden had supported strengthening links with the United States following the Roosevelt initiative aimed at building international cooperation on worldwide disarmament, while opposing further deals with the dictators. Eden was unhappy with Chamberlain's pursuit of an Anglo-Italian agreement and his apparent endorsement of its conquest of Abyssinia, which followed previous reservations over Italy's robust support of the nationalist side in the Spanish Civil War. In the House of Commons debate that followed Eden's resignation, Winston Churchill, still in the 'wilderness', came to the former Foreign Secretary's defence while offering a prescient warning to Chamberlain, asking: 'Is the new policy – I hope we shall hear more about it – to come to terms with the totalitarian Powers in the hope that by great and far-reaching acts of submission, not merely in sentiment and pride, but in material factors, peace may be preserved?'[11]

Back at the *Sunday Times* Lakin was uneasy and frustrated at the situation at the newspaper. Friends on the staff, including Alexander Werth, its foreign correspondent in Paris, and Sir John Keane, its Dublin correspondent, had made clear their concerns and support for Eden's position. Lakin was also sympathetic to Eden, whose brand of Conservatism he much admired. He took steps to broaden Kemsley's circle of advisers by introducing Sir Robert Vansittart, a strong opponent of Nazism and the drift towards appeasement before Chamberlain had removed him from his post as Permanent Under-Secretary at the Foreign Office. Three months before, Lakin had welcomed Winston Churchill (still in relative political obscurity) to open the *Sunday Times* book exhibition, and he now started to mix with other Tory reformers like

Henry Longhurst. It was at this point (according to Leonard Russell) that his disillusionment with the *Sunday Times* set in and he started to consider a political career himself.

Eden's resignation evoked some sympathy among the population and much criticism of Chamberlain from liberal anti-fascist opinion, even if, at this point, Lakin still retained some faith in the prime minister. Through the course of his work he had often got to know leading politicians, among them Austen Chamberlain, Neville's half-brother. While still at the *Daily Telegraph*, Lakin had persuaded him to write a leading article on the Anglo-Irish Treaty, in which the latter had been a participant more than a decade earlier. Austen Chamberlain, a former Conservative Party leader and Foreign Secretary in Baldwin's government, had also helped negotiate the Locarno Treaties, aimed at preventing war between Germany and its European neighbours through the implementation of a new territorial settlement. Now reflecting on his role in the Anglo-Irish Treaty, which had 'dragged on for weeks', he recalled that it was hard bargaining and the prospect of 'ruin' that won over reluctant Irish delegates in the end.[12] Until his death eighteen months before the Munich Agreement, Austen Chamberlain had maintained a strong anti-appeasement position drawn from this experience, which may have resonated with Lakin once the weaknesses of the government's position became apparent. The government's attempts to placate Germany by encouraging that country's colonial aspirations when its real ambitions were in Austria and Czechoslovakia were failing. Germany's annexation of Austria in March was regarded as inevitable by some, while the attitude towards Czechoslovakia and its Sudeten German population only perpetuated the ambiguity over the British government's position.

These dilemmas continued throughout 1938, but after Chamberlain's protracted discussions with Hitler and Mussolini over a series of meetings in Munich in the autumn, the relief at reaching agreement – 'peace for our time' as the British prime minister announced at a rainswept Heston Aerodrome on his return – was evident around the country, and it seemingly had the support of public opinion. This extended to Wales where, in Cardiff, exuberance at Chamberlain's diplomacy even extended to parading the swastika over City Hall on the orders of Oliver Cuthbert Purnell, the lord mayor, who thought it would 'symbolise the joy of the Welsh people at the signing of the pact' while at the same time 'show[ing] the world that we are anxious for the friendship of Germany'.[13] Indignant Labour councillors eventually succeeded in removing the flag, though the desire for 'friendship with Germany' at this critical time was widely shared. Indeed, Sir Ernest Bennett, the National Labour MP for Cardiff Central, had been one of Germany's strongest advocates in House of Commons debates. Bennett, a former Liberal MP for Woodstock, Oxfordshire, had won Cardiff Central for Labour in 1931 when he defeated both the sitting candidate and Barney Janner (then standing as a Liberal). He was an eccentric former Oxford don and Victorian war correspondent whose accounts of his observations in Palestine, Crete and the Mahdist and South African wars brought charges of 'sensationalism', and whose political discourse was often conducted in Latin. Most of his parliamentary interventions and indignant letters to *The Times* from the mid-1930s concerned either the Palestinian question, in which he supported restrictions on Jewish immigration to Palestine, or, increasingly, the appeasement debates, in which he defended German actions in Austria and

Sudetenland, which in his view befitted Germany's natural colonial aspirations. He continued to support the Munich Agreement even after it had been seen as a humiliating act of weak diplomacy, on the grounds that 'there was every reason for national pride and satisfaction over our Prime Minister's action in averting a senseless war, and securing a settlement, without bloodshed, of the obviously just claim of the Sudeten Deutsch to . . . self-determination'.[14] Although concerned not to appear overtly anti-Semitic, his warnings over 'cosmopolitan financiers', and complaints that Germany's treatment of Jews was being used against them unfairly in order to undermine their just claims, put him in the same camp as many more-militant anti-Semites. Indeed, Bennett had been a supporter of the Nordic League, regarded as the 'British branch of international Nazism', which held large meetings of mainly middle-class members and often culminated in the anti-Semitic chant of 'Perish Judah' (or 'PJ'). He voted for Captain Archibald 'Jock' Ramsay's Alien Restrictions Bill of 1938 and followed Ramsay (one of the Nordic League's main speakers) when the latter formed the Right Club, a secret society founded in May 1939 to rid the establishment of Jewish influence. His name was in the 'Red Book' compiled by Ramsay of Right Club supporters, and Bennett was regarded as a 'prominent fellow-traveller'.[15] His support was frequently invoked by Ramsay who, known for his violent anti-Semitism, was in 1940 the only MP interned under defence regulations. Pro-Franco and a virulent anti-communist, Bennett claimed that the people of Cardiff had supported non-intervention in Spain and that Chamberlain's appeasement position was being undermined by journalists and politicians who were making 'frenzied attacks on dictatorships and totalitarian states'.[16]

Some of the strongest opposition to appeasement in Wales came from the South Wales miners, whose exceptional ideals of internationalism had grown from support for the Spanish Republic to broader European anti-fascism. A long-standing 'Welsh Jacobinism', Nonconformist religious dissent and a 'cosmopolitan coalfield' had been succeeded by unprecedented class militancy during and after the General Strike in 1926.[17] Under its communist leadership, its internationalism was evident in early opposition to fascism in Greece, Spain and Italy. The Welsh miners were among the first to sign up to the International Brigades in defence of Madrid in December 1936 and in all sent 174 volunteers to Spain. This political maturity, sharpened during their involvement in the hunger marches in the same year as well as through other forms of extra-parliamentary activity, was partly shaped by the ideological convictions of the CPGB, which had deep roots in the mining villages in the Rhondda and Merthyr valleys.[18] The CPGB's endorsement of the Popular Front against fascism (after 1936), shared by wider cohorts of workers and intellectuals, as well as among left-wing MPs like Aneurin Bevan, meant implacable opposition to appeasement. They viewed Chamberlain's negotiations with Hitler as right-wing accommodation of fascism. This position was maintained throughout 1939 until the disastrous Molotov–Ribbentrop Pact, though the miners' leader Arthur Horner cautiously pursued a 'war on two fronts' strategy in defiance of the CPGB leadership.[19]

The Munich debate in Parliament – where former Labour leader George Lansbury echoed Chamberlain's call for 'reasonableness' in negotiating with Hitler and Mussolini – suggested that appeasement would become less of a left–right issue. For different reasons, this was borne out in the coming months, with pacifist groups like the Peace Pledge Union strengthening their opposition to conflict and the *New Statesman* under Kingsley Martin's editorship adopting a pro-appeasement position. The Cliveden Set of rich pro-German advocates consistently pushed the appeasement line, while the pro-German right-wing organizations virulently campaigned against war. In Wales, the small Welsh Nationalist party (Plaid Cymru) also supported the Munich Agreement, with many members and supporters continuing to oppose the conflict either on strong pacifist grounds or on the basis that it was a 'clash of rival imperialisms from which Wales, like the other small nations of Europe, has nothing to gain but everything to lose'.[20]

The Times under Geoffrey Dawson's editorship remained the most vigorous defender of Chamberlain. In the immediate aftermath of Munich, the press was generally supportive of the prime minister, with only the *Daily Herald* maintaining outright criticism of the deal. *The Times* and the *Daily Mail* were the most demonstrative in their praise, with the former commending the resolute statesmanship of the prime minister and the latter seeing it as the basis for a permanent 'Anglo-German understanding'.[21] The *Sunday Times* saw the agreement between Hitler and Chamberlain as 'awakening from a nightmare',[22] while the *Western Mail* saw in it 'the hope that a less barbarous and more humane spirit may now begin to animate the Nazi regime'.[23] Among the few sceptical papers was Camrose's *Daily Telegraph*. While it was keen to 'acknowledge the enormous debt we owe to the lofty and indefatigable endeavour of a single man', Chamberlain's efforts had not resolved the ultimate question of 'what sort of peace' had been secured. 'Is it too high a price?' it asked. Over the ensuing months the paper would make clear it believed that, indeed, the price was too high.[24]

Although Lakin later came to recognize Chamberlain's policy of appeasement as a 'miserable failure', he maintained some outside hope that war could be averted. During the tense and turbulent months that preceded the outbreak of war, Lakin spent half an hour alone with the prime minister in the Cabinet Room at 10 Downing Street (possibly standing in for Hadley). At this 'heart to heart' (as he recalled later in a BBC broadcast), with Lakin perched alongside Chamberlain at his usual place in the middle of the long table, he found the prime minister impenetrable: 'You would feel, as I frankly felt, that you couldn't make any impression on this man at all.' Nevertheless, he empathized with his predicament: 'From the first day of his premiership one anxiety was with him in every waking hour [with] Europe and the world drifting towards war and he knew that he could never justify himself if he failed to do everything in his power to stop it.' The only time Lakin got beneath the surface of this 'simple, straight-forward and non-aggressive man' with 'cold, unblinking eyes' was at the mention of Erdington in Birmingham – where it had all started for the Lakins, and the city that Neville Chamberlain, along with his father and half-brother, had represented as an MP. At that point, the older man's 'face lit up with a lovely smile'.[25]

In the months following the Munich Agreement, public opinion towards Chamberlain altered as Hitler's aggressive expansionism continued. Nevertheless, there were concerted efforts in the form of 'peace feelers', often on the initiative of pro-German sympathizers who attempted to act as mediators. There were also 'covert operations' involving peers and other people of influence who saw Hermann Goering as the 'channel for peace' within the Nazi hierarchy.[26] At the same time, Hadley had continued to meet and support Chamberlain and communicate his latest whims to Kemsley, one of which was to try and establish a rapport between British and German newspapers. Kemsley had heard of an approach made to an American newspaper group by Dr Otto Dietrich, head of the German press office, whereby the latter would provide material for articles in an American newspaper about the current situation in Germany. This approach had been turned down by the Americans, but Kemsley, 'urged on by Hadley, who in turn, it was said in the office, was urged on by Neville Chamberlain',[27] now suggested an exchange of articles in the German and British press – a process he would facilitate through the *Daily Sketch*, one of his own papers. The British articles were originally to be written by one of his main writers, Herbert Sidebottom, an experienced former *Manchester Guardian* leader writer who wrote for the *Daily Sketch* under the pseudonym 'Candidus'. However, on the recommendation of Downing Street, Sidebottom was replaced by Arthur Bryant, a popular historian of Britain and biographer of Samuel Pepys who had just produced a hagiography of Stanley Baldwin, the former prime minister. Bryant was a stalwart supporter of appeasement and a pro-German activist with links to anti-Semitic organizations. He was trusted by Lord Halifax, who had succeeded Anthony Eden as Foreign Secretary, but was regarded by many as being too deferential to German interests.

At the end of May, Kemsley received a reply from Dietrich in which certain conditions were imposed to protect the German side before an exchange of articles could be considered. Kemsley quickly adhered 'unequivocally' to the points made and, apparently oblivious to the way in which Dietrich sought to use any meeting for propaganda purposes, agreed to travel to Germany at the end of July to meet him, Hitler and his entourage, where the agreement could be finalized. This visit, which had the backing of Chamberlain, was more official than Kemsley would let on to the Germans (or during the brief public announcement of the trip). He needed an adviser and a trusted right-hand man competent enough to produce a report of the meeting, and to that end Cyril Lakin became the second journalist from Barry to have an appointment with the Fuehrer.

Chapter 10

Meeting Hitler

Once Kemsley opened the dialogue with Dr Dietrich, arrangements were set in place to travel to Berlin by train and boat in late July. Being courted by the Nazi hierarchy was not a new experience for Kemsley. In 1936, during the Berlin Olympics, he had enjoyed the hospitality of the Ribbentrops at their luxury villa, and though his appreciation did not match the euphoric praise heaped on the regime by Chips Channon, another dinner guest on that occasion, he was comfortable in their company.[1] He departed with the backing of the prime minister, while Permanent Head of the Civil Service and Chief Industrial Adviser to the Government, Horace Wilson – who had accompanied Chamberlain to Munich the previous autumn – confirmed that Kemsley 'has promised to stick closely to the line' in any discussions with Hitler.[2] A few weeks earlier, in a more secretive approach made through Wilson, Sir Ernest Tennant, a financier and leading member of the Anglo-German Fellowship, had been authorized to hold talks with Ribbentrop, by now Germany's foreign minister.

Despite Tennant's optimism, those talks at the beginning of July came to nothing, with Ribbentrop denouncing Britain's elite and declaring that any British defence of Poland would be futile.[3] Unlike Tennant's mission, Kemsley's was made public and included a brief statement of its purpose in his own *Daily Sketch*:

> It has behind it not the surreptitious and disturbing secret circulation of propaganda considered by either party to be lying and mischievous, but the free and fair exchange and the open publication through the whole of the German press on the one hand, and through as many English newspapers as care to print them on the other, of the respective views of German and British policies.[4]

They arrived in Germany in pouring rain at 8.30 a.m. on Tuesday 25 July and were met at Friedrichstrasse station by Otto Meissner, 'Chief of the Presidential Chancellery of the Fuehrer and the Chancellor', before being driven in two large black Mercedes to the Adlon on Unter den Linden, a luxurious hotel of Neo-Baroque architecture with all modern on-site facilities. Originally opened by the kaiser in 1907, its patrons included film stars and politicians, while it was situated close enough to the British Embassy to host regular functions in its palatial lounges and dining rooms. Here, as Lakin recorded in his diary of the trip,[5] they were treated 'like royalty & conducted in state to our rooms'. After he had 'unpacked every blessed thing',[6] Lakin was initially disappointed that their stay at the Adlon would be cut short as they were required to move on to Bayreuth the following morning.[7] However, it was known that Hitler attended the annual Wagner festival there every year and the prospects of a direct meeting between him and Kemsley were improved by the news.

Shortly after their arrival in Berlin, Lord Kemsley made the short distance to the embassy for a meeting with the British ambassador, Nevile Henderson, followed by lunch with Alfred Rosenberg at his home in Dahlem, a leafy district in the south of the city. Henderson had been well briefed in advance of the meeting and was aware that a meeting with Hitler was the main purpose. Also present at lunch were Professor Karl Boemer, director of Germany's foreign press department (who two years later would be imprisoned for treason after confirming Germany's intention to invade Russia); Frau Scholtz-Klink, the leader of the National Socialist Women's League (the 'Reich's Women's Fuehrerin'); Arno Schickedanz of Rosenberg's office; and Meissner. From these early talks it became apparent to the British party that the Germans held wider ambitions for the meetings that went beyond the publication of newspaper articles. The precise programme of meetings for the visit was never finalized and constantly subject to change while they waited for decisions from Hitler's office. After 'much coming and going from the propaganda ministry',[8] hopes of the meeting were raised as talks continued after lunch with Rosenberg, Ernst von Weizsaecker (Germany's Secretary of State for Foreign Affairs, and an opponent of war) and Boemer, though it was Rosenberg who did most of the talking on the German side.

Dr Alfred Rosenberg was one of the main ideologues of the Nazi party, whose theories of racial superiority promoted the Aryan, Nordic race to the top of a hierarchy that relegated Jews, black people and homosexuals to inferior status. He was also a significant proponent of anti-Semitic conspiracy theories.

Since his visit to Britain in 1933, where he placed a swastika at
the cenotaph, he had long advocated closer links with British
governments. As a senior official in the German regime, he was
known to be close enough to Hitler to carry influence while
given to outspoken comments. The terms of their discussion
were important in deciding whether a meeting with Hitler
would go ahead. Rosenberg started off by expressing his anger
at the letter addressed to the German people by Stephen
King-Hall, a war veteran and naval officer (he would win the
Ormskirk by-election for National Labour two months later).
In his newsletters to thousands of German individuals, King-
Hall attempted to correct the impression of British public
opinion that had been given to the German people by its
leaders. This act of 'personal diplomacy' had irked Germany's
propaganda machine and incurred the wrath of Goebbels and
others (who claimed he was acting on behalf of the British
Foreign Office), while for different reasons it also upset the
Italian and British foreign ministries, who felt it had not helped
their own diplomatic channels. At their meeting, Rosenberg
told Kemsley that they held the British government responsible
for King-Hall's intervention, while he also warned him of the
implications for Anglo-German relations if Winston Churchill
replaced Chamberlain as prime minister. Kemsley, as he did
throughout the discussions, continued to state his belief that
an agreement could be reached with Germany that would win
support in the House of Commons and on which Chamberlain
would fight a new election. Testing the limits of credibility,
he added that any successor would then be obliged to 'stand
by' that agreement. Kemsley attempted to reassure Rosenberg
that Churchill and the opposition were not a serious threat.
'In England we have freedom of speech and a free press. You

will never understand England,' he went on ill-advisedly, 'unless you think of Neville Chamberlain as our Fuehrer'. 'I wish you would tell that to the Fuehrer,' Rosenberg replied.[9] Throughout the discussion Rosenberg seemed perplexed by Chamberlain's conclusion that Hitler had broken the Munich Agreement, and remained unconvinced by Kemsley's assertion that criticism of Germany in Britain was due to the situation in Czechoslovakia. Nevertheless, the talks were recorded as 'vigorous' with a 'frank exchange of views', held in a 'friendly atmosphere' with 'happy impressions created on both sides'.

The talks with Rosenberg carried on until 3.45 p.m., at which point the Kemsley party was escorted to the Hitler Youth HQ where they were presented to leaders of its girls' section. That evening, while the Kemsleys dined with Henderson (who was eager to be involved in some of the discussions), Lakin worked on the programme and made telephone calls home to inform Vera of their arrangements. His wife then phoned the Foreign Office to update them using a pre-agreed code (relating to the health of their daughter Bridget).

The following morning, they set off by car for Bayreuth, stopping off on the way to visit a labour camp, before lunch in Leipzig with Boemer and Meissner. With Boemer accompanying them, they finally arrived in Bayreuth at 8.30 p.m. where they met the gauleiter (the regional head of the Nazi party) for dinner and more talks and were put up for the night in his private residence. Shortly after they arrived, Boemer received a phone call and, on returning to the party in an excited manner, informed Kemsley that he would 'see the leader at noon tomorrow and it is to be a serious talk'.[10] The following morning in the gauleiter's summer house the group held their first formal talks when Kemsley was joined by Dietrich, Paul Schmidt (Hitler's interpreter), Boemer and Meissner. Prior to their visit, negotiations with Dietrich, Hitler's head of press, were couched in cautious tones: Dietrich, an experienced propagandist, clearly came to the meeting with a strong brief. From Dietrich, Lakin had the impression that the German side were happy to use the discussions as a 'direct line' in political negotiations with the British government. At the same time, he observed that 'they are obviously prepared down to the last button for war'.[11] Dietrich was grateful for the 'personal contact' with Kemsley: 'It is essential to have a direct wire between you and me,' he told him, while reassuring him that Hitler appreciated his decision to travel to Germany as he 'had been making every effort to fight "press lies"'. For his part, Kemsley attempted to reassure Dietrich that the criticisms of the German government by the British press were no worse than those directed at its own politicians like Chamberlain and Churchill. They both declared their support for further Anglo-German cooperation and even contemplated the possibility that such discussions could help resolve big political decisions. However, in the first indication to the British party that the German leadership did not attach the significance or seriousness to the proceedings that their counterparts had assumed, Dietrich suggested that any exchange of articles would need to wait until 'the atmosphere is better' and the possibility that 'there is going to be a rapprochement between the two countries'. 'I must say that I looked on these articles as being a means to the beginning of a rapprochement,' Kemsley replied. Dietrich would not commit to any predictions in advance of the meeting with Hitler: 'On political matters, I will not anticipate what the Fuehrer will say to you.'[12]

At noon, as agreed, Hitler arrived with his entourage to meet Kemsley for the first time. Lakin was not present at this meeting but was later given a summary by Paul Schmidt, who had acted as interpreter during the conversation and was well acquainted with Hitler's whims and mannerisms. Schmidt had interpreted for Hitler and Neville Chamberlain during the Munich discussions the year before, and two years later he would be the interpreter for Hitler in the meetings with Romanian dictator Ion Antonescu, as the two leaders discussed the planned invasion of the Soviet Union as well as their joint mission to exterminate mass numbers of Jews. Schmidt told Lakin – rather pompously – that he had been impressed by the length of the interview (which lasted an hour and ten minutes rather than the customary twenty minutes or so), the candour on both sides and the good-natured atmosphere. Hitler, he told Lakin, had insisted that between Britain and Germany 'there must either be close contact or conflict [with] the danger that the spark may be lighted at any time'. 'You think you will win that conflict,' Hitler had told Kemsley, 'and we think we will win. But we know that the real winners will be Japan in the East and America in the West.' (Kemsley later denied to Lakin that Hitler had referred to America.) In the meeting, Schmidt continued, Hitler had told Kemsley he 'wanted colonies' but not necessarily the 'old colonies'. Schmidt then shared with Lakin his own impressions of the meeting and prospects for taking the discussions further:

> Although the atmosphere today was so favourable, we must not underrate the difficulties between the two nations. The differences are mainly ideological. We must first "agree to differ" about those matters. But "agreeing to differ" is especially difficult

for a young nation like ours. It is easier for you, and you as the
older nation must have patience with us because we are young.[13]

According to Kemsley's detailed recollection to Lakin later,
Hitler welcomed Kemsley's approach and 'hoped some good
would come of it as he personally had never been anything
but friendly towards Britain'. Hitler referred Kemsley to his
speech in the Reichstag on 28 April in which he argued that
the agreement forged with Chamberlain at Munich would
continue 'in a friendly spirit of consultation'. The 'desire for
Anglo-German friendship and cooperation' was derived both
from 'the racial origins of our two peoples but also to my
realization of the importance of the existence of the British
Empire for the whole of mankind'. Yet his speech had started
as a diatribe against the injustices of the Treaty of Versailles,
and 'the cowardly democratic peace dictators', 'Jewish parasites'
who had 'ruthlessly plundered the nation', and the 'Jewish press'
that had 'confused' public opinion. While admiring the British
Empire, Hitler expected the British to adopt a similar attitude
to 'the freedom and preservation of the German Reich' as it
set about restoring its own empire. He regretted that, since
Munich, a different view had prevailed that saw war between
the two countries as likely if Germany continued to expand
its territorial ambitions, but had left open the possibility that
further negotiations could be held.

That was still his position three months later, though he
conceded that the two countries were 'drifting' towards war.
Kemsley made clear his own wish for conciliation and used the
strange comparison of the differences between the two sides
as analogous to the competition between his newspaper group
and the papers owned by Lord Rothermere. This allusion to

his own empire – which earned some appreciative comment from Hitler – was followed by an exchange of views on the respective prospects for victory that would not have been out of place in the prelude to a gentlemen's duel or a conversation between two cup-final managers politely previewing the forthcoming encounter. Hitler thought Germany would win but he accepted that Kemsley would think Britain's armed forces would be enough to secure victory. Kemsley told him he thought Britain would triumph, but on the other hand recognized Germany's military strength.

Kemsley, perhaps enjoying being feted by the German hierarchy, and with the ear of its dictator, explained to Hitler that as a large newspaper owner he had used all his influence with the British prime minister immediately following Munich and was 'absolutely convinced that Mr Chamberlain attached tremendous importance to the document which had been signed by Herr Hitler and himself'. Chamberlain, Kemsley told Hitler, saw the Munich Agreement not only as a way of settling the Sudeten dispute but as 'the forerunner of a different relationship with Germany in the future'.

Kemsley maintained that if an agreement with Germany could be reached even at this late stage then war could be avoided. The British people did not want war and Parliament would be only too ready to give 'enthusiastic' approval of a new settlement if a consensus could be found on a reduction in armaments. On the other hand, the country was ready to go to war if necessary. In his response Hitler was more concerned with Chamberlain's opponents in Parliament, notably Winston Churchill with whose speeches he was now familiar. Kemsley played down Churchill's influence, pointing out to Hitler that 'far more notice was taken abroad of the opposition' and that while Churchill was an accomplished writer and speaker, his previous political 'campaigns' had not been successful.

Hitler then raised the question of Britain's 'unfair' and 'unreasonable' position on Poland and reiterated two points on which he would not compromise: Germany must be permitted to have colonies and the Treaty of Versailles needed to be cancelled. He argued that each country should set out their positions in writing. It seemed clear that those were his conditions for any further negotiations between the countries.[14]

Schmidt, outwardly friendly and hospitable, accompanied the Kemsley party for the remainder of the day until his return on the night train to Berlin. The talk with Hitler was followed by lunch at the Schloss Fantaisie, a castle on the west side of Bayreuth, with Dr Joseph Goebbels, Hitler's director of propaganda and one of the leading proponents of Germany's expansionist policies in Czechoslovakia and Poland. Goebbels, with his 'acid wit', contributed to a 'friendly atmosphere' among the group while further inconclusive talks took place.

After lunch Lakin accompanied Lord and Lady Kemsley to the Bayreuth Festspielhaus, the festival theatre built by Richard Wagner in 1876, for a performance of *Parsifal*, his last completed opera, staged in three acts. Here they bumped into Unity Mitford, Hitler's 'Storm Troop Maiden', who had insisted on staying on in Germany in the shadow of war. Unlike the other 'sloppy English girls who were always having affairs with dreadful SS types',[15] Mitford was a 'full-blown Hitlerite': an ideologue who was unable to keep her hatred of Jewish people out of general conversation and who greeted visiting friends with a clicking of her heels and a '*heil* Hitler!' salute. Back in England her father, Lord Redesdale, had just been made a warden of the Right Club, while her sister Diana was married to Oswald Mosley, the leader of the BUF (another sister, Jessica, was a communist whose lover was Esmond Romilly, Churchill's 'Red nephew'). After trailing Hitler and looking out for him in the Osteria Bavaria, his favourite Munich restaurant, she succeeded in attaching herself to his informal entourage of admirers, while he was flattered by the attentions of the daughter of a British aristocrat whose 'Nordic' features symbolized his ideal race. In May that year Hitler's office had offered her the choice of a new apartment in the centre of Munich that had been requisitioned from its Jewish owners; in her visits to view the flat and measure up for refurbishment, she was oblivious to the plight of the existing owners who had opened the door to her. A regular at the Bayreuth Festival, she had just returned from lunch with Hitler when she encountered Lakin and Lord and Lady Kemsley and was keen to impress upon them Hitler's agreeable response to their discussions and his hope of further cooperation between the two countries.[16] During the interval the Kemsleys and Lakin were introduced to Hitler again, this time in the midst of concert goers and supporters.

Following the concert, the gauleiter escorted the party on an inspection of the new Nazi headquarters in Bayreuth, before a tour of the town's slum clearance measures and a visit to the 'Hall of German Motherhood'. Finally, they were taken by the gauleiter to dinner at a country restaurant. On their last day – Friday 28 July – they had further inconclusive talks with Boemer and were accompanied by Meissner to Nuremberg where they set off for Ostend.

Kemsley left Germany pleased with what he felt he had accomplished. Downing Street was informed that he had secured a commitment that would follow in writing. It was the indication that Chamberlain sought to keep alive his hopes of pursuing a 'different relationship' with Germany. Realistically, the talks had barely kept to the government's 'firm and friendly' position on which Kemsley had been briefed, while 'the dreams of the pure spirit of appeasement were still the dominant feature'.[17] On the British side there was an overeagerness to placate the Nazi leaders – 'only the Jews wanted to bring about a war between Germany and England', Lady Kemsley is reported to have commented[18] – with a naive assessment of their counterpart's motives. For Hitler's side, it was little more than a propaganda exercise. In Dietrich's (albeit unreliable) memoir, he noted Hitler's 'marked reserve' during the one-hour talk with Kemsley.[19] While they were happy to fete their guests for any useful publicity that portrayed them in serious negotiations, Hitler had shown little interest in pursuing other official channels that may have been open to him and Nevile Henderson, Britain's beleaguered Ambassador to Germany, who was not trusted by the regime. ('That idiot Henderson', Unity Mitford called him.[20]) Despite being entrusted with the Kemsley party, Henderson's attempts to present himself as an important point of liaison came to little. After setting off to join them at Bayreuth, his car broke down and his delayed arrival prohibited any chance of meeting Hitler (who continued to ignore him in the coming weeks).[21]

Lakin returned home dejected and unconvinced by the outcome of the talks. While he accepted there was a desire for contact with Kemsley and through him a 'direct line' to Chamberlain, Hitler was quite prepared for war and he did not hold strong hopes that it could be avoided. The Germans 'feared' Churchill and at the same time found it 'increasingly difficult' to understand the British system of parliamentary democracy that might facilitate his route to power. Among the Nazi officials they met, he described the younger ones as 'Clever, and mostly cultivated, zealots; with great faith in Hitler and the utmost confidence in Germany's future.' As far as policy was concerned, all the Nazi officials 'told the same story', though he also noted that 'one or two of them expressed doubts (in their more expansive moments) as to the wisdom of the last Jewish purge, and the protectorate of Czecho-slovakia'. The Nazi party, he concluded 'had made immense strides in power and popularity. There is no doubt that skilful propaganda about "encirclement" had made the country practically 100% fervently pro-Hitler'.[22]

Back in the *Sunday Times* office, Leonard Russell found his colleague reluctant to discuss the talks, observing that Lakin had 'returned to England a scared man' who believed that war was only weeks away.[23] Any optimism on Kemsley's part that the talks would be a prelude to serious negotiation and even an exchange of articles was soon dashed. On 18 August Dietrich sent him the draft article in German he had promised (and for which Kemsley had campaigned for so long). Kemsley, however, was on holiday in Normandy when it arrived and by the time he had seen it and returned to London intending to respond, Germany and the Soviet Union had entered into their non-aggression (Molotov–Ribbentrop) pact that divided Poland between them. In the meantime, Kemsley received a visit from the German press attaché in London, acting on Dietrich's orders, who insisted a German article should be published in the British press before a British one in the German newspapers. The culmination of these events only confirmed the failure of the mission and its objectives.[24]

Lakin's doubts over the value of the visit were heightened

by the knowledge that Camrose's *Daily Telegraph* was taking an increasingly critical position of Chamberlain and appeasement. At the time of the Munich Agreement it had carried several critical articles by Churchill and others; when the Germans invaded Czechoslovakia in March it stated that Hitler had 'dropped the mask',[25] and by the beginning of July, shortly before the Kemsley visit, it had published a long editorial demanding that Churchill be brought into the government. Politically the *Daily Telegraph* was strongly anti-appeasement, while on a personal level Camrose would become a close friend and ally of Churchill. As he reflected, Lakin must surely have looked back at the choice he had made three years earlier when the two brothers had divided up their press interests.

When war was declared on 3 September following Germany's invasion of Poland, Unity Mitford walked into the Englischer Garden in Munich and shot herself in the head, carrying out a threat she had made to friends and family in the event of war between her two countries. The bullet which lodged in the back of her skull did not kill her but ensured permanent disability and an early death.

Arthur Bryant, the author of the ill-fated articles (which never appeared in the British press), had made his own private visit to Germany (with Chamberlain's knowledge) just weeks before the Kemsley visit. On this visit – the details of which were only made public many years later – he met leading Nazi officials including Walther Hewel, a close friend of Hitler and Kurt Blohm of the Nazi's foreign affairs section at Nazi Party Headquarters, but despite his evident pro-Hitler sentiments returned without any agreement. The extent of his pro-Nazi convictions, which together with his dubious reputation as a historian went unnoticed by successive British prime ministers, increased in subsequent months. Shortly after the outbreak of war, a verbatim account of the articles intended for the Kemsley press appeared in the introduction to his book, *Unfinished Victory*. The book was 'as pure an apologia for Nazism as it is possible to imagine being published at such a time'.[26]

Chapter 11

BBC Broadcaster

Ivo Geikie-Cobb was a Harley Street surgeon who during the interwar years had built up a successful practice in the exclusive Marylebone district noted for its rich clientele as much as the skill of its practitioners. However, he was an unusual doctor who held literary ambitions that would take him beyond the confines of his surgery. During the 1930s, under the pseudonym Anthony Weymouth – adapted from a combination of his son's first name and the thoroughfare that accommodated his home and practice – he had published a series of detective stories, starting with *Frozen Death* in 1934. In these Inspector Treadgold mysteries he was able to draw on his extensive medical knowledge in setting up the plots and dangling the evidence before the readers as his unlikely police detective, fond of fast cars, quoting Latin and defying his superiors, went about solving the riddles behind the untimely deaths of unfortunate aristocrats. These literary excursions did not always impress Lakin's regular *Sunday Times* fiction reviewers, including Dorothy L. Sayers and Milward

Kennedy, the civil servant-turned-crime writer, who were underwhelmed by Weymouth's plots and characters, though his history of leprosy and other non-fiction works were well regarded as he became better known as a writer. It was through his novels and literary connections at the *Sunday Times* that Lakin and Weymouth first became acquainted and it was through Weymouth that Lakin was introduced to the BBC as a potential broadcaster.

The war had brought financial insecurity for Geikie-Cobb's practice, and he needed to supplement his income. Since 1937 he had done a little broadcasting as an occasional BBC consultant on medical questions, and now sought to bring his specialist knowledge – he was an expert on shell shock among other conditions – to the wider public. At the beginning of the war – a time when producers and contributors worked without the 'red tape' that was characteristic of its later stages – BBC editors were looking to recruit more staff to produce programmes for their rapidly increasing audiences in the colonies and across the 'dominions' (notably Canada, Australia and New Zealand). Being a wartime broadcaster appealed to his sense of patriotism and what he called the 'English spirit', a theme he developed in a later collection of essays.[1] He had already made his own stand against Nazism by driving an Austrian Jewish boy and his uncle over the mountains and across the border to safety, one of several adventures that earned the admiration of his BBC colleagues, who saw him as a kind of 'modern Scarlet Pimpernel'.[2] Impressed by his contributions and by his facility for conducting discussions, Weymouth was appointed as a part-time talks assistant in its Overseas Service department (the forerunner to the BBC World Service, which was still often known by its former name of 'Empire Service').

Under the tutelage of Margery Wace, the outstanding Empire
Talks Organizer, he was 'initiated into the mysteries of the
microphone', and encouraged to adopt a conversational style
while imagining himself broadcasting to 'a lone man in the
Australian bush switching on his wireless'.[3] His main job
as a talks assistant was to select important news items and
recruit speakers who could describe them evocatively, adding
insight and humour where necessary. Ideally, speakers had to
be well informed and confident enough to perform in front
of the microphone, as well as capable of producing material
themselves: 'getting scripts out of them' was a constant refrain
from Weymouth's bosses.

He was well connected and he soon impressed BBC
superiors as a noted talent scout – a description often applied
to Lakin himself. In April 1940, shortly after taking up his
role, Weymouth brought Lakin to the BBC. He knew that
the latter had wide editorial experience and followed world
affairs closely while enjoying good contacts with politicians
and other public figures. Two months before, on Weymouth's
request, Lakin had helped to put Kemsley on the air to explain
(from his own recording studio) the reasons for his approach
to Dr Dietrich and what he felt could still be achieved through
more negotiations.

For Lakin, working for the BBC was a welcome diversion
and marked a new beginning in his life. Frustrated at his lack
of advancement at the *Sunday Times* and still reeling from the
shock of the botched Hitler visit – a disagreeable experience
all round for him – he now had the opportunity to break free
from the shadow of the Berry brothers. In a meteoric rise
he had served them faithfully as personal assistant, editorial
secretary, literary editor and assistant editor, but now he had

been handed a more public role of his own. He could draw on his curiosity in world affairs as well as apply editorial judgment in producing succinct talks, while his well-worn skills of persuasion would be crucial in the propaganda battles ahead. Broadcasting also became a vehicle for his patriotism and a growing, latent anti-fascism that had now replaced any prior concerns he had over his country going to war for a second time in a quarter of a century. His BBC career, which would last six years and subsume over 150 programmes, would show him to be a smooth-talking, engaging and authoritative voice; an informed commentator on world events who was comfortable with the new medium of radio.

He joined the BBC at a propitious time. It was the latter period of the 'phoney war', when despite limited conflict big changes at the top of British government were expected. The Ministry of Information (MOI) had been founded at the beginning of the war – after years of secret preparation – and from its base at Senate House in Bloomsbury was assigned the role of regulating relations between the BBC and government. Anthony Weymouth thought Lakin could be put to good use in commenting on government policy and on the critical ongoing discussions in the Cabinet. His first programmes focused on the Cabinet changes that would lead eventually to Winston Churchill taking over as prime minister. In his opening seven-minute broadcast delivered on the afternoon of 5 April from the Empire News studios, a former department store building located at 200 Oxford Street and a short walk from Broadcasting House, he informed overseas listeners of a significant reshuffle. Though more 'a game of musical chairs'[4] in which some ministers merely swapped places, the biggest change saw Churchill (he had been a member of Chamberlain's War Cabinet as First Lord of the Admiralty since September 1939) replace Lord Chatfield as chairman of the Military Coordinating Committee, a role he had long coveted, in April 1940. Churchill's first initiative, made on the day of Lakin's broadcast, was to give the green light to Operation Wilfred, a British naval mission to the Norwegian ports of Stavanger, Bergen and Trondheim, where two minefields were to be laid off the coast. It was not until three days later that British forces set off, though initially Churchill was unperturbed, doubting that Germany had the intention of invading Norway. News of the arrival of German destroyers in the ports and the takeover of Copenhagen and Oslo was an unwelcome revelation to Britain's complacent politicians, and the Germans were able to exploit weaknesses in the British government's (and Churchill's) strategy. Their propaganda messages that they were acting in defence of Norwegian neutrality against British aggression produced celebrations in Germany.

Over forthcoming weeks Lakin had the task of describing the failed British mission under Churchill's command, the significant losses and capture of personnel (which included Churchill's nephew Giles Romilly, a *Daily Express* correspondent), and the eventual withdrawal of British forces from Trondheim. At the same time as keeping listeners abreast of ongoing debates in the House of Commons, it needed tact on his part to avail them of the necessary facts while countering German propaganda. 'In all these Empire talks,' Margery Wace had stressed to producers and contributors at the outset, 'we are, as it were, doing propaganda for England and the English way of life'.[5]

Despite the challenges he faced in keeping up with the

disturbing, fast-moving events while maintaining an optimistic front, he was soon in demand. His crisp delivery and the quietly confident tone he adopted while conveying the latest parliamentary speeches to listeners overseas were admired by his superiors. If he looked ten years younger, then his voice carried the authority of an older man grounded in experience of world politics. His BBC commitments multiplied, and soon after joining he found himself in the studios four days a week for talks and news commentary at lunchtimes, early evenings and late nights. On the night of 2–3 May he was in the Oxford Street studios from 9.30 p.m. to 2 a.m., assigned the formidable task of explaining how a promising scenario – one in which the government was driven by Churchill's insistence that Hitler had made a strategic error in taking Norway and Denmark – was now on the verge of collapse. Chamberlain's statement to the House of Commons, reported by the BBC, was the first inkling to the public that things were not going well. The 'wireless' was the means by which they were kept informed of developments as tensions mounted and fears escalated. Now, as Chamberlain notified the nation of the withdrawal from Trondheim, there was more reason to distrust the messenger and therefore more pressure on Lakin to deliver accurate information in the right tone while empathizing with rising public concern. This was the moment when the war became serious with the possible threat of invasion.

The government was in trouble and faced more scrutiny once Labour leader Clement Attlee called for a full debate on its conduct of the war, which took place from 7 to 9 May. Although Chamberlain did not lose the vote, its majority was threatened and there were calls for a national government. The following day, on 10 May, German armies invaded Belgium, the Netherlands and Luxembourg with clear intentions to move into France. Chamberlain's attempts to form another government failed after Labour made clear that it would not serve under him, and Churchill was chosen ahead of Lord Halifax, whose membership of the House of Lords and closeness to Chamberlain would have precluded an effective cross-party alliance.

Lord Camrose, a mild critic of Chamberlain's appeasement policy who had remained loyal to the government until this point, was one of those to whom Churchill confided regularly in the days before he succeeded Chamberlain. Churchill had told Camrose on the eve of the debate that Chamberlain had made the mistake of not including his critics – 'Duff Cooper, Amery and others' – in his Cabinet, which had enabled them to 'become fierce critics and rallying points for opposition' (thus strengthening Churchill's own position).[6]

Camrose's long friendship with Churchill made him an important ally and he continued to have the ear of the new prime minister in the difficult years ahead. For Lakin, these developments added an urgency to his early broadcasting and he devoted a week of talks to it, starting with 'Withdrawal from Trondheim', progressing to 'The Debate' and 'Reactions to the Debate', and ending with 'Mr Churchill's New Cabinet'. His coverage of Churchill's accession to the premiership, the resulting Cabinet changes and the new prime minister's priorities was extensive, detailed and delivered with a solid understanding of the political context. Throughout his talks there was an appreciative recognition of the cross-party nature of the new government; among Churchill's new Cabinet were Labour's 'big three': leader Clement Attlee, Ernest Bevin, the Minister of Labour, and Herbert Morrison, the Minister of

Supply. His War Cabinet included Attlee, along with Arthur Greenwood (Attlee's deputy), Lord Halifax and Chamberlain, who was now ill with the cancer that would kill him by the end of the year. Lakin's sympathy for the new coalition and ease with its composition would serve him well over the next five years.

From his first broadcasts, he was quickly regarded as a 'very good' speaker and assiduous in his approach to work. This prompted Michael Barkway, the Empire news editor, to request that he now contribute a short daily comment after the main news summary each evening so that 'listeners should get in the habit of waiting for Mr Lakin's comments'. Lakin took the invitation as a compliment, while raising concerns about the pressure it would put him under given the *Sunday Times* editor had been absent on grounds of ill health and that he found the production of scripts – though rewarding once they had been delivered – something of a drudge. 'I have never written with facility & ease (in fact I hate it!),' he told Barkway, 'and it is the writing that causes me most strain and not the actual broadcasting'.[7]

If he could not broadcast seven days of the week, then his BBC schedule still meant irregular hours with both pre-recorded and live broadcasts occupying much of the day, as Churchill set about his strategy for war. As Barkway had hoped, in the ensuing months Lakin's voice did become familiar to listeners through its Pacific Service in Australia and New Zealand as he guided them through Churchill's new Cabinet, addressed the threat of invasion and described the evacuation from Dunkirk.

'During the difficult period after Dunkirk,' one listener recalled, all Australians and we English temporary residents hurried home to hear what Lakin had to say in his news commentary. His grasp of the realities of the situation, his sound forecasts, his humour and his friendly reassurance were qualities which kept us confident despite our extreme concern about the Homeland.[8]

If he did not have the prominent role in the BBC's subtle propaganda campaign given to the writer and playwright J. B. Priestley, whose ten-minute *Postscripts* for the Home Service every Sunday evening from June to October 1940 proved to be so popular as to warrant him the unofficial title of 'voice of the nation', then his broadcasts provided a similar service to the dominions. Priestley's *Postscripts* was broadcast live after the evening news bulletin, which was then peak listening time. 'The Epic of Dunkirk', his commentary on the evacuation of British troops from northern France, drew on an idealized view of the nation in making the connection between ordinary British virtues and the bigger questions facing the country, which, he surmised, amounted to 'snatching glory out of defeat'. Extracts from his broadcasts would appear in the following day's newspapers. Alongside the *Britain Speaks* series given by Priestley and the actor Leslie Howard (who would die in a Luftwaffe attack in 1943), Lakin's news commentary – 'a short talk built on the news of the day at short notice' – had become a 'popular feature', according to *The Listener*.[9] Lakin, like Priestley, drew to some degree on romantic imagery combined with a serious and comforting message that truth and justice would prevail in the end. His message to listeners, perhaps influenced by the liberal anti-fascist outlook of Ernest Barker,[10] was always couched in moderate tones and never wavered from the official government position, indicative of both his strong sense of loyalty and easy access to government. Once more he appears as a dependable lieutenant, while he was trusted sufficiently to come up with original and expansive ways of getting the message across. Over the next year this would distinguish his commentary from Priestley's more critical comments, and would come to reflect the political divide between defenders of the national government and the growing opposition among fellow broadcasters like Priestley and Vernon Bartlett.

As the war got serious during the summer of 1940, Lakin now spent more time at the Oxford Street studio and other BBC buildings than he did in the offices of the *Sunday Times*, though suppers at the top of the building it still shared with the *Daily Telegraph* with Leonard Russell and Alexander Werth became a regular event during the Blitz until the sirens sent them underground. Werth, now a war correspondent who had come to prominence with his reports on the fall of France, was an invaluable source on the progress of the war, and soon after he would depart for Russia following the German invasion.[11]

Constantly in demand and now divided between the different branches of the Overseas Service, Lakin was given the responsibility of communicating the latest critical happenings in Parliament while combatting pro-German propaganda – including that of 'fifth columnists'– to larger audiences, which now extended to Asia and the Middle East. His attempts to set the record straight inevitably incurred the wrath of pro-German propagandists like Lord Haw-Haw (William Joyce), who in one of his *Germany Calling* broadcasts included 'Little Cyril' among his targets.

But for others he remained a calm voice of quiet humour and reassurance. The wife of a British diplomat in the Middle

East, who described herself as a 'lonely and anxious exile', was another who wrote in to commend Lakin's broadcasts.

> I have just listened to him talking about ordinary English things, and thoughts and I am thrilled . . . His voice is like my father's and Uncle Bernard's [and] has that slow, self-confident homesy delivery that I know so well. That man does me more good and gives me more courage with his firm simple Englishness than all the observers and Wickham Steeds and others . . . [he has made me] cry with pleasure and memory and laugh with recognition and fierce resolve.[12]

A growing postbag and commendation from other broadcasters and BBC bosses made him a recognized name for overseas listeners, while he remained as well connected as ever, even if these contacts were now among foreign correspondents and reporters as much as writers and literary editors. He was fortunate in his friendship with Howard Marshall, by now one of the most familiar voices on British radio. Marshall was already known as the expert cricket commentator, but after more restrictions on sporting events he took on new duties as a popular host of current affairs discussions and debates. For BBC producers, Marshall's soothing, mellow tones made him an ideal 'crisis talker' who could prepare the British public for air raids, reassure them on food supplies and pull apart unfounded rumours.[13] Marshall's experience as a broadcaster was invaluable to Lakin and if their visits to Lord's Cricket Ground had been curtailed by the war, they met regularly for dinner and drinks, with ample time to exchange views on fast-changing events.

In agreement with Barkway, Lakin supplemented his news

commentary with a weekly ten-minute review – a 'careful summing-up' – of the week's news on Saturday evenings. His broadcasts normally ranged from two or three minutes to a quarter of an hour. In short broadcasts that went out on the different networks to Canada, New Zealand and Australia, he updated listeners on the 'Subtleties and Dangers of Rumour', 'The capitulation of France', the threat of invasion and 'local war preparations'. In a busy month of broadcasting through July and August, he provided a mixture of scripted talks on 'German Propaganda', 'Famine in Europe', the 'Anniversary of World War 1' and 'Air Raids'.[14]

In fact, air raids were a now a fixture of nightly routine once the Blitz on British cities began in September. After nights of heavy bombings had disrupted his sleep and made him feel he was 'living in the road', he, Vera and Bridget moved from their Hasker Street home to temporary accommodation at the Hyde Park Hotel. He preferred his home comforts and didn't relish the increased costs of living in the hotel, but he knew the French hotel manager and they agreed a price of thirteen guineas per week. The Hyde Park Hotel was packed with forces personnel, including soldiers and officers from the Free French, which added to the sense of drama and urgency. One Saturday evening when Lakin was at the BBC, the hotel was hit after a delayed action (time) bomb fell in the hall. Regarded as a 'dead' device, its shell remained for some weeks after it had been pushed between two sofas in the main body of the hotel, only to be removed later when it was deemed 'active'. General conditions in the plush hotel were relatively luxurious for wartime, however, and the Grill Room and bar were normally packed to the sound of animated chatter; even if the fare on offer was more limited than normal, there was always the Slaters restaurant opposite. For the teenage Bridget Lakin on visits to London from Berkshire, where she had been temporarily evacuated, it was an exciting time of evenings with her parents in the West End or listening to the conversations in the lounges, with the sound of gunfire and bombings in the background. For Vera, it was a busy time. Always industrious and independent-spirited, she and her friend Molly Mercer volunteered at the armed forces charity SSAFA (Soldiers, Sailors, Airmen and Families Association) to support overseas servicemen and their families.

Lakin's BBC offices were also damaged, but this did not stop him broadcasting from another studio during a particularly heavy fortnight of bombing in London's West End in mid-September. The following month a 500 lb delayed action bomb fell through the newsroom into the music library on the fifth floor of Broadcasting House and exploded just as Bruce Belfrage was reading the nine o'clock news. Seven BBC employees were killed when they tried to remove the bomb (which also destroyed the switchboard). 'It was a bad business,' Anthony Weymouth noted in his diary. Weymouth was in his office on the floor below, but despite the large jagged hole in the fourth and fifth floors he had a lucky escape.[15]

Throughout the autumn Lakin's messages of reassurance and hope in an increasingly desperate situation went out to his audiences in the dominions who now depended on his broadcasts. His knowledge of political events and personal connections to politicians enhanced his authority. In November he was asked to do an obituary for Neville Chamberlain on *Questions of the Hour*, a prime Sunday evening slot, after a couple of other candidates were unavailable and Churchill too busy – and perhaps an inappropriate candidate – to do it.

'What we obviously want is a well-known voice and a speaker with sincerity and judgement,'[16] he was told by Ronald Boswell, the Talks Booking Manager, by now well acquainted with Lakin's facility for broadcasting. His thirteen-minute tribute combined warm words about Chamberlain's personality and patriotism with criticism of the failures of his foreign policy.

He used his contacts with politicians to add weight to his talks and his assessments of the changing situation, and was always mindful to end on an optimistic note. This was what happened after the King's speech to the House of Lords on 21 November, in which the head of state restated his faith in his people and armies. In another speech on the same evening the prime minister situated the current challenge within Britain's proud historical role of defending liberty.

In reflecting on the two speeches in his broadcast the following evening, Lakin picked out what he regarded as significant phrases from each. The King was 'confident that victory is assured', while Churchill referred to 'the inspiration of old days and the splendour of our political and moral inheritance'. According to Lakin, these words 'epitomise to my mind, how we feel in London and in Britain and indeed in the whole great British commonwealth of nations'.

The two important 'watchwords' to be taken from these speeches, Lakin impressed upon his audience, were 'confidence' and 'inspiration'. These he emphasized time and again in his attempts to dismantle the claims of the Axis powers. The Italian campaign in Greece in the late autumn of 1940 brought one of Lakin's strongest attacks on Mussolini and Italian fascism: 'It would indeed be hard to estimate the far-reaching results of Mussolini's crime and blunder. We are only just seeing the beginning of them – and you may be sure they will go on growing in volume.' Despite his bluster, 'Mussolini,' he continued, 'had been badly beaten by a small nation. News of these hard knocks – which even in a totalitarian country cannot be entirely suppressed – will only make their [Italian people's] heart searching more profound and bitter.'[17]

The following week, on news of the resignation of the Italian naval chief Cavagnari, he reflected on his own time in the Mediterranean:

> I thought at once of people I knew in Europe – not statesmen or diplomats but just ordinary people – in various cities in Europe, and I wondered how these men would be feeling today. I thought of two people particularly. I thought about the little beetle-browed waiter in Floca's café in the square in Salonika. I am quite certain that in his pride and excitement he's spilling his drinks and coffee all over the place. Then I thought of Beppo ... a mad taxi driver whose cab rank was just outside the Grand Hotel in Rome. If he's only allowed, like any other Italian to know half the truth: let alone the whole of it, he must have lost all his exuberance by now. I'm sorry for him, for he loved Rome, every stone of it, and Italy too, and once not so long ago he adored his Duce. He must be disillusioned now, because even he must know that things have gone very wrong in this war he never wanted.[18]

At the end of 1940 and into the new year, as the Blitz intensified, Lakin sought to maintain a balance between countering Nazi and Italian fascist propaganda and communicating a hopeful message that avoided over-optimism. 'What we are now threatened with,' he predicted on 6 December, 'is a large-scale assault on the morale of the civilian population.'[19] This amounted to a 'sadistic destructive mania' on behalf of the German ideologues, with whom he had dined the previous year. On 22 December he went further:

> If there is anything more ruthless than totalitarian war, it is totalitarian diplomacy. That is, if you can call this axis game of blackmail, bluff and double-crossing anything like diplomacy. A game of strip-poker with a crowd of gangsters sitting in would be a pleasant Sunday afternoon's nursery game, compared with the game Hitler is now playing.[20]

His unrelenting tone continued in his New Year broadcast, in a week when the air raids had targeted St Paul's Cathedral and the area he knew so well from his earliest days as a journalist. This clearly hurt him and provoked one of his strongest attacks. The Germans had now

> thrown off the mask. They are the enemies of all that makes life worth living. They are the barbarians who are threatening to destroy human and Christian civilisation, as the other night they destroyed eight Wren churches, among them the lovely church of St Brides, in Fleet Street, as they destroyed Guildhall.[21]

At the same time, he warned against complacency and reiterated the importance of sharing known facts with the public as the war escalated. He disagreed with Lord Beaverbrook's view that some elements of the British press were over-confident:

> In these commentaries I try to give you as fairly and objectively as I can the truth as we see it here in London, and what I do want to impress on you is that at the back of all our minds is

the knowledge that the next months are going to be critical, that they are going to be very unpleasant, that they are going to be as bad as anything we have gone through hitherto. So, there is no false optimism, no wishful thinking.[22]

This balance of realism and optimism was one he recognized in government and during the critical months of 1941: 'The days are approaching when the supreme battle will begin between Germany and England. Mr Churchill has told us what to expect for some time to come: sweat and blood and tears; untold suffering; hardships. Until the days when we are ready with American help to kill Nazidom.'[23]

Lakin's broadcasts were now closely attuned to the aims of Churchill's government and its cross-party coalition, which matched the former's own desire to steer clear of partisan party politics. 'Who would have thought even a few months ago that we in Britain should be seeing a socialist minister?' he asked in a talk on Ernest Bevin's plan to increase production in vital industry and the intentions to utilize the capacities of women workers. This was a 'terrific step forward' that 'shows the determination of every one of us – all classes and all parties – to do everything in our power to overcome this threat to human freedom and human decency'.[24] The breadth of his sympathies extended further after the Soviet Union entered the war in June, with the potential for more alliances on the ground.

There was more opportunity for spreading the messages of resistance in his fortnightly *Inside Nazi Europe*, a widely reported series that ran through the summer and early autumn of 1941. This was his most in-depth investigation into the nature of Hitler's rule, and was helped by witness accounts of the behaviour of the Germans in the occupied territories. He recounted stories of German soldiers in Patissia in Greece who, from their balconies, ate from large loaves of bread before dropping scraps to the crowds below, and, in another case in the same country, of Italian soldiers pretending to distribute bread while on camera, only to retrieve the loaves after the recording ended.[25]

Earlier in the year, the BBC had launched the 'V' campaign – an initiative of Belgian programme organizer Victor de Laveleye to encourage Nazi opponents to paint unifying symbols of resistance. For his broadcast on the 'V' campaign, Lakin had benefited from the advice of the BBC's European producers in Bush House, who were well versed in the sabotage techniques used by resistance movements in the occupied territories. He received further useful detailed summaries of daily life in the occupied states from other listeners. Writing from Tangier, under occupation from Franco's forces where Germany's influence was growing daily, Alan Houghton Brodrick, author and historian, and an acquaintance of Lakin, told him that 'Your daily talks are one of the few things that make life in this appalling hole just bearable.'[26] He also looked for moments of humour or mild satire to emphasize the resistance to occupation. In one case a Norwegian, on being stopped by a Nazi gauleiter, was asked what he thought of the English. 'I'd sooner work for you than the English,' came the reply. 'That is very gratifying,' the gauleiter responded. 'What is your work?' 'I'm a grave-digger,' the Norwegian answered.[27]

At the end of 1941, he moved from his temporary base in the Hyde Park Hotel to Chiltern Court, a prestigious, stylish apartment block, complete with central heating, refrigerators and in-house restaurant, that had been the home of Arnold

Bennett and H. G. Wells at the beginning of the 1930s. From there it was a short walk to Regent's Park and Broadcasting House, while Anthony Weymouth, who lived nearby, often popped round for informal get-togethers and BBC gossip. Bridget was the same age as Weymouth's children Anthony ('Hod') and Evie, and they often had dinner together as families. Lakin still maintained his editorial role at the *Sunday Times*, often standing in for its editor, while his own indifferent health was not helped by constant late-night broadcasting. However, he was now an important part of the Overseas Service set-up.

'I don't know if I've ever told you formally how consistently good I think your commentaries are,' Barkway had congratulated him earlier in the year. 'I marvel how you keep it up day in and day out.'[28] To his bosses Lakin was an excellent broadcaster 'in a robust kind of way', had proved to be very popular and was 'very pleasant to handle'.[29] His performances behind the microphone were earning him a broader profile, and he was invited to present occasional discussions on books and writers, and the role of the press. His political knowledge and commitments continued to take priority and in February 1942 he was asked to give a talk on the 'Political Animal' to the overseas Eastern Service, which was an opportunity to set out his own thoughts on politics:

It is my business in life to watch the practical side of politics. I know that man is, as Aristotle called him, a political animal. I am not a learned professor. On the contrary, as I say, I have spent my life watching theories put into practice; observing politicians and statesmen and electors. What has interested me most is how man has argued about his form of society all through the ages and how he still persists in arguing about it as long as any form of freedom is left in any part of the world.

He was 'wary of utopias' and saw political life in the space between freedom of the individual and totalitarian governments.[30] This was a summation of his moderate philosophy, but his talk was deemed by BBC bosses to be less palatable to an audience in India where the independence movement was growing and the 'political animal will not swallow what the political animal in Britain will'.[31] Lakin was still committed to the Empire, and in that regard his rare contributions to the Eastern Service were no match for those devised by Orwell, who knew 'educated Indians would switch off overbearing British propaganda, and that a more implicit celebration of democracy was required'.[32]

Beyond the Eastern Service more offers came his way, and by early May, Barkway had written to him again telling him that he had put his name forward to present talks on the BBC Forces Programme, which given Lakin's own previous military service would make it an attractive opportunity. However, this new project did not materialize. At about the same time as Barkway made his offer, Patrick Munro, the Conservative MP for Llandaff and Barry, died at the House of Commons during a mock 'Invasion of London' exercise. The 'enemy' were represented by the Scots, Irish and Welsh Guards, and in carrying out the 'realistic incidents' converged on areas of Central London, left a time bomb at a government office, used 'fifth columnists' dressed as a chaplain and a chauffeur and attempted to storm Parliament. Munro, a former Scottish international rugby union captain, was a private in the Home Guard who were defending the Palace of Westminster. Though 'the defenders were very keen and energetic ... and to be found everywhere, on roofs, at windows, behind barricades', the event was too much for Munro, who had been up most of the night preparing for the activity: he collapsed and died in the Liberal Whips' Office.[33]

The vacancy came at an opportune time for Lakin, whose politics and sense of patriotic duty were ideally suited to the government's approach to the war. And, of course, he was the local boy.

Chapter 12

The Barry By-Election

Much had changed in the years since Lakin had moved away from Barry. Its status as the leading coal-exporting town had declined, having been badly hit by the Depression of the 1930s, and once again it had to adjust to wartime restrictions. In the interwar years it had lost some of that late Victorian–Edwardian 'progressivism' that, in the making of the modern, prosperous town, had very successfully married entrepreneurialism with impressive social mobility. There were fewer 'quick fortunes', 'elevations' and 'sudden breakthroughs'.[1] Instead, Barry of the 1920s and 1930s had had to grapple with stagnant docks, economic crisis, large numbers of unemployed and a long-term housing crisis.

Lakin had also changed. He had left as a product of Barry County School, a war casualty and an Oxford graduate in search of new prospects. He had returned as a well-known broadcaster and Fleet Street editor, member of the Athenaeum and a 'man of affairs', with impressive links to government and the literary world. Of course, in the intervening years he had visited Barry regularly. His father, after relocating his family to Highlight Farm – in what had eventually turned out to be another shrewd move and wise investment – passed his time as a man of independent means: the former butcher now liked to present himself as a gentleman farmer, cane in hand, who was content to peruse his land while it was farmed by his two younger sons.

Harry was proud to welcome his eldest son back in such circumstances. Despite the many changes in local politics in the thirty-three years since he had represented Cadoxton Ward, some familiar faces remained in office. Dudley Howe, a former Vere Street neighbour who had first been elected onto the Urban District Council in 1913, had served time as an influential chairman of the Finance Committee and, having overseen its transition to the status of a municipal borough, became Barry's first mayor in 1939. That change in status, following the charter of incorporation granted by King George VI, was formalized in a ceremony at the memorial hall presided over by Lord Plymouth (the charter mayor), at which tribute was paid to the early councillors for creating the civic culture and infrastructure of the new town.[2]

Howe was a director of J. C. Meggitt's timber importer (Meggitt and Jones Ltd), and his family and business connections were more significant for the town than his Liberal Party allegiance. Meggitt himself, the first chairman of Barry Urban District Council (and a former council colleague of Harry Lakin), had been a major contributor to Barry's civic life and was regarded as the elder statesman of the town, having by this time reached his ninth decade. He was a lifelong Liberal, while his son Arthur was the chairman of the local Conservative Association and thus closely involved with Lakin's campaign.

Since the early 1930s, Dudley Howe's deputy mayor had been Dan Evans, the son of Ben Evans, the Baptist minister with whom Lakin senior had clashed on the education authority. As owner of the town's renowned department store on Holton Road (close to the council offices on King Square) Evans was an influential voice within Barry's Chamber of Trade and Commerce. Throughout the 1930s Howe and Evans were the two dominating figures in Barry politics at the forefront of attempts to revive the town's flagging prospects, ensuring that the town 'passed into the era of modern local government in the hands of a small group of well-known leaders whose careers had been spent in local management and business'.[3]

Yet by May 1942 when Lakin arrived as parliamentary candidate, they were perceived as the 'old guard': heads of a cabal of independents, Liberals and Conservatives who seemed to have been running the council since the days when Lakin senior and others had warned of 'hole-and-corner' meetings. While respected for their long commitment to the town, they had also become the butt of local jokes and satirized as 'Dan and Dudley'. It was an indication that things had changed. The Labour Party had earlier made significant inroads into the constituency and in 1929 had elected its first Labour MP, Charles Ellis Lloyd. An author and popular figure, Lloyd had been unable to hold his seat after his party had split, losing in 1931 to Patrick Munro, who was elected as a national government Conservative. In the mid-1930s Labour had come close to taking control of the council, with its future MP Dorothy Rees prominent among those working for change. Though they didn't succeed in gaining a majority, Labour's strength and new importance ensured that when Howe left office as mayor, he would be succeeded by two working-class leaders. William Butcher, who served from 1940 to 1941, was a former seaman and coal trimmer, educated by the National Council of Labour Colleges and the Workers' Educational Association. He was followed by former dockworker and trade union official Stan Awbery, a popular figure with a keen interest in the history of the town, who would be elected as a Bristol MP in 1945.[4]

The rise of the Labour Party had brought more openness to local politics, and some of this filtered into the Barry by-election once candidates had been announced. Lakin first had to be adopted by the Llandaff and Barry Conservative Association. On 20 May he comfortably saw off competition from Ronald Bell, a Cardiff-born barrister who had unsuccessfully contested Caerphilly in a pre-war by-election in 1939. At this point there was no formal indication that Lakin would face a serious opponent, though John Emlyn-Jones a former Liberal MP and shipowner, was still considering whether to stand. From the start of the war the three main parties had agreed an electoral truce in order to maintain national unity, a position Lakin had long supported and endorsed through his BBC broadcasts. Under this agreement the party that had previously held the seat would be unopposed in the event of a by-election. However, various independent candidates, initially on a mix of anti-war platforms and latterly on the back of discontent with the national government, had won unexpected victories. In the three months prior to the Llandaff and Barry by-election they had defeated the national government candidate on three occasions: at Grantham, Wallasey and Rugby – the latter the former seat of David Margesson, who had just been relieved of his position as Secretary of State for War. In April, the Independent Labour Party's Fenner Brockway had lost to a Conservative in Cardiff East, but the timing of the Barry by-election enabled a broader gathering of supporters to be galvanized behind a strong independent candidate.

Days after Lakin's adoption, Ronald ('Kim') Mackay, an Australian-born lawyer with good links among left-wing intellectuals, announced he was relinquishing his position as Labour's candidate for Frome, Somerset to take on Lakin as an independent socialist. 'The electoral truce must go and there must be a general election,' Mackay told his supporters as he declared his candidacy.[5] Officially, the Labour Party withdrew from the by-election in deference to the agreement between parties, but it was soon clear that Mackay enjoyed support among ordinary Labour members as well as some prominent public figures. Though the local management committee of the Labour Party had expressed its support for the truce, this fell short of explicitly endorsing Lakin's candidature and left ordinary members and activists to make up their own minds. 'The broad fact,' reported the *Manchester Guardian*, 'is that the local leaders are keeping to their tents while the rank and file have extemporised a fighting machine on Mr Mackay's behalf.'[6]

The main vehicle for Mackay's campaign was provided by members of the 1941 Committee, shortly to become the Common Wealth Party. Its leading advocates were J. B. Priestley and Sir Richard Acland, a former Liberal MP and landowner who was in the process of selling his estates to the National Trust to help fund his electoral machine. They could count on the support of other well-known figures, including Vernon Bartlett, another of Lakin's former BBC colleagues, who in 1938 had won a by-election as an anti-appeasement Popular Front candidate, and Victor Gollancz, whose Left Book Club had helped to publicize aspects of the 1941 Committee's Nine

Point Plan, which included common ownership of property, democratic renewal and upholding political morality. In the years since Gollancz had courted the *Daily Telegraph*, his Left Book Club had been a pivotal influence on left-wing culture in Britain but had waned in the aftermath of the Molotov–Ribbentrop Pact (many of its members and key employees were CPGB members), while Gollancz's own communist links had been questioned; among other things, he had refused to publish George Orwell's *Homage to Catalonia*. 'Thank you so much for trying to save me from being a Gollancz author,' Rebecca West, a consistent critic of Soviet communism, had written to Lakin in 1940.[7] At the time, she was finishing her major book, *Black Lamb and Grey Falcon*; part-history, part-political reportage and part-travel memoir, it explored Yugoslavia on the verge of war, set against, as she saw it, the double menace of fascism and communism.

Gollancz was initially impressed by the Labour left's attempts to challenge the electoral truce, and though he had misgivings about Acland's ability to inspire large audiences, by the beginning of May 1942 he was 'urg[ing] those members of Left Book Club groups who are members of the Labour Party to do everything in their power, through their organisations, to get the truce renounced'.[8] In his campaign, Mackay was therefore able to draw on significant resources on the left of the Labour Party.

In the vote at the party's conference in May, it only narrowly failed to end its support of the electoral truce. Two weeks after the Llandaff and Barry by-election, this assemblage of socialists and left-inclined liberals carried Tribunite and *Daily Express* columnist Tom Driberg to an unlikely victory in Maldon.

Once it was clear that a straight contest was under way,

Emlyn-Jones pledged his support for Lakin, who quickly received the backing of other local politicians, including their most prominent figure J. C. Meggitt, who in an article for the *Western Mail* was happy to draw on his long knowledge of the Lakin family in promoting his candidature. The first British Party to declare its support for Lakin, however, was the CPGB, which quickly booked committee rooms and advertised meetings to make their case. Following the entry of the Soviet Union into the war twelve months earlier, British communists had reversed their original denunciation of it as an imperialist conflict to strongly endorse military action and call for a second front in Europe in support of Russian forces. That May, in a conference in London, Harry Pollitt, the CPGB's general secretary, described the demand for a second front as 'the decisive issue upon which victory or defeat depends', and argued that communist backing for Churchill (who had recently added Stafford Cripps, former British ambassador in Moscow, to his War Cabinet) with that aim in sight was now crucial.[9]

There was genuine public enthusiasm for Russia's involvement in the war and the CPGB's own membership reached a peak of 53,000 during this period. In Wales, where its influence in the unions was bolstered by anti-fascism and pragmatic leadership, Arthur Horner, the leader of the SWMF, had never gone along with the Molotov–Ribbentrop Pact, though his criticism of the party line was muted. He was now able to be more open and urged Barry communists to support Lakin. Leonard Finch, a former Labour councillor, was quick off the mark in asserting the CPGB's support for Lakin as the national government candidate. From a socialist family in Barry – his father was the town's first Labour county councillor and his elder brother the future Labour MP for Bedwellty – Finch established a critical engagement with Lakin himself that he would continue for the remainder of the war.

In Barry, the Communist Party was eager to endorse Lakin. In its statement on the by-election, where it made its demand 'for a united people to defeat the Fascist menace', it clarified what it perceived as the main issues:

> The Communist Party has presented a series of questions to the Government candidate Cyril Lakin. In order to be assured that he will stand, if returned, for national unity behind the Churchill Government in fullest military cooperation with the Soviet Union and other Allied nations for the complete defeat of Hitlerite Germany and against all appeasement. These questions he has answered in the affirmative.
>
> In view of these answers, and in view of the Prime Minister's support for Mr Lakin, the Communist Party recommends that he should be supported as the representative of national unity behind the Government for the defeat of Fascism. A vote for the Government candidate is a vote for national unity and not for any particular party.
>
> The Communist Party warns the electors in the strongest terms against giving any support to the ambitious individuals who present themselves under the guise of independents, responsible to no-one but themselves.[10]

Lakin needed broad support. The constituency at that time included not only industrial, working-class Barry, but the leafier and more salubrious Lisvane and Llandaff, as well as isolated rural areas. The backing of senior Conservatives like Lord Plymouth at St Fagan's Castle or Charles Rhys (the future 8th Baron Dynevor), former Parliamentary Private Secretary to Stanley Baldwin, was to be expected and no doubt helped, but his agent and campaign organizers were keen to present him as a figure who enjoyed the widest appeal. He was a 'Barry boy', unlike his opponent (an 'outsider' and 'London barrister'), with deep roots in the constituency. Old Barry friends came to his aid, writing to wish him well or volunteering to deliver election material. 'The family Longdon feel that I must send you a few lines to wish you luck in your political venture and to tell you what real joy it will give us to feel that our old parish of Cadoxton Barry is represented in Parliament by an old friend whom my husband loved,' Zoe Longdon wrote.[11] Another 'old Barrian' and 'staunch Liberal' who remembered him from their days together at Barry County School wrote to offer her support and promised to 'muster as many of my old friends as I can to do a spot of work in any part of the constituency where special help is needed'.[12]

At the same time, voters were informed that he was a 'man of great experience in the commercial and newspaper worlds', with great 'knowledge of men and affairs'. In trying to be helpful, W. W. Hadley, editor of the *Sunday Times*, suggested to Lakin that biographical references to his roles as both assistant editor and literary editor 'depreciated' each, and that in an 'industrial constituency' the former 'perhaps cuts more ice'. Hadley's other advice to 'be bold – and yet prudent' was well meant, even if the first virtue had been noticeably lacking in his own editorship of the newspaper.[13] His supporters also talked up Lakin's army experience: he had seen war 'at first hand' and thus knew the seriousness of the military campaign, which gave a clear purpose to his election addresses. 'The common man's great part in the war' was a regular theme and he was often accompanied by former soldiers.

Above all, he was 'Churchill's man'. That of course marked a change from his previous position as the 'Berrys' right-hand man' and reflected this new public persona. In fact, his speeches were almost a seamless continuation of his BBC talks: in Fairwater, where a huge banner reminded them of Churchill's endorsement, he urged voters to

> Reflect on the great battle being fought now by our troops and allies. Think of the encouragement Mr Churchill has given each and every one of us through those perilous days and nights and ask yourself whether it is not human that such a man should at times call for reciprocal encouragement from the people of this country to carry him forward with new zest and life.[14]

Two weeks before the election, Churchill, in a letter to Lakin, had sent a clear signal to the voters of Llandaff and Barry. The prime minister told him that he stood 'for the cleansing of the world from Hitlerism . . . You are the candidate who stands for the completion and execution of the plans for victory that have been developed by the National Government.'[15] It was a message Lakin could repeat time and again as he set off from his agent's office in Queen Street, Cardiff to tour the vast parameters of the constituency. More placards and posters adorned with Churchill's message appeared, and this remained at the forefront of his appeal to the electorate as he made his pitch, often from the loudspeaker van accompanied by Vera, Bridget and his organizers. Unlike his mother Annie, who had been a loyal Conservative, active on the various committees and in the women's association,

Vera had little interest in politics – 'she didn't get it at all'[16] – and, as someone who enjoyed socializing with friends of different political persuasions, found partisan allegiances disagreeable. This ecumenical outlook combined with her easy sense of humour can only have helped Lakin in reaching out to different people. His daughter Bridget, given time off as a fourteen-year-old schoolgirl to join her father's campaign, had a keener interest in politics and, having attended the *Sunday Times* book exhibitions, was used to hearing her father speak.

Beyond Churchill, Lakin ensured that voters were reminded at every opportunity that Mackay did not have the backing of the Labour Party and was pursuing a different agenda at odds with the priorities of the national government. In this Lakin was aided by the *Western Mail*, his former employer (and a loyal stalwart of Welsh Conservatism), which helped drive home the message of national unity. Now aware that Mackay posed a serious threat, it sought to remind Labour voters of their party's own position:

> It is very necessary as Mr Churchill insists, that the so-called independent socialist who has thrust himself uninvited on the constituency shall tell us exactly what he stands for. In what does his independence consist? Why does he flout the authoritative decisions of his own party which has laid it down definitely that no loyal socialist should break the electoral truce?[17]

The questioning of Mackay's motives went well beyond party loyalties. Jack Jones, an ex-miner and former communist from Merthyr Tydfil, and an organizer during the General Strike, was one of those who accompanied Lakin on his street tours. Jones was also a First World War veteran who had once stood for Parliament as a Liberal. He was also an author who two years earlier had written the dialogue for the film *The Proud Valley*, starring Paul Robeson as an African-American sailor who finds work and comradeship in a South Wales mining community. Speaking with Lakin at a public meeting in Llanishen (chaired by Arthur Meggitt), Jones denounced Mackay's candidature as an 'insult to the courage of men and women who were dying for the freedom of the world'. Where had Mackay come from? he asked the audience. 'Out of the blue,' he told them. He reminded them that 'National Government with party independence is impossible'.[18]

Mackay, an effective campaigner who later galvanized the Common Wealth Party's support sufficiently for it to triumph in three by-election victories over national government candidates, sought to exploit the vacuum created by the electoral truce at a time when the government's handling of the war was under scrutiny. Japanese advances in the Far East and defeats in North Africa had raised more critical, dissenting voices. The public mood was changing. An opinion survey two months earlier had indicated sympathy for the decision of independent candidates to stand in open contests against the national government representative.[19] Tighter wartime restrictions and shortages had also produced more opposition and a growing belief that social problems would need to be addressed by more radical measures once the conflict was concluded. Though it was a national government, it was an administration dominated by the Conservatives (who effectively had a majority of over 200), and Mackay and his supporters detected a new anti-Tory feeling. He feared that once the war was concluded there would be a 'coupon' election, not unlike the one arranged by David Lloyd George after the First World War, which would recommend only those candidates who had been loyal to the government.[20] Following Churchill's letter to Lakin, Mackay reiterated his support 'for ending the electoral truce and for a general election'.[21] It was a position shared by some Labour MPs and growing among its rank-and-file membership, who were becoming increasingly critical of the party's leadership for their deference to Churchill. At the same time, Mackay portrayed Lakin as a stooge of Churchill – too close to offer any critical judgement and with a narrow base of supporters.

This was also the view of the only other candidate to put himself forward. Malcolm Ritson Paton was a Herefordshire farmer, the son of an ironmaster, and a Welsh nationalist who decided to enter the race at a late stage so that 'the constituency might like a Welshman to put up for a Welsh seat for a change'.[22] Either unaware of Lakin's origins or dismissive of his London connections, Paton generally found Barry an unconducive environment for his Welsh nationalism. Mackay's campaign, on the other hand, was far more serious. He fought the election on the need for an alternative. This included a new vision of what post-war Britain could become. The Australian lawyer's campaign slogan, 'For Democracy! Socialism! Federation!', reflected the beliefs of an avowed European federalist, a supporter of proportional representation and, like Richard Acland, an advocate of the common ownership of land. His election literature included a programme to 'nationalise the key industries', a policy that would be a central component of Labour's 1945 campaign. This concern with extending democracy, devolution and an idealistic vision of a new fellowship among peoples and nations was intended to be the basis for a wartime mass movement that could shape the Labour Party in a socialist direction.

In Barry, a town where much of its industrial core was absent on military duty, the appeal to constitutional reform may have resonated more in the suburbs and among the idealistic and professional middle classes. The core appeal of Common Wealth throughout its short life would remain with more affluent voters, but the breadth of the Llandaff and Barry constituency meant it was the home of different classes and social groups with varying outlooks on life. As a port, the town's biggest contribution to the war effort was at sea – with regular harrowing reports of Barry casualties dominating local news – and this strengthened the notion of a 'People's War', which probably aided Lakin in his campaign. After some hesitation and complaints of inadequate Anderson bomb shelters in Cadoxton, 500 volunteers were recruited to the Home Guard, a dummy fort was constructed and information offices set up, a Spitfire Fund was established, roadblocks were put in place and mock air raids were organized.

It seems clear that Barry's cosmopolitanism helped foster a community spirit that brought people together in these years. After earlier cases of racism just after the First World War and during the period of Oswald Mosley's rise in the 1930s, Barry's black community was well established by the 1940s. In the language of the time, its Coloured Society and Colonial Club, headed by Abby Farah, a Somali seaman and entrepreneur, were integrated into the civic life of the town. It was not helped by the internment of members of the Greek and Italian communities but months later would be enhanced by the arrival of American troops, who under US regulations resided in segregated camps on the outskirts of the town, including one next to Highlight Farm.

Barry's multiculturalism, a legacy of the tolerance towards different communities brought together by its docks, almost certainly strengthened the fight against fascism. Not everyone was endowed with Barry's cosmopolitanism or committed to the war effort. Gwynfor Evans, Dan Evans's son and the future leader of Plaid Cymru, regretted what he believed was a dilution of the town's Welsh identity, did not feel he was part of a 'truly rooted community', and had left Barry in 1939 to live on his family's farm in Llangadog, where (in the words of his biographer) 'at last, he could live among naturally cultured people'.[23] On the outbreak of war, Evans, along with other Peace Pledge Union supporters and Welsh nationalists, opposed the conflict, with his pacifism at this point matching his nationalism. He opposed not only conscription, but the sequestration of Welsh land for military purposes at the Epynt mountain, while warning of the effect of evacuee children on Welsh-speaking communities; to these ends, in March 1940 he joined others in supporting the Committee for the Defence of Welsh Culture. In Barry his orations against the war in King Square had brought some embarrassment for his father (a staunch unionist and supporter of the war), whose vans and store windows were daubed with 'Spy', 'Traitor' and 'Fifth columnist', and a mild rebuke from his uncle who pleaded with him to desist in the interest of family unity and to preserve the reputation of his father.[24]

Lakin, on the other hand, was used to Barry's diverse communities and had enough political nous to know how to engage small shopkeepers, workers and members of the political classes. He was helped by friends in the press and more declarations of support from public figures across parties. He already had the elder Meggitt, who was happy to add his voice in support. Now he won an endorsement from the national leader of the Liberal Party. Writing from the Air Ministry in Whitehall, where he was Secretary of State, Sir Archibald Sinclair, who had served under Churchill in the First World War, told Lakin 'that the electors should show to the world through our democratic machinery that the country stands united . . . Your election, therefore, would clearly indicate the determination of Llandaff and Barry to wage the war with vigour and confidence until victory has been won'.[25]

It was becoming clear that attempts by Mackay to portray Lakin's support as dependent on a narrow base were inaccurate. He had the backing of Churchill, and now the Liberal Party, with some Labour figures adding support as well as a vociferous band of communists who held placards proclaiming 'Joe Stalin Backs Cyril Lakin', and with whom Lakin enjoyed very cordial relations. 'They were very sincere . . . everybody was pulling together. The left wing was very patriotic.'[26]

As the election day of 10 June approached, meetings became more frenetic as both the main candidates attempted to reach all parts of the constituency. In the last week of campaigning they addressed several meetings a day, many in the open air in public squares, outside churches or on the common, as well as in halls and cinemas, with Lakin revisiting the places of his youth in Cadoxton and Barry's town centre. He was an accomplished speaker, able to talk off the cuff, while respectful towards opponents and critics. 'You have to be careful not to bully people,' he would tell his daughter. 'The minute you leap to your friend, you've got to hold on to yourself.'[27] On the final weekend, he covered Cyncoed, Llanishen, Lisvane and Sully in one afternoon, before addressing a packed meeting in King Square outside the old council offices. Accompanied by Vernon Bartlett, Mackay arrived at the same venue shortly after to put forward the counterarguments. Lakin, Mackay argued, was merely the Churchill candidate and had no vision of Britain, while alternatives for a different future based on the common ownership of industry and a federate Europe should now be discussed.

The last days were fought out along similar lines. The *Western Mail* warned of the 'confusion' that would be generated by a general election, while reminding voters that Mackay did not have the support of the divisional Labour Party or the Liberals and was a divisive figure – a message Arthur Meggitt reiterated by warning of the dangers of complacency and voter apathy. Albert Bugler, member of the National Union of Railwaymen and lifelong socialist, warned a packed meeting at Barry Dock against the 'interloping intruder' who wanted to 'create national disunity and ultimately oust Mr Churchill from leadership'.[28] Lakin himself told voters that 'Mackay is sneaking [in] the Labour Party programme and trying to slip in the House of Commons by the back door.'[29]

Though Lakin had the official backing of the national government, Mackay, with the help of Acland and Bartlett, was still able to bring in speakers with links to both main parties for his final day's campaigning, which took in nine separate public meetings across the constituency. One of the meetings, chaired by a Conservative schoolteacher, was hosted in the Barry Liberal Club, which added to the feeling that he was winning some mainstream support. Lakin, in his final tour of the constituency, was accompanied by the Conservative MP and BBC governor Sir Ian Fraser, who after being blinded in the First World War had become chairman of St Dunstan's, the blind servicemen's charity. Fraser put forward the case that voting for Lakin was to support the military effort and what he assumed would soon be a second front. His last public backer was Sir Walter Womersley, the Minister for Pensions, a working-class Yorkshireman and former mayor of Grimsby. The patriotic message and the 'duty' and 'responsibility' of all classes to vote was repeated by his supporters in speeches and in the press until polling day, while Lakin made clear to the voters that he 'would stand or fall by Churchill . . . I was born and bred in this constituency. It is my home. I am one of you,' Lakin told them in his final message.

The outcome was regarded as very tight up until election day, when big efforts were made to transport voters from rural parts of the constituency to one of the fifty polling stations. 'Barry expects narrow margin,' the Labour-supporting *Daily Herald* reported, while on the eve of the poll the *Daily Mirror* predicted a victory for Mackay, claiming he had 'the undivided support of Labour'.[30]

The result, which was announced on Thursday 12 June at Glamorgan County Hall in Cardiff, brought a majority for Lakin of 5,655 over Mackay, with Paton, the Welsh nationalist, receiving less than a thousand votes and losing his deposit (he would stand in subsequent by-elections as a Liberal). Though Mackay lost, he did not give up his campaign and was himself later returned to Parliament in 1945. For Lakin, there were congratulations from the different quarters of his life and work. Lord Camrose was 'more pleased than I can tell you to see you as a Member of Parliament. I know it has been your ambition for many years and that you have now achieved it gives me a real thrill'.[31] 'No sooner do I go away for a bit on holiday than you get yourself into mischief and become an MP,' Nancy Pearn, the literary agent, teased him.[32] One of his

mother's relatives wondered if Stanley Baldwin's rise from a
Bewdley MP to prime minister would be repeated by another
Conservative with family links to the area.[33] Arthur Watson,
the editor of the *Daily Telegraph*, looked forward to the days
when with his 'long beard you will still be sitting on the green
benches as Father of the House'.[34]

Chapter 13

Politician

Cyril Lakin arrived at the House of Commons in unusual circumstances. The Palace of Westminster had been severely damaged by a German Air Force raid on 10–11 May 1941 – the biggest Luftwaffe attack on London during the war – which destroyed the Chamber of the House of Commons and left other buildings in pieces. For the duration of his time as an MP, House of Commons business was conducted in the House of Lords chamber, while the Lords were temporarily moved to the Robing Room.[1] He joined the House at a difficult time for the government, which was facing ongoing criticism of its war strategy. Within three weeks of his election, John Wardlaw-Milne, a right-wing Conservative MP, had moved a motion of no confidence in the 'central direction of the war' under Churchill, proposing instead that one supreme commander-in-chief – he suggested the unlikely figure of the Duke of Gloucester – should replace him.[2] Aneurin Bevan, left-wing Labour MP for Ebbw Vale and by now a constant critic of the Churchill government, in one of his powerful wartime parliamentary speeches supported the motion on the grounds that the 'main strategy of the war was wrong . . . the wrong weapons have been produced and third, those weapons are being managed by men who are not trained in the use of them and who have not studied the use of modern weapons'.[3] Although the motion was heavily defeated it had brought some anxiety to Churchill and the government, which, after a string of defeats to independent candidates in by-elections, was already under scrutiny. Lakin's victory therefore offered some relief to the government, and he was greeted on arrival with the congratulations of many well-wishers. It was the beginning of a new career – one that, with his various attributes and influential contacts, he may have reasonably expected to lead into a future Churchill government. He was a good speaker, was effective on committees and had the additional merit of being a skilled broadcaster; he would continue to flourish behind the microphone for larger audiences than before.

As an MP he was engaged, industrious and prepared to intervene on causes important to him, such as the role of the wartime BBC, the plight of war pensioners and, in particular, the future of school organization in Barry, which along with other education authorities was under review in the Butler Education Bill. It was Rab Butler who on 16 June formally welcomed Lakin to the House, with Sir James Edmondson, Banbury MP and government whip, seconding the introduction. Perhaps appropriately, Lakin's first speech, which came three weeks later, was a fifteen-minute contribution to a motion on government use of propaganda, namely information that had been authorized by the MOI and broadcast on the BBC. In the debate, opened by Ernest Thurtle, Parliamentary Secretary to the MOI in the absence of Minister of Information and

Churchill acolyte Brendan Bracken, Lakin was able to draw on his specialized knowledge as a wartime broadcaster. He offered insight into the important work of the Overseas Service in keeping listeners informed, while defending the BBC and MOI against charges that there was too much, ineffective or – in some cases – untruthful propaganda. The ensuing debate included several of Lakin's former BBC colleagues or others he had met through journalism. Vernon Bartlett, his fellow broadcaster, independent MP for Bridgwater and recent political opponent in Barry, argued that the MOI's role in suppressing material or stifling its coverage meant that it was 'not using this very good opportunity of educating our people so that they will be really worthy of democracy and able to make the machinery of democracy work in all circumstances'. Harold Nicolson, one of Lakin's *Daily Telegraph* reviewers and the MOI's former Parliamentary Secretary and official censor, refuted Bartlett's claims, arguing that the MOI was there to support the press.[4] Tom Driberg, like Bartlett, elected as an independent MP (for Maldon), also questioned the value of British propaganda. Driberg, who like Lakin was making his maiden speech in the debate, was well versed in the subject, having been an MI5 informant until the previous year (in the mid-1950s, while in Moscow visiting his friend Guy Burgess, he would be recruited as a KGB agent[5]).

In his speech, Lakin was typically cautious and moderate, avoiding the more contentious parts of the arguments while noting sympathetically that Thurtle had 'received a *damnosa hereditas* . . . and the longer I listen to this debate the more I feel sorry for him'. Rejecting the 'parochial' complaints of Thurtle's critics he argued that 'relations between Fleet Street and Bloomsbury [where the MOI was based]' had 'never been more affectionate' and that the main focus should be on how news of what was going on in Britain reached readers in America, now that it was a crucial ally. He felt that some American newspapers had not reported accurately, partly due to the inadequate press resources in London that were provided for their journalists. He argued that the BBC had been unfairly criticized, and he rejected Bartlett's view that more direction (or 'interference') was needed in the dominions and the colonies from the Overseas Service, which, in his experience, was doing 'brilliant work' and would 'have a tremendous effect in holding together this British Empire'. Home Guard duties meant Bartlett missed most of the speech, but he later wrote to Lakin to congratulate him and comment on it. Had he been in the chamber, he would have felt obliged to intervene, he told him, and went on to express surprise that 'you have not experienced interferences with your talks. You must be a model of tact!'[6]

While generally supportive of Thurtle and the government line, he had some reservations. The responsibility for European news, he felt, should be under one authority as

No newspaper can really control its actual man on the spot at midnight, who decides what goes into the paper and is responsible for it, but as regards news and comment surely it ought to be comparatively easy, to see that the right thing is being said to Germany and the rest. I urge upon my right hon. Friend to consider carefully whether we cannot make some rule whereby our foreign broadcasts are under one authority, and one authority only.[7]

In a lively debate, Lakin was able to share his experience as a broadcaster with fellow members. His 'large audience included most of the Welsh members', the *Western Mail* reported, 'and he impressed and pleased the House by his clear voice, easy style and well-mannered case'.[8] His 'reverence' for Parliament was noted, and he received the usual praise that followed maiden speeches. Over the course of the next three years he would be an active member, sitting on committees and making several contributions to parliamentary debates. He was among a loose, growing cohort of reform-minded progressive Tories who in these years attempted to set out visions of a Conservative Britain.

It was broadcasting that claimed his initial attention in the weeks following his election. The BBC, aware of his ability behind the microphone and keen to provide space for new discussion programmes on politics and current affairs, invited him and Labour-supporting Maurice Webb, vice-chairman of the Parliamentary Lobby Association and political correspondent of the *Daily Herald,* to co-present *Westminster and Beyond*, a new half-hour radio series aired at peak time. Throughout the series, *The Listener* gave it prominent space, previewing the first edition by citing Thomas Jefferson on the importance of 'frugal, wise and good government'. Following the failures of world politics over the previous decades, *The Listener* reminded its readers, there was a need for governments not only to cooperate with each other but to enable its citizens to take a role in running affairs:

> Since we are democrats and have a duty, whether we like it or not, to 'meddle with' government, it behoves us to equip ourselves as best we can for the task. The purpose of these talks is to give a simple account of our system of government as it now exists. Each week men and women actively concerned with

government – MPs., civil servants, election agents, policemen,
borough councillors – will be brought to the microphone to
answer the questions that the ordinary citizen wants to ask. It is
sometimes alleged that controversial issues cannot be discussed
over the wireless; enough, we trust, has been said about this
series to show how much – or rather how little – there is in
this contention.[9]

Lakin and Webb, who became a firm friend,[10] introduced
the programmes and convened the gatherings, taking it in
turns to chair or lead discussions. In the first programme on 28
September, sandwiched in the Home Service schedule between
Ladies' Man (starring Henry Ainley) and Shakespeare's *Julius
Caesar*, Maurice Webb chaired a talk entitled 'Politics and the
Ordinary Man', which featured two taxi drivers, a publican,
a shoemaker and an insurance agent and had been partly
prompted by Webb's encounter with a group of teenagers
on Harrow Station who were lamenting the state of the
political system and those who ruled it. Only one of the
participants in the programme was active in politics (prompted
by unemployment in the Rhondda Valley), and the question
of why more people did not get involved and what they could
change if they participated was a theme of the following
weeks.[11] In his conclusion to the discussion Lakin, according
to Tom Harrisson in *The Observer*, 'wound up forcefully with
an admirable theme. The machinery [of the state] is nothing.
It's got to be *worked* and it's we ordinary people who have to
make it work.'[12]

Harold Nicolson was a guest for the programme on freedom of speech, while Lakin's old adversary Vernon Bartlett
appeared in the 'Do We Need Parties?' episode on 9 November.

Bartlett was keen to continue his argument that even at times of war, voters needed to be given clear choices between parties. After all, there was a 'profound difference – almost a biological difference – between the Left and the Right, the Progressives and the Conservatives, or the Reds and the Blues', which was reflected in the contrasting voting habits of the 'comfortably off' and the 'have-nots'. Nevertheless, Bartlett saw that party discipline could be a 'curse' and a 'danger' during wartime: 'that's why I have got no party'. Lakin, in bringing him back to the question, pointed out that despite the party whip system, 'an MP has plenty of opportunity of making his views and convictions felt'.[13]

The weekly series continued to involve a mix of experts and politicians up and until its last programme, 'Where Do We Stand Now?', was broadcast in December. The programme had a wide audience and was well received:

The BBC has reason to believe that on the serious side of its work, *Westminster and Beyond* edited by Cyril Lakin and Maurice Webb, has broken all records. Hundreds of discussion groups are pursuing the themes raised in the Monday night political talks, and the flood of letters is amazing.[14]

The Listener carried the scripts of the programmes, while William Emrys ('Bill') Williams, its talks critic and editor-in-chief of Penguin Books, regularly praised the series. In his 'Critic of the Hearth' column, he commended its 'robust quality' and the absence of 'opiate' or 'sanctimonious adulteration', while admiring its timely contribution to the future of the country at a critical time: 'Despite overtime and the black-out and the perils of falling off the tram before it stops, British citizens are still assembling in public libraries or community centres or each other's parlours to hammer out their ideas of what is and what ought to be.'[15]

Westminster and Beyond put Lakin in the eyes of the public and suggested to him that another career in broadcasting was in the offing. George Orwell, in his role as a BBC talks assistant (employed as Eric Blair) in its Eastern Service based in the Oxford Street studios, recommended Lakin, along with Labour MP Edith Summerskill, to do five-minute talks on current politics in *The Debate Continues* series.[16] This amounted to a contribution by Lakin for the Overseas Service on Churchill's speech in March 1943 in which the prime minister, recently recovered from flu and with the progress of the war at a more favourable stage than six months earlier, outlined his ideas for a 'Four-Year Plan' of 'transition and reconstruction that will follow the downfall of Hitler'. Orwell, who resigned from the BBC six months later, was more critical than Lakin had been of the way the corporation handled propaganda – though he himself had been 'allowed very great latitude' and had not 'been compelled to say anything on the air that I would not have said as a private individual'.[17] Over the next few years Orwell drew on this experience for his book *Nineteen Eighty-Four*, with its Ministry of Truth resembling the Senate House base of the MOI, and its 'Newspeak' partly inspired by BBC bureaucratic jargon, while the cubicles in the Oxford Street studios where he and Lakin had delivered their scripts were refashioned as Winston Smith's Records Department.

The success of the *Westminster and Beyond* series held a wider significance for Lakin. Its topics reflected his own belief that the values of citizenship and democracy had assumed a new urgency in an era that was likely to be defined by the greater involvement of ordinary people in the running of their affairs. At a meeting in St Mary's Church Hall, Barry Dock in the new year he gave a lecture on citizenship, with the large audience perhaps augmented by some of his regular radio listeners. At the Conservative Party conference in May, the only resolution to come from South Wales was his motion on reviving the Conservative and Unionist Association's junior movement, which had been suspended at the beginning of the war:

> Unless we as a forward-looking progressive Conservative Party help these young men and women, give them full partnership and give them the benefit of our long experience in making them fit for their tasks, we shall fail in our duty not only to our party but for our country and our empire. I believe the time is ripe. As I go about the country, I have the distinct impression that there is a spiritual resurgence and a wider interest in political problems.

Contrary to a Board of Education White Paper on young people's lack of awareness of politics and public affairs, he had found the reverse was the case in Barry and elsewhere, which suggested to him that young people were 'realists not sentimentalists, and will not be taken in by totalitarian ideologies'.[18]

Lakin continued with his progressive theme throughout his short time as MP. In an article in *The Onlooker*, the Conservative Party's official organ, in August 1943, inspired by David Stelling's pamphlet *Why I'm a Conservative*, he expounded his brand of modern, patriotic values as befitting for the

> inquiring new generation. It will do no harm to the old generation itself to re-think and re-feel and re-state that [Conservative]

faith. Our very strength as a party lies in the fact that we approach new problems with an open mind and have no prejudices or antipathies inherited from pre-war days. Progressive Conservatism wants to provide the conditions which will enable us to give our best and to get the best out of life. Given an informed and intelligent electorate, Conservatives have no need to fear the verdict of the ballot box.[19]

The one-nation and pragmatic rather than ideological blend of Conservatism that he set out in *The Onlooker* carried echoes of Ernest Barker's lectures, where the latter had argued that democracy was best developed in broad-based discussion forums and community associations and through civic participation, while he had remained sceptical of doctrinaire programmes. They now struck a chord with wider developments in the Conservative Party. In the following months, the voices of some fifty reform-minded backbench Conservative MPs became more familiar in Westminster corridors as they 'coordinated parliamentary activities, published bulletins and pamphlets', founded groups such as the Tory Reform Committee and the Progress Trust and held informal dinners in the Athenaeum, in search of a 'new Conservatism'. Centrist in its leanings, it proposed a Keynesian mixed economy and state intervention in welfare and social policy.[20] From Lakin's speeches and occasional writings he undoubtedly shared these values, even if he was not a formal member of any of the groups.

In fact, his time in Parliament was fully occupied with work on other committees and in interventions in some of the big debates of the time – including the readings of the Beveridge Report and the Butler Education Bill. The Beveridge Report, after the public became aware of its contents in December 1942, became, according to surveys and post office censor reports, the most talked-about domestic policy, with great enthusiasm for its ambition to install a new social security system aimed at tackling the five giant evils of want, squalor, ignorance, idleness and disease. In Barry, Labour and trade union representatives saw the Report as a strong demonstration of the new post-war society they wanted to create and Lakin was pressured to make clear his full backing (in light of the reluctance of some Conservatives to wholly endorse its findings). He promised his 'wholehearted support' for the reform, and in fact the measures largely reflected the reformist outlook that he and some of his Conservative colleagues were proposing.

His other parliamentary commitments included his membership of the 'Post-War Policy' group of MPs and peers that had been given the task of developing a post-war policy towards Germany. The group endorsed President Roosevelt's call for unconditional surrender of the German military, which

> must be followed by the effective occupation of Germany and the setting-up of an inter-allied council of control. This council should be charged with the duty of preserving order, of carrying out the immediate demobilization of all German armed forces, and with many other problems. The only condition for the cessation of hostilities should be unconditional surrender. This should be followed by a peace treaty which, however, could not materialise for several years owing to the many different questions to be settled.[21]

His knowledge of Germany and the ruthless ambition of its regime may have helped inform that group's ideas for post-war solutions, and another issue where he could draw on personal experience was the predicament encountered by wounded or disabled soldiers. In June 1943 he co-sponsored a bill that made clear that in the case of all active members of the forces who are invalided, disabled or dying, the death or disability should be put down to their war service unless any other evidence is presented. This bill, in its second reading, was introduced by Sir Walter Womersley and contained a proposal from another friend, Sir Ian Fraser, for a select committee. Since his own evacuation from military duty in the First World War and his subsequent battles with the pensions department, ensuring soldiers received fair pensions had been a cause close to his heart. It was wrong, he told the *Western Mail*, that the onus is put on disabled soldiers to have to demonstrate their pension entitlement; rather, the presumption must be that the war is the cause of the disability.[22]

It was his intervention in the Butler Education proposals that brought him most prominence. Rab Butler's bill offered free secondary education for all pupils and would amount to a transformation of the education system, with particular significance for Wales. Butler, in his speech, emphasized 'my interest in the Welsh language, a special interest in Welsh problems, and I trust that over this year as we are framing our plans every opportunity will be given for the development of the national self-expression of Wales within the framework of our education proposals'.

In general, Lakin praised the proposals on 'educational reconstruction' in the White Paper:

We think this scheme is bold and progressive, and for that reason we welcome it. If the White Paper's proposals are eventually translated into an Act, we shall in due course change the face and mind of British civilisation ... My right hon. Friend the President of the Board of Education has realised that education must be carried into adolescence and beyond, that education can be unified without uniformity and, best of all, he has realised that there must be equality of opportunity. I think that is most essential.

Teachers were going to have a more crucial role under the new legislation:

They are the most important thing of all; they are the master key of the White Paper. If you get the right teachers, I think the syllabuses can almost look after themselves. How many of us owe so much to one or two particular teachers who have inspired us in our early life? This is a great opportunity for teachers. We must treat them right and with fairness, we must give them self-respect and must respect them. After all, teaching is one of the greatest vocations to which any man or woman can be called.

However, while grateful that Butler recognized that 'Wales is indeed a special problem [and] the offer of an Advisory Committee goes some way towards meeting Welsh aspirations ... I am afraid it does not go nearly far enough.' Lakin took issue with the intended removal of democratic control over Barry's highly regarded education system from local council to a district committee:

Whenever I hear the term 'district committee' I think of gas and water undertakings. This, surely, is a matter of human life and destiny and cannot be treated as a commodity like gas, water or electricity. Who is going to take any notice of the

Mid-Glamorgan or South Glamorgan district committee?
How will it be constituted? Who will take the trouble to look
after it, and how can it deal with different places with the same
interest that it should? . . . The real trouble with the proposal is
that it is really a revival of the ad hoc principle: a school board,
without responsibility. Will these district committees have the
right of inspection? Clearly not. Yet inspection, surely is the very
key to all educational administration . . . What I am afraid of is
that these district committees will have no life in them at all,
and teachers and managers do not want a lifeless third body
interposed between them and the authority.

He then made an impassioned plea for Barry, no doubt with
the memory of his early schooling and inspirational teachers:

I think I can give an unanswerable case that a place like Barry
must have its full control of elementary, and indeed of higher,
education. My right hon. Friend realises the place that education
takes in Wales. I think he knows that in many of the newer
Welsh industrial towns the real landmark of the town is the
school. There are not many others, and it is like the shadow of
a great rock in a weary land very often. Barry is one of the best
of those authorities. It has a population of 40,000 and a school
population of 5,000 . . . It has always been a progressive town in
its education. Before the Burnham scale was adopted nationally,
Barry paid probably the highest salaries in the Kingdom. The
result is that it has always had the best teachers. It has never
been asked to increase the number of teachers, but on occasion
it has been asked to reduce the number. Already it has two
nursery schools, whereas in the whole county of Glamorgan
there are only four.

... the people of Barry feel that the new education will be administered by people who are to be appointed by the county council and they will not be directly elected by the people. That in itself is a most undemocratic proceeding. Keenness will suffer, because they know that they will have to report, not to a body exclusively concerned with education, but to a body with multifarious interests which cover the whole public administration. Most serious of all, they have the feeling that such is the constitution of the Glamorgan County Council that there is great danger, as they have learned from past experience, that party politics will play too great a part and the real interests of education too small a part in the future. Therefore I appeal to my right hon. Friend. This is not an appeal *ad misericordiam* but an appeal to fairness. Is he going to throw over an authority such as that, which has the record and the financial resources to deal with elementary and higher education? Is it right and fair, and will it be in the interests of education? I say 'No.'[23]

Lakin's contributions to the debate over Butler's reforms reawakened his firm belief, borne from his own experience, that education was central to changing lives and rebuilding communities. During the same period of his parliamentary interventions, he attempted, in the *Sunday Times* offices, to persuade Lord Kemsley to commission a regular column from the classicist, author and educational administrator Richard Livingstone. Lakin had always shared the view that solutions to modern problems could be found in the classics, and Livingstone, a classical scholar who supported adult education for workers, had recently published *The Future in Education*, a critique of the limitations of the existing education system, which advocated continuing education beyond school.

He was 'obviously a remarkable man, great scholar, humanist and, I should think wields one of the most vivid pens of the day. He can even make education vivid', Lakin continued. 'It strikes me that this is just the sort of man who ... would be of immense value to the right kind of newspaper.' [24]

Lakin's robust defence of Barry's education system, which had done so much for him in his early years, enabled a closer bonding with fellow Welsh MPs, and in general his short period as an MP seemed to strengthen his Welsh roots. Among his Welsh colleagues was an impressive gathering of individuals across parties whose voices were heard regularly on the airwaves, to the extent that over a third of all broadcasts by MPs (excluding ministers) were made by Welsh members. In addition to his own regular contributions, Megan Lloyd George, Liberal MP for Anglesey and the first woman member of a Welsh constituency (as well as an opponent of the electoral truce), was the most prominent, with Jim Griffiths (Llanelli) and Dai Grenfell (Gower) also contributing regularly, with the latter one of numerous broadcasters in the Welsh language; others included Moelwyn Hughes (Carmarthen), Sir Henry Morris-Jones (Denbigh), William Henry Mainwaring (Rhondda East), D. O. Evans (Cardiganshire), Will John (Rhondda West), Professor W. J. Gruffydd (University of Wales) and Goronwy Owen (Caernarvonshire). The Welsh politicians were commended by the BBC for their lucidity and style: 'There is, I suppose, something in the Welsh language which teaches Welsh speakers to look after their consonants and allow the vowels to take care of themselves.'[25] This, at least, was a welcome development given earlier criticisms of the BBC's coverage of Wales, which had drawn complaints over the exaggerated and inaccurate dialects and accents that caricatured Welsh people, and had led to representations to the BBC's Welsh regional director and the Welsh Advisory Committee of Post-War Reconstruction.[26]

Though his time in the constituency was constrained by his various commitments – he usually made fortnightly visits that he combined with seeing the family – he had strengthened his links with his hometown. As well as dealing with constituency business, he welcomed Barry visitors at Westminster. Among his guests was J. C. Meggitt, his father's old friend and fellow Midlander who had given wise counsel during the by-election. Meggitt had seen every prime minister since Disraeli (whom he had heard as Lord Beaconsfield) deliver speeches in the House: an impressive list of Gladstone, Balfour, Campbell-Bannerman, Asquith, Lloyd George, Bonar Law, Baldwin, Ramsay MacDonald and Chamberlain, but was yet to hear Churchill. After showing him the remnants of the House of Commons chamber, Lakin took him off to the Lords to hear Churchill's speech on the German counteroffensive in North Africa.[27]

In the constituency, relationships with American servicemen remained cordial and friendly and there were further attempts to ensure that the strong bonds forged during the war – Barry would become an important embarkation point for the Normandy 'D-Day' landings – would continue afterwards. At a farewell meeting in Cardiff for Commander Claudius Pendill of US Naval Headquarters, it was proposed that the British government ought to put aside several million dollars against Lend-Lease to facilitate costs of family exchanges between Britain and the US. Lakin praised Pendill's work in strengthening the Anglo-American relations on which so much of future world affairs would depend.[28]

His various commitments and the intensity with which he pursued them, at what was now clearly the apex of his life's work, was beginning to tell. At the end of September 1944 he was put under doctor's orders to take a break from Parliament due to 'overwork'. In fact, as well as exhaustion he was suffering from tuberculosis, its symptoms a remnant of his earlier malaria and made worse by smoking. Away from the office in London, he spent some of the time reading, taking out books from the W. H. Smith lending library below Chiltern Court in Baker Street Station – often choosing Westerns, which he pretended were for his daughter – while most of his convalescence took place in Brighton. Once war had started, they had moved their weekend retreat from the Sussex countryside to the more easily accessible Brighton (which Vera knew well), taking a stylish new apartment in Embassy Court, an art deco block close to the seafront. He stayed in Brighton for the next three months before being deemed fit enough to return to Parliament in the new year. With the war reaching its conclusion, the nature of the post-war settlement was hotly debated, with Lakin initially assuming the national government would continue. Churchill sent a letter to the Welsh MPs with draft proposals for a new Welsh office that would be under the authority of a Secretary of State for Wales, a position advocated by the Labour and Liberal parties. This met with some support from Welsh members, though Churchill himself appeared only lukewarm in his commitment.

Once the general election was announced Lakin expected, like many, that it would be a comfortable victory for Churchill. Once more he was adopted as Barry's candidate and looked forward to extending his career as its representative.

Chapter 14

The Lost Worlds of Cyril Lakin

Cyril Lakin often appeared in his various worlds as a *modern* protagonist; a Barry boy who rose from humble origins to the citadel of journalism, politics and the literary scene. In Fleet Street, he was an ambitious but thoughtful modernizer where, taking on board the remit (and trust) afforded him by the Berry brothers, he drove forward changes to the production, appearance and content of the paper, helping, in the case of the *Daily Telegraph*, to produce a transformation in its content and style. As editor, he was a cautious advocate of new writing while retaining good relations with those of earlier traditions, and introduced new forums to bring together authors and the public. As the BBC became the modern medium for conducting the war in providing propaganda, news and commentary, he became one of its more successful proponents; his crisp delivery offered up-to-date insight that had been informed by his excellent political contacts. His less privileged background was no barrier to his career, or his wide circle of friendships and acquaintances in Fleet Street,

Westminster, the BBC and the Athenaeum. He knew that in the modern world, 'getting on' was about new opportunities and fewer restrictions on those with talent, but also about who you knew and what you belonged to. 'If you have got brains,' he told Bridget, 'you will get on anyway but if you haven't you need influence. I've got influence.'[1] Of course, he had brains and was a particularly astute judge of character, with the faculty to assess fast-changing events and to look beyond parochial concerns. But he was also a man of influence, a smooth operator, with access to those in power and an aptitude for getting things done.

This changed after 1945. As the year began, and he returned to Westminster after his bout of tuberculosis with the war nearing its end, the future of British politics still had to be resolved. Once Germany had been finally defeated in May, Churchill hoped to continue with the coalition beyond the war, but the Labour and Liberal parties demanded an election, and a new caretaker national government composed of Conservatives and a few National Liberals remained until the July general election. It was still widely believed that Churchill would be the likely victor in an early election. Britain was still at war with Japan, and the Conservative Party manifesto, Winston Churchill's 'Declaration of Policy to the Electors', was still focused on Britain's role in that conflict and its status as a leading power: it warned that the time when 'all foreign enemies are utterly defeated ... will not be the end of our task. It will be the beginning of our further opportunity – the opportunity which we snatched out of the jaws of disaster in 1940 – to save the world from tyranny and then to play our part in its wise, helpful guidance.'

Proposals for rebuilding health, education and housing

were set out under the 'Four-Year Plan' he had introduced
two years earlier on the back of the Beveridge Report and
the Butler Education proposals, while there were hints of
the Conservative suspicions of state bureaucracy. Lakin could
easily have written the last paragraph, which concurred closely
with his outlook on life: 'Our programme is not based upon
unproved theories or fine phrases, but upon principles that have
been tested anew in the fires of war and not found wanting.'[2]

Though Lakin had perceived a shift in outlook among the
people and, as usual, was alive to the need for the Conservative
Party to modernize its appeal, like the rest of his party he
misread the extent of the public mood for change. Having seen
off an avowedly socialist candidate in the by-election, he did
not believe that socialism, including large-scale nationalization,
would have wide appeal. In fact, he made the mistake of
comparing Labour's plans for nationalization to totalitarian
systems of state control. He was by now adept at pulling apart
the ideologies that legitimized totalitarian regimes, as well as
dismissing utopian schemes for change at home. He was not
alone in his preoccupation with totalitarianism. Churchill and
his Conservative candidates routinely characterized Labour's
proposals for a greater role of the state in economic and social
life as the first step on a slippery path to draconian rule. The
previous year, Friedrich Hayek's *The Road to Serfdom* denounced
what he saw as the new tyranny of centralized economic
planning and state control, with its dire consequences for
individual freedom. In 1945 George Orwell published *Animal
Farm*, his satirical portrayal of how societies (like Soviet
Russia) founded on egalitarian idealism can quickly become
manipulated into a system of totalitarian dictatorship. His
next book, *Nineteen Eighty-Four*, would take his assault on

totalitarianism to another stage. These were warnings of regimes that would expand once the Cold War took shape.

Lakin's error of conflating Labour's policies with totalitarianism also underestimated the desire for change and 'reconstruction' that had grown in the armed services and among a younger generation, which would help bring Labour to power. Crucially, he discovered that the mantle of patriotism, on which he had spoken so eloquently and persuasively in his BBC talks and in the Barry meeting halls, was not the exclusive preserve of Churchill and the Conservative Party. Apart from the fact that Labour had played a full part in the wartime coalition its manifesto contained more references to 'nation' and 'people' than it did to 'socialism'.[3]

Once notice was given for the election, Lakin was now the official Conservative candidate, no longer the comfortable consensus politician backed by a broad coalition of parties and groups. Used to being the conciliator and working alongside colleagues and friends of differing political viewpoints, he was required to adopt stronger partisan views in what amounted to a straight fight with the Labour candidate. Lynn Ungoed-Thomas, the son of a Welsh Baptist minister from Carmarthen, was a barrister, privately educated (like his party leader, Clement Attlee, as well as Hugh Lunghi, the first British soldier to reach Hitler's Berlin bunker) at Haileybury College, who had previously played rugby for Leicester, narrowly missing a call up to the Wales national side. More than ten years younger than Lakin, Ungoed-Thomas had reached the rank of major in the war and campaigned in his army uniform. This, together with Labour's optimistic portrayal of a brave new world, gave him the edge. Labour's message resonated with the servicemen returning to Barry, who were determined to find a better future in civilian life. Barry had given a lot for the war – its victory was celebrated long into the night on King Square on VE Day – but people wanted change, with housing at the top of the list of demands. There was a major shortage of council houses and some residents were forced into temporary accommodation in prefabs and bungalows. A different atmosphere prevailed during the election, with a large and more impatient electorate bolstered by the returning soldiers ensuring a large turnout, and more clashes were evident. Lord Beaverbrook, owner of the *Daily Express*, was particularly vituperative in denouncing the threat represented by Labour's plans to hand powers to the state (Churchill had stoked the fire in an election broadcast by claiming that a Gestapo would be needed to impose Labour's version of socialism). Labour leader Attlee, visiting Barry in the early days of the campaign, countered by arguing that 'there was a whispering campaign by little, mean-minded people who crept around old women and little children telling them that wicked Socialists would take up their savings'.[4]

Lakin's relations with his Labour opponent remained civil, however. His public meetings in the streets, squares and public halls – in 'the last old-fashioned party-political campaign before the television era changed the nature of politics forever'[5] – were well attended and sometimes overflowing. This reinforced the misleading impression that Churchill's message was winning and that his government would be re-elected. The *Western Mail*, once again a strong advocate of a friend and former employee, was upbeat on the eve of the poll as it reported 'Churchill's Message for Wales'. Apologizing for not visiting Wales during his election tour, the prime minister spoke of the work that still needed to be done in defeating the

Japanese and restoring the 'ravaged' and 'occupied' countries.
'The Man for To-day and To-morrow' called on voters to
support government candidates, which the paper helpfully
listed as 'The Men Behind the Man'. On his last major speech
to the Barry electorate, Lakin warned that Churchill's 'reform
plan' would be jeopardized if the 'dictatorial' intentions of
the socialists were endorsed by the voters. Many difficulties
remained, he told the crowd, but they needed to be addressed
in practical ways by strong government leaders rather than
by Cabinet diktat derived from abstract academic concepts.[6]

After the election on 5 July, the country had to wait
three weeks for the ballots to be counted, with Churchill,
accompanied by Attlee, spending the latter part of that time
at the Potsdam conference of international leaders called
to decide how to govern Germany now it had surrendered.
Churchill remained confident about his chances of winning.
Right up until the result of the election was announced, the
stock market, Conservative Central Office and most of the
press were expecting a Conservative victory, and many Labour
MPs (including Attlee) did not expect to win, while the
Manchester Guardian believed the best hope was for another
coalition. Lakin, too, after the poll had closed, was upbeat
about his and the government's chances, noting the 'largest
poll we have had for many years', and the 'splendid' turnout
from women voters. 'The indications are that the National
Government candidates have done well. I think the prospects
are very bright.'[7]

His defeat by over 6,000 votes to his Labour rival in a
turnout twice as high as the by-election three years earlier
precipitated a wider sense of loss. In its 'Demob' summary
on the future of the defeated Welsh MPs, the *Western Mail*

announced that he would return to 'important work in journalism and literature'. In fact, he would have a reduced role at the *Sunday Times,* one that was limited by further bouts of illness. But he had not given up on politics just yet. He did not expect Labour to be in office for long, he told his local Conservative association at its annual general meeting in October, where he was adopted once more as their candidate. Predicting that the Labour government would soon 'find itself in serious difficulties' he warned members to 'be prepared for an early election'. In the meantime, having witnessed developments in other parts of Europe, he reminded them that it was the role of Conservatives (and Liberals) to ensure that 'Totalitarianism does not happen in this country.' The electorate had been won over to 'extravagant promises' without realizing the consequences that would arise from the 'full shackles' of nationalization. In place of sectional interests of the trade unions and more nationalization schemes, Progressive Conservatism had to provide a new vision and strong leadership in line with the 'national character'.[8] His misreading of the situation – Labour after all had a strong majority and enjoyed popular support in its first years – was not unusual. His friend Ivo Geikie-Cobb (writing once more as Anthony Weymouth), in a 'One Year Later' postscript to his *Journal of the War Years*, remained incredulous at the ingratitude shown to Churchill and could only see 'unrelieved' and 'bitter' disappointments, a notable decline of Britain's prestige and standing in the world, and dark days ahead under Labour.[9]

These mistaken, immediate assessments of Labour's policies ignored the fact that the government led by Clement Attlee, an undemonstrative, upper-middle-class Englishman with a social conscience nurtured by many years working in the East

End of London, was building on a consensus first forged in 1940 when the Labour Party joined the national government: 'It completed and consolidated the work of the Coalition by establishing a peacetime managed economy, and the expanded welfare state envisaged by Beveridge.'[10] Many of its nationalization measures were endorsed by business and included public utilities in need of investment. Aneurin Bevan, on the left of the party, was more radical in delivering the National Health Service and council housing, but its socialism was conciliatory and reformist rather than an ideological assault on British institutions.

With its broad support and the continuing difficulties of rationing notwithstanding, Labour's victory represented a much bigger deal than Lakin originally imagined, and if it built on an existing consensus it was also a rejection of the old order associated with the Conservative-led governments of the 1930s. He might have felt a little aggrieved at being regarded in that way given his recent election and modern image and outlook, but Labour's landslide was unforgiving. Overall, it won 393 seats, with 47.7% of the vote. The party took twenty-five out of thirty-six seats in Wales, many with large majorities.[11] In Barry, the rejection of the 'old guard' was emphatic, with Ungoed-Thomas's general election victory followed four months later by an outright Labour majority on the council after the party won eighteen out of the twenty-one seats. Dudley Howe was among the defeated independents, while the election of six women councillors marked a further significant change, with Mary Holland elected as Barry's first female mayor.[12] These developments, combined with a mixture of illness and despondency, meant Lakin formally withdrew his candidacy in the new year.

At the *Sunday Times* he continued to attend the weekly Tuesday editorial meetings, often travelling up from Brighton for the day. Lord Kemsley, recently ennobled as a viscount, was in the process of bringing in a new cohort of directors and courtiers (including the Canadian politician and businessman Sir Beverley Baxter, a close associate of Lord Beaverbrook at the *Daily Express*). Circulation had reached half a million by the end of 1945 – twice what it had been ten years earlier – and despite the political limitations of the Kemsley–Hadley partnership, the quality of its literary and cultural sections, which owed much to Lakin's earlier groundwork in drawing in good writers and reviewers, now appealed to an educated middle-class readership. Desmond MacCarthy was still reviewing books, Dilys Powell was writing on film and Jimmy Agate remained its drama critic. Under the much-vaunted 'Kemsley Newspapers', the title he had used for his empire since 1943, Lord Kemsley hosted a lavish dinner at The Dorchester in November 1945 for 120 of his executives, including representatives beyond his inner circles at the *Daily Sketch*, as well as the *Western Mail* and the *Aberdeen Press and Journal*. Lakin was there with Leonard Russell, who had succeeded him as literary editor, W. W. Hadley and others, but a 'brave new breeze was sweeping through Kemsley House'[13] and a younger coterie would take over Lakin's mantle as a dashing protégé of the owners. These included Ian Fleming (seated with the Kemsley family at the Dorchester dinner), fresh from an impressive wartime career in naval intelligence, who was appointed as foreign manager – a role he maintained while writing his early James Bond books. H. V. Hodson, a former fellow of All Souls and another handsome figure known for his charming ways, was the paper's new assistant editor.

William (later Lord) Mabane had briefly been a minister in Churchill's caretaker government but, like Lakin, had lost his seat; he became one of Kemsley's close political advisers.

Now a more peripheral figure who was occasionally consulted for advice and to help out with reviews, Lakin's last major contribution as a talent-spotter at the *Sunday Times* was his recruitment of Jack Lambert, who would go on to be the paper's arts and literary editor. Lambert met Lakin in May 1946 after being recommended by Robert Webber, telling him that 'I have an ambition to be a theatre critic and in due course critical capacity, on a paper or periodical which deals with the theatre, films, books, music and "art".' Though disappointed at not being offered the chance to take up a recent vacancy as understudy to drama critic Jimmy Agate, Lambert still entertained 'hopes of meeting the right chap at the right time'. Lakin duly brought him on board, initially to write on a rather dull topic ('A comparative analysis of provincial newspapers can hardly fail to be interesting', the eager Lambert responded), but it was the first step for a career in press and broadcasting that had some similarities with his own.[14]

His weekly visits to London normally meant more time at the Athenaeum, where he lunched regularly with old friends Alec Waugh, Ralph Straus and the Egyptologist and historian Stephen Glanville. Now a member of the Library Committee of the club, a position he shared with R. N. Carew Hunt (author of *The Theory and Practice of Communism*), Stanley Morison, typographer and editor of the *Times Literary Supplement*, the Anglican priest Walter Matthews, and Sir Stanley Marchant, organist and composer, he was still able to exert a little influence. Among those he nominated for membership was Arthur Watson, the *Daily Telegraph*'s editor, who had been recommended by Lord Camrose. His effective withdrawal from public life – his broadcasting had also dried up apart from a solitary review of the papers in 1946, where he was introduced as a representative of Kemsley Newspapers – meant more time with his family. In London they were still visited by Vera's brother Mervyn, by now beginning to see some hope for a promising career as translator of German and French literature (he would go on to translate the novels of Hermann Hesse, as well as accounts of Second World War battles). Lakin was always wary of his brother-in-law, while Vera, knowing that he was still buying affection, continued to help him and was supported in her endeavours by Mervyn Savill's Romanian literary agent Rosica Colin, who recognized what she saw as the gifts of an unacknowledged talent, despite his constant clashes with publishers.

More time with family and fewer days at the *Sunday Times* and the BBC meant he lost touch with some of his friends, other than those he met at the club. Howard Marshall, whose wartime career at the BBC reached a peak on VE Day when he reported on the cheering crowds outside Buckingham Palace as they waited for the Queen and the two princesses, suddenly left his wife for Nerina Shute, a writer, socialite and film critic. The unlikely affair between the upstanding Marshall (who had sent his family abroad for the duration of the war) and the bisexual Shute, who carried on with a semi-bohemian lifestyle, left Lakin unimpressed and the two old friends drifted apart. In Brighton, where Vera took charge of his regular periods of convalescence, he spent occasional lunchtimes in the Norfolk Hotel next door to Embassy Court (drinking Guinness on doctor's orders), where his usual companion was the comedian Bud Flanagan. After spending the war entertaining the troops,

Flanagan had starred in the 1946 comedy film *Here Comes the Sun*, which tells the story of a sports reporter on the run after a rich newspaper owner passes away in mysterious circumstances and the businessman who takes over the ownership of the paper (after forging the will) lays the blame at his door. Lakin would have enjoyed discussing the storyline and sharing his knowledge of the newspaper world with Flanagan, for whom the film – notable for the song 'Tomorrow Is a Beautiful Day' – was the last occasion he partnered Chesney Allen.

He made fewer trips to Barry after his election defeat. As an MP he had been assiduous in keeping up with requests for meetings and participating in public events, but the demands on his time had taken a toll on his health. His father visited him in London and Brighton during his convalescence but his main contact with the family was now through correspondence where he reiterated his concern for the future of the farm and the welfare of his father. Harry, now in his late seventies, divided his time between Highlight Farm in the summer and his sister and relatives in Birmingham in the winter, when harsh weather conditions meant Highlight Lane was often inaccessible, and he was dependent on his sons for financial support. His elder son had paid him a regular amount each month since Annie died, but he was still short of money and needed a further allowance from Stan, who now ran the farm with the help of his own three teenage sons. Lakin's own finances had diminished after the loss of his seat and the reduction of his *Sunday Times* employment and he could not increase Harry's allowance substantially. After a visit from his father in July 1946, Lakin wrote to his brother Stan and his wife to 'settle' Harry's maintenance: 'This will take money and the question you must decide is what is due to him & what it is worth in present sacrifice to you.' He suggested selling some land and using money gained from rentals, but now advised against the sale of Highlight: 'For your family's sake you ought to hold on to Highlight. Certainly, for years to come there ought to be good money in it.'[15] Lakin was concerned that Harry wrote a will so that future financial arrangements between the brothers could be resolved.

His father had given the Lakins an ambitious, purposeful start in Barry, but he knew that his own rapid rise across the different worlds of journalism, literature and politics owed much to the two Berry brothers, by now press barons in control of their own empires. In 1945 the *Financial Times*, originally bought by the brothers in 1919 but under the control of Camrose since their division of ownership, merged with the *Financial News*, which was under the chairmanship of Brendan Bracken, the Anglo-Irish businessman and politician, and close confidante and follower of Churchill. The two papers had only small readerships – the *Financial Times* in the interwar period was a mainly dull paper with a limited appeal to 'uniformly bowler-hatted readers'. Camrose, by now not in the best of health and who, unlike Lakin, had anticipated a Labour victory, was keen to sell so that he could focus his energies on the *Daily Telegraph*. His 'capricious decision'[16] to sell to Bracken was also, in part, to reject any claims from his brother; Camrose was thought to be irritated by his brother's use of the term 'Kemsley Newspapers' on the head of the paper he had originally purchased (Kemsley 'always insisted in later years that he rather than Bracken should have been given the first option to buy'[17]). The suggestion of a split resurfaced in the *Financial Times* (now under Bracken's control) in the spring of 1948. Lakin, still employed by Kemsley, was disturbed by an article in the 'Observer' notes column in the *Financial Times* that had downplayed Camrose's role in the partnership. He wrote to Camrose to reiterate his loyalty to both:

> There is one thing you will never doubt – that I am as loyal to you as I am to Lord Kemsley. I was very annoyed and angry at the omission of a word about your partnership . . . It sounds deliberate – & those who do this are, to my mind, enemies of you both. I may be suffering from illusions of grandeur in my old age, but I felt I could not let it pass without some comment.

With his note to Camrose, Lakin enclosed a letter he intended to send to the *Financial Times* to set the record straight:

> The main credit for this achievement [the early success of the *Daily Telegraph*] must of course be given to Lord Camrose who is editor-in-chief. It is rare for a newspaper proprietor to be a superb business manager and a first-rate editor . . . One day, inevitably, the full story of one of the remarkable partnerships of our times will have to be written; a story that may well become part of the romantic family and business history of this century . . . I write with special knowledge of the matter for it was my good fortune to be a personal secretary to both the Berry brothers (as Lord Camrose and Lord Kemsley were then known in Fleet St.) when the *Daily Telegraph* was purchased by them. No one (except perhaps his brother) knows more assuredly than I how great a journalist Lord Camrose is . . . No one, on the other hand, has been more ready and insistent than Lord Camrose himself in acknowledging the part played by his brother in their long and unique (for truly they acted as

'one') partnership . . . And to me, owing equal loyalty to both, it would be unforgivable to overlook their joint achievements as partners over thirty memorable years.[18]

It was a poignant reflection on both the influence of the Berrys and his gratitude to them for what they had done for him at an early crossroads in his life. One month later, in June 1948, Lakin, along with his wife, daughter, and friends Bill Stanley and Colonel and Molly Mercer, was holidaying in the Burgundy wine region in the hills of the Côte-d'Or. Driving through Beaune on the way back to Dieppe with Stanley at the wheel – Lakin had never been a good driver – the steering failed, the car spiralled out of control and hit a tree. Lakin was killed instantly, ending up on the lap of his daughter seated behind. Stanley died within twenty minutes with the steering wheel lodged in his stomach. Vera, accompanying her friend Molly Mercer in the car behind, witnessed the accident, while Bridget suffered minor injuries, losing a tooth and sustaining some cuts and bruises.

The shock at his death at the age of fifty-four suggested a life that ended too early and was unfulfilled. By the time of his death, of course, illness had curtailed his career. But as his friends, colleagues and family reflected at his memorial meeting, held at the church in Belgravia (St Michael's) where he and Vera had been married twenty years earlier, his life had been full and rich in variety. The breadth of his friendships was indicative of an urbane and amiable character that enabled him to draw admiration and loyalties across wide circles, politically of left and right, irrespective of class backgrounds and newspaper rivalries. 'He was someone quite apart,' Susan Ertz, the Anglo-American writer told Vera. Camrose was 'deeply grieved' for 'a loyal and affectionate character' with whom he 'treasured a great friendship'. Viola Garvin, for many years the literary editor at the rival *Observer*, was one of many who rallied to Vera's support in the immediate aftermath of his death. For Robert Lynd, the essayist and literary host, 'He was the most charming man whom I or anybody has ever met.' Leonard Russell, whom Lakin had rescued and promoted from a mundane job in the depths of the *Daily Telegraph* library ('I owe practically everything to him'), was 'terribly moved' by the memorial service. Others from politics and literature praised his 'adventurous ways', 'fine achievements', 'spirit of generosity', 'companionable gaiety and charm', while commending the closeness of the couple and the strength of their marriage.[19] After his death, Vera returned to her favoured district of Belgravia, taking lodgers and using her creative endeavours to establish a catering business.

This was 'the literary man in London', as relatives and friends from his hometown often remembered him in the years before he fell into oblivion. In Barry, Harry (who, along with Lakin's brother Harold, attended the memorial service) outlived his eldest son by seven years. Highlight Farm, which Lakin had helped support since his father first purchased the property in 1921, remained in the family to be farmed by later generations. A nephew became a local councillor, while his early sporting interests, notably in rugby and running, were carried on by later Lakins.

His brief political career was over before he had the chance to see his one-nation Toryism come to fruition in the 1950s under the influence of Rab Butler, whom he could count among his political friends at Westminster. Yet his brand of Conservatism, originally shaped by a combination of the Anglican Church and the entrepreneurial values of Birmingham tradesmen, had in the years after disestablishment of the Church of England grown out of those limitations, and was now sufficiently appraised of Welsh political culture to be at ease with its Nonconformist political tradition. At the same time, his politics had been informed by his wider experiences in journalism, his editorial work and broadcasting, which had left him strongly committed to the union while ecumenical enough to find common cause beyond party. These values, and his moderate pragmatic Toryism, suggest he may have been part of the 'hidden potential' of Welsh Conservatism in the interwar period.[20] If viewed as a Welsh Conservative, then Lakin would now be considered, in the years before a Secretary of State for Wales and devolution, to be part of the 'English-Wales' variant, even if his background in industrial South Wales differed from the archetypal Welsh Tory. At a time when 'Englishness' and 'Britishness' were used interchangeably, he was certainly in the tradition of Stanley Baldwin's 'civic nationalism' (as Matthew Cragoe has put it[21]), a kind of unitary Englishness based on a UK-wide 'state patriotism', the primacy given to common civic institutions and constitutional freedoms, and the exercising of 'moral leadership in the world'. As a BBC news presenter broadcasting at a time of war, his patriotism was unquestionable, while his 'Welshness' was always subordinate to his Britishness. His interest in citizenship, in looking for new ways of strengthening democratic institutions, was evident in *Westminster and Beyond* and his attempts to get his party to appeal to new generations. This left a mark on his daughter, who after being sent by her mother to Malta for eighteen months to get over the shock of his death (which occurred a month before her twenty-first birthday) began working for the Progress Trust, the influential group of reform-minded Conservative MPs. She would go on to run its administrative side and look after its archive for over fifty years.

His life experience as a war veteran, as well as the knowledge and rising influence he gained from his various public roles – in a seamless rise that he seemed to relish at every step on the way – was much broader than the backgrounds of more recent generations of 'career' politicians: the ex-lobbyist or full-time adviser and spin doctor. Had he lived and been in better health, a return to Barry and a possible role in government might have been attainable in later years at the height of reform-minded Conservatism. After the constituency was reorganized for the 1950 election, Dorothy Rees was elected for Labour as the first woman MP in South Wales; a year later she lost to Raymond Gower, who would serve as a one-nation Tory for over thirty years. He was, like Lakin, a faithful servant, committee man and columnist for the *Western Mail,* though perhaps without the style and panache of his predecessor.

Endnotes

Chapter 1. A Man from Somewhere

1   Iorwerth W. Prothero, 'The Port and Railways of Barry', in Donald Moore, ed., *Barry: The Centenary Book* (Barry: Barry Centenary Book Committee, 1984), 220–21.

2   Andy Croll, *Barry Island: The Making of a Seaside Playground, c.1790–c.1965* (Cardiff: University of Wales Press, 2020), 79.

3   Brian C. Luxton, 'Ambition, Vice and Virtue: Social Life, 1884–1914', in *Barry: The Centenary Book*, 272.

4   Daryl Leeworthy, *Labour Country: Political Radicalism and Social Democracy in Wales 1831–1985* (Cardigan: Parthian, 2018), 76–7.

5   Cited in Luxton, 'Ambition, Vice and Virtue', 271.

6   Luxton, 'Ambition, Vice and Virtue', 289.

7   As reported in the *South Wales Star* (SWS), 28/4/1893.

8   The SWS published profiles of some of the leading Barry figures under its 'Darius Dare' column. Meggitt appears in the edition dated 21/10/1892.

9   SWS, 28/10/1892.

10   As reported in the *Barry Dock News* (BDN), 26/2/1892.

11   SWS, 16/9/1892.

12   Bridget Lakin, interview with author.

13   *Barry Herald*, 25/6/1897.

14   Though the entry in the Cadoxton School register gives his date of birth a year later. Cadoxton School records are held in the Glamorgan Archives (GA), C/SE 13/1/2.

15   Leeworthy, *Labour Country*, 77–8.

16   Highlight Farm Papers (HFP), Lakin to parents, 25/11/1924.

[17] GA, C/SE 13/1/2.

[18] BDN, 25/5/1906.

[19] GA, Lib/31/1, Brian C. Luxton, *St Cadoc's: A History of the Old Village Church Cadoxton-Juxta-Barry* (Cadoxton: self-published, 1980).

[20] BDN, 6/6/1902.

[21] Frank Bright, *Sketches Around Cardiff*, 141, cited in Luxton, *St Cadoc's*.

[22] BDN, 21/11/1902.

[23] Times Newspapers Ltd (TNL) Archive, ST/ED/CL/2/1, Zoe Longdon to Lakin, 24/5/1942.

[24] BDN, 12/2/1904.

[25] Some of the paintings are kept at Highlight Farm. Christine James, interview with author.

[26] Bridget Lakin, interview with author.

[27] BDN, 21/7/1905.

[28] Elsie Janner, *Barnett Janner: A Personal Portrait* (London: Robson Books, 1984), 4–5.

[29] BDN, 15/12/1905.

[30] John Dickie, *The Craft: How the Freemasons Made the Modern World* (London: Hodder and Stoughton, 2020), 7.

[31] L. N. A. Davies, *The Centennial History of Barry Lodge No. 2357 1890–1990* (London: The Lodge, 1990). Held at Museum of Freemasonry, Freemasons' Hall.

[32] Davies, 'Frontispiece', in *The Centennial History of Barry Lodge*.

[33] BDN, 6/1/1905.

[34] BDN, 15/9/1905.

Chapter 2. The Lakins: Making a Mark in Barry

[1] BDN, 30/3/1900.

[2] BDN, 30/3/1900.

[3] Leeworthy, *Labour Country*, 107.

[4] Peter Stead, 'The Language of Edwardian Politics', in Dai Smith, ed., *A People and a Proletariat: Essays in the History of Wales, 1780–1980* (London: Pluto Press, 1980), 153.

[5] BDN, 6/4/1906.

[6] BDN, 18/5/1906.

[7] BDN, 9/3/1906.

[8] *Barry Herald*, 6/4/1906.

[9] BDN, 6/4/1906.

[10] BDN, 1/6/1906.

[11] BDN, 30/8/1901.

[12] Cited in BDN, 9/11/1906. Details of Urban District Council meetings are held in the GA at GB 214 BB. Details of the meetings were described in depth in the BDN.

13 BDN, 10/5/1907.

14 BDN, 18/5/1906.

15 BDN, 24/4/1908.

16 BDN, 24/4/1908.

17 BDN, 24/4/1908.

18 Barnett Janner, unpublished memoir, cited in Elsie Janner, *Barnett Janner: A Personal Portrait*, 11.

19 The National Library of Wales (NLW), A/1, Gareth Vaughan Jones Papers (Major Edgar Jones). Former Barry County School master in letter of appreciation to Edgar Jones on his retirement.

20 *Western Mail*, 28/4/1945. Speech to Conservative women in his Llandaff and Barry constituency.

21 Pupil reminiscences in 'Barry County Schools 1896–1946', GA D513/1.

22 Lady (Ruth) Morris (Barnett Janner's daughter), correspondence with author.

23 Edward David, 'Illtyd David and the Extra-Mural Community 1920–81', Centenary Essays, Swansea University 1920–2020 (2020), https://collections. swansea.ac.uk/s/swansea-2020/page/illtyd-david, accessed 30 Apr. 2021.

24 Elsie Janner, *Barnett Janner: A Personal Portrait*, p. 10.

25 GA, D513/1, 'Barry County Schools 1896–1946'.

26 Lakin's Barry County School notebook in the HFP.

27 GA, D513/1, 'Barry County Schools 1896–1946'.

28 BDN, 1/5/1908.

29 Peter Stead, 'The Town That Had Come of Age', in *Barry: The Centenary Book*, 368.

30 GA, D513/1, Edgar Jones, 'Barry County Schools: The First Four Decades'.

31 W. M. Davies, *Ystrad Meurig Grammar School 1757–1957: Outline History of the School* (Aberystwyth: Cambrian News, 1957), 13. I am grateful to Nicky Hammond, Special Collections Archivist at the University of Wales Trinity Saint David for this and for advice and information on the history of the school.

Chapter 3. Oxford

1 Herbert Armitage James, Obituary, *The Times*, 16/11/1931.

2 Obituary, *The Times*, 16/11/1931.

3 NLW, GB 0210 WAITES ARCH/MSS, David Lloyd George Papers, 1–42.

4 NLW, GB 0210 WAITES ARCH/MSS 9/10/1912, W. Watkin Davies Papers, 1–47, file 45.

5 Information provided by Oxford University Archives.

6 HFP.

7 NLW, GB 0210 WAITES ARCH/MSS 17/10/1912, file 45.

8 Ernest Barker, *Age and Youth: Memories of Three Universities and Father of the Man* (Oxford: Oxford University Press, 1953), 40.

[9] NLW, GB 0210 WAITES ARCH/MSS 9/6/1913, file 45.

[10] See Andrzej Olechnowicz, 'Liberal Anti-Fascism in the 1930s: The Case of Sir Ernest Barker', *Albion*, 36 (2004), 636–60 for a good discussion on the evolution of Barker's political thought.

[11] NLW, GB 0210 WAITES ARCH/MSS 14/1/1913, file 45.

[12] NLW, GB 0210 WAITES ARCH/MSS 14/6/1913, file 45.

[13] Bridget Lakin, interview with author.

[14] St John's College Archive (SJCA), MISC II.114 8/5/1914.

[15] C. F. G. Masterman, 'Preface to New and Popular Edition', in *The Condition of England* (London: Faber and Faber, 2008). See also David Selbourne, 'The Condition of England', *New Statesman* (19 Nov. 2009), https://www. newstatesman.com/books/2009/11/masterman-england-times-world, accessed 30 Apr. 2021.

[16] Masterman, 'Postscript' in *The Condition of England*, 234.

[17] Barker, *Age and Youth*, 40.

[18] Mo Moulton, *Mutual Admiration Society: How Dorothy L. Sayers and Her Oxford Circle Remade the World for Women* (London: Corsair, 2019).

[19] NLW, GB 0210 WAITES ARCH/MSS 30/11/1913, file 46.

[20] SJCA, MISC II.114 29/5/1913.

[21] NLW, GB 0210 WAITES ARCH/MSS 4/2/1913, file 45.

[22] She reappeared in Swansea a few days later. 'Sensational Disappearance from Cadoxton, Barry: Young Lady and Young Tradesman Missing', BDN, 21/11/1913.

[23] NLW, GB 0210 WAITES ARCH/MSS 20/5/1914, file 46.

[24] Members of the Oxford Faculty of Modern History, *Why We Are at War: Great Britain's Case* (Oxford: Oxford University Press, 1914), 5. The authors were Ernest Barker, H. W. C. Davis, C. R. L. Fletcher, Arthur Hassall, L. G. Wickham Legg and F. Morgan.

[25] Oxford Faculty of Modern History, *Why We Are at War*, 29–30.

[26] Oxford Faculty of Modern History, *Why We Are at War*, 109.

[27] Oxford Faculty of Modern History, *Why We Are at War*, 116.

[28] Oxford Faculty of Modern History, *Why We Are at War*, 14–5.

[29] Oxford Faculty of Modern History, *Why We Are at War*, 117.

[30] SJCA, MISC II.114 8/10/1914, 7/11/1914.

[31] SJCA, MISC II.114 24/11/1914.

Chapter 4. Lieutenant Lakin

[1] Nigel Fisher, *Harold Macmillan: A Biography* (London: Weidenfeld and Nicolson, 1982), 5.

[2] Oxford Faculty of Modern History, *Why We Are at War*, 117.

[3] His army notebook with details of training exercises is in the HFP.

[4] HFP, James Laycock to Lakin, 2/7/1915.

5 NLW, GB 0210 WAITES ARCH/MSS 3/4/1915, 201–30, Ernest Willmore to William Watkin Davies, correspondence series 68–339.

6 NLW, GB 0210 WAITES ARCH/MSS 30/7/1915, 201–30, Ernest Willmore to William Watkin Davies, correspondence series 68–339.

7 HFP, Stan Lakin to Cyril Lakin, 5/8/1915.

8 The War Diary of the 8ᵗʰ South Wales Borderers is held in the National Archives (TNA), WO 95/2166/29.

9 TNA, WO 95/2166/29, Appendix 2: 'Report on operations during the night of 21 Sept. 1915 in the CHUIGNES sector'.

10 Alan Wakefield and Simon Moody, *Under the Devil's Eye: The British Military Experience in Macedonia, 1915–18* (Barnsley: Pen and Sword, 2011), 3.

11 Testimony of Iorwerth Miles Davies in Stuart Sillars, 'A Welshman in Salonika, 1916–1919: Iorwerth Miles Davies (1893–1981)', *Llafur*, 3 (1983), 66–75.

12 Richard Harding Davis, *With the French in France and Salonika*, (New York: Charles Scribner's Sons, 1916), 121–2.

13 TNA, WO 95/4857.

14 Part one of the letter was published in BDN, 14/1/1916, with the second part in the following week.

15 BDN, 'Barry Boys at Salonika', 21/1/1916.

16 HFP, Cyril Lakin to his parents, 21/8/1916.

Chapter 5. Recuperation: New Horizons

1 Bernard Brabin, 'Malaria's contribution to World War One – the unexpected adversary', *Malaria Journal*, 13 (2014). doi: 10.1186/1475-2875-13-497.

2 John Keegan, *The First World War* (London: The Bodley Head, 2014), 306, 308, cited in Brabin.

3 Brabin, 'Malaria's contribution to World War One'.

4 Bridget Lakin, interview with author.

5 Bridget Lakin, interview with author.

6 John Postgate and Mary Postgate, *A Stomach for Dissent: The Life of Raymond Postgate, 1896–1971* (Keele: Keele University Press, 1994), 90.

7 Duncan Bowie, *Reform and Revolt in the City of Dreaming Spires: Radical, Socialist and Communist Politics in the City of Oxford 1830–1980* (London: University of Westminster Press, 2018) has a good discussion of these issues.

8 Jonathan Hicks, *Barry and the Great War 1914–1918* (Barry: Fielding Publishing, 2007), 10, 257.

9 Steve Duffy, 'How Spanish Flu Epidemic Devastated Wales in 1918', BBC News (12 Oct. 2018), https://www.bbc.co.uk/news/uk-wales-45577611, accessed 30 Apr. 2021, drawing on relevant medical reports, death certificates and Registrar-General data, estimates the death toll in Wales from Spanish flu as being approximately 11,400.

[10] BDN, 14/12/1917. The play was written by the Canadian author Sara Jeannette Duncan.

[11] BDN, 15/2/1918.

[12] Lakin's Medal Card is held at TNA, WO372/11/223635.

[13] Leeworthy, *Labour Country*, 214–5.

[14] HFP, Ministry of Food correspondence, 1/6/1918, 31/3/1920.

[15] HFP, 8/7/1920.

[16] Luxton, 'Ambition, Vice and Virtue', 329.

[17] Neil Evans, 'The South Wales Race Riots of 1919', *Llafur*, 3 (1980), 13.

[18] Jacqueline Jenkinson, *The 1919 Riots in Britain: Their Background and Consequences* (Edinburgh University, 1987) [unpublished PhD], 241, https://era.ed.ac.uk/bitstream/handle/1842/6874/D086172.pdf?sequence=1&isAllowed=y, accessed 30 Apr. 2021. Jenkinson provides a detailed account of the Barry riots.

[19] Jenkinson, *The 1919 Riots*, 261, 264.

[20] TNL Archive, ST/ED/CL/3/3.

[21] John Ruskin, 'Lecture 5: Crystal Virtues', in *The Ethics of the Dust: Ten Lectures to Little Housewives on the Elements of Crystallization* (London: George Allen & Co, 1883).

[22] *Western Mail*, 17/6/1922.

[23] Bridget Lakin, interview with author.

[24] HFP, Lakin to parents, 25/7/1923.

[25] HFP, Lakin to parents, 6/7/1923.

[26] HFP, Lakin to parents, 15/10/1923.

[27] HFP, Lakin to parents, 21/11/1923.

[28] HFP, Marjorie Davies to Mrs Lakin, 8/10/1923.

Chapter 6. The Berry Brothers

[1] Joe England, *Merthyr: The Crucible of Modern Wales* (Cardigan: Parthian, 2017), 18.

[2] Duff Hart-Davis *The House the Berrys Built: Inside the Telegraph, 1928–1986* (London: Hodder and Stoughton, 1990), 12.

[3] Robert Smyly, private papers, 'The Berry Brothers', 5.

[4] Harold Hobson, Phillip Knightley and Leonard Russell, eds., *The Pearl of Days: An Intimate Memoir of the Sunday Times 1822–1972* (London: Hamish Hamilton, 1972), 67.

[5] *The Pearl of Days*, 70–71.

[6] *The Pearl of Days*, 105.

[7] Hart-Davis, *The House the Berrys Built*, 20.

[8] 'Personalities and Powers: The Berry Brothers', *Time and Tide*, 28/3/1924.

[9] Hart-Davis, *The House the Berrys Built*, 22.

[10] 'Personalities and Powers: The Berry Brothers', *Time and Tide*, 28/3/1924.

[11] HFP, Lakin to parents, 31/3/1925.

12 HFP, Lakin to parents, 1/1/1925.

13 HFP, Lakin to parents, 19/2/1925.

14 HFP, Lakin to parents, 14/3/1925.

15 HFP, Lakin to parents, 28/6/1925, 29/6/1925.

16 HFP, Lakin to parents 3/6/1925; Owen Picton Davies, 'DAVIES, Sir WILLIAM (1863–1935), journalist and editor', *Dictionary of Welsh Biography* (1959), https://biography.wales/article/s-DAVI-WIL-1863, accessed 30 Apr. 2021.

17 HFP, Lakin to parents, 28/29/6/1925.

18 Bridget Lakin, interview with author.

19 Bridget Lakin, interview with author.

20 Hart-Davis, *The House the Berrys Built*, 46.

21 *The Pearl of Days*, 135.

22 *The Pearl of Days*, 187.

Chapter 7. Vera: An English Marriage

1 Felicity Peake, *Pure Chance*, (Shrewsbury: Airlife Publishing, 1993), 3.

2 Peake, *Pure Chance*, 6.

3 Bridget Lakin, interview with author.

4 Bridget Lakin, interview with author.

5 *Western Mail*, 23/1/1926.

6 Bridget Lakin, interview with author.

7 Christine James; Bridget Lakin, interview with author.

8 D. J. Williams, *Capitalist Combination in the Coal Industry* (London: Labour Publishing Company, 1924), 99, cited in Hywel Francis and Dai Smith, *The Fed: A History of the South Wales Miners in the Twentieth Century* (Cardiff: University of Wales Press, 1998), 138.

9 Hart-Davis, *The House the Berrys Built*, 54.

10 Hart-Davis, *The House the Berrys Built*, 57.

11 *The Pearl of Days*, 188.

12 *The Pearl of Days*, 189.

13 *The Pearl of Days*, 189.

Chapter 8. Fleet Street Editor

1 BBC Written Archives (BBC WA), L1/289/12, Marshall's BBC file.

2 Howard Marshall, 'Novels of the Year', *Daily Telegraph*, 30/12/1930.

3 *Daily Telegraph*, 15/1/1931. Her first review was published the following day.

4 Lorna Gibb, *West's World: The Extraordinary Life of Dame Rebecca West* (Macmillan, 2013), 133.

5 'Miss Rebecca West looks at some of the new books', *Daily Telegraph*, 16/1/1931.

6 Rebecca West, 'Aldous Huxley on man's appalling future', *Daily Telegraph*, 5/2/1932.

7 Rebecca West, 'What can Mrs Sidney Webb mean by this?', *Daily Telegraph*, 18/3/1932.

8 Rebecca West, 'What is T. S. Eliot's authority as a critic?', *Daily Telegraph*, 30/9/1932.

9 Rebecca West, 'What will posterity think of Priestley and Maurois?', *Daily Telegraph*, 1/7/1932.

10 Carl Rollyson, *The Literacy Legacy of Rebecca West* (San Francisco: International Scholars Publications, 2007), 106.

11 Bridget Lakin, interview with author.

12 TNL Archive, ST/ED/CL/3/4, Leonard Russell to Vera Lakin, 6/7/1948.

13 TNL Archive, ST/ED/CL/1/1/133.

14 D. J. Taylor, *The Prose Factory: Literary Life in England Since 1918* (London: Chatto and Windus, 2016), 34.

15 Taylor, *The Prose Factory*, 35. Taylor has an extended discussion of J. C. Squire, 34–42.

16 I am grateful to Jennie De Protani, the Athenaeum's archivist, for this information.

17 Taylor, *The Prose Factory*, 89.

18 TNL Archive, ST/ED, Rebecca West to Lakin (no date).

19 Rebecca West, 'An autobiography that sparkles', *Sunday Times*, 27/1/1935.

20 TNL Archive, ST/ED/CL/1/3, Lakin to Camrose, 29/1/1935.

21 TNL Archive, ST/ED/CL/1/1/1/93, Warner to Lakin, 18/7/1933.

22 I am grateful to D. J. Taylor for sharing his thoughts on other literary impresarios of that era.

23 Harold Nicolson, *Diaries and Letters 1930–39*, ed. Nigel Nicolson (London: Collins, 1966), 147, 157.

24 *Daily Herald*, 20/10/1937.

25 *Illustrated London News*, 6/11/1937.

26 His file is in TNA, KV 2/1385. MI5 continued to monitor him, on and off, for the next twenty years.

27 TNA, KV 2/1385. MI5 memo, 20/9/1938.

28 TNL Archive, ST/ED/CL/1/2, Lakin to Arthur Watson, 30/6/1937. This was written on Lakin's last day at the *Daily Telegraph*.

29 Andrew Lycett, *Dylan Thomas: A New Life* (London: Phoenix, 2003), 158.

30 *Sunday Times*, 15/11/1936.

31 *Sunday Times*, 'Letters' ('A New Poet: Miss Sitwell's Review'), 22/11/1936.

32 *Sunday Times*, 'Letters' ('In Defence of a New Poet'), 29/11/1936.

33 George Orwell, *Seeing Things as They Are: Selected Journalism and Other Writings*. Ed. Peter Davison (London: Penguin Classics, 2016), 44.

34 Orwell, *Seeing Things as They Are*, 48.

35 Orwell, *Seeing Things as They Are*, 49.

36 Papers held by Bridget Lakin, Cyril Lakin to Dorothy L. Sayers, 15/10/1934; TNL Archive, ST/ED/CL/1/3/1, Cyril Lakin to Camrose, 13/10/1936.

37 *The Pearl of Days*, 199.

38 *The Pearl of Days*, 201.

39 TNL Archive, ST/ED/CL/3/4, Camrose to Vera Lakin, 7/7/1948.

40 *Western Mail*, 9/1/1937.

Chapter 9. Appeasement: Divided Loyalties

1 *Western Mail*, 28/2/1933.

2 Tim Bouverie, *Appeasing Hitler: Chamberlain, Churchill and the Road to War* (London: The Bodley Head, 2019), xi.

3 NLW, GB 0210 GARNES 19/4/1932, Gareth Vaughan Jones Papers, correspondence file 13, Gareth Jones to parents.

4 Bouverie, *Appeasing Hitler*, 49.

5 NLW, GB 0210 WAITES ARCH/MSS 2/6/1937, 1–42, correspondence, David Lloyd George to William Watkin Davies. Watkin Davies was then an academic at Birmingham University.

6 *Daily Telegraph*, 16/10/1937 carries report of the trial ('20,000 damages in Lord Camrose's Libel Suit').

7 Francis Beckett, *Fascist in the Family: The Tragedy of John Beckett M.P.* (Abingdon: Routledge, 2017), 2.

8 *Daily Telegraph*, 16/10/1937.

9 Cited in Bouverie, *Appeasing Hitler*, 149.

10 *Sunday Times*, 13/2/1938; *The Pearl of Days*, 207–08.

11 Hansard, HL Deb 22 February 1938, vol 107, cc796–801.

12 Austen Chamberlain, 'How Ireland's Treaty Was Negotiated', *Daily Telegraph*, 29/3/1932; Austen Chamberlain to Lakin, 27/3/1932 (author's private collection).

13 Nathan Bevan, 'The Shocking Moment A Swastika Flew High Over Cardiff Before World War II', WalesOnline (18 Oct. 2018), https://www.walesonline.co.uk/lifestyle/nostalgia/shocking-moment-swastika-flew-high-15283230, accessed 30 Apr. 2021.

14 Sir Ernest Bennett, letter to *The Times*, 10/3/1939.

15 Richard Griffiths, *Patriotism Perverted: Captain Ramsay, the Right Club, and British Anti-Semitism, 1939–1940* (London: Faber and Faber, 2010), 146–9.

16 Speech to South Wales National Labour Conference at Port Talbot, reported in *The Times*, 13/2/1939.

17 See Hywel Francis, *Miners Against Fascism: Wales and the Spanish Civil War* (London: Lawrence and Wishart, 2012), 29–41.

18 Francis and Smith, *The Fed*, 350–75.

19 For a detailed account of Horner's views and his difference with the CPGB's official position see Nina Fishman, *Arthur Horner: A Political Biography, Volume 1: 1894–1944* (London: Lawrence and Wishart, 2010), 410–54.

[20] In the words of its president, Professor J. E. Daniel, *Western Mail*, 5/8/1940, cited in, among others, Martin Johnes, *Wales Since 1939* (Manchester: Manchester University Press, 2012), 25, which has a good discussion of Plaid's attitude to the war.

[21] W. W. Hadley summarized the various press responses in *Munich: Before and After* (London: Cassell and Company, 1944), 96.

[22] Hadley, *Munich: Before and After*, 98.

[23] Hadley, *Munich: Before and After*, 108.

[24] Hadley, *Munich: Before and After*, 95.

[25] BBC WA Script Library, Cyril Lakin's personal file, 'Neville Chamberlain', 10/11/1940.

[26] Griffiths, *Patriotism Perverted*, 212.

[27] *The Pearl of Days*, 211.

Chapter 10. Meeting Hitler

[1] Chips Channon, *Henry 'Chips' Channon: The Diaries 1918–1938*, ed. Simon Heffer (London: Hutchinson, 2021), 559–60.

[2] TNA, PREM 1/332; see also Adrian Phillips, *Fighting Churchill, Appeasing Hitler: How a British Civil Servant Helped Cause the Second World War* (London: Biteback, 2019), 312–6 for a good discussion of the political context and ramifications of Kemsley's visit.

[3] Phillips, *Fighting Churchill, Appeasing Hitler*, 312.

[4] *Daily Sketch*, 24/7/1939. It was also announced in the previous day's *Sunday Times*.

[5] His diary of the visit is held in TNL Archive, ST/ED/CL/1/1/4, 'Trip to Germany with Lord Kemsley'.

[6] TNL Archive, ST/ED/CL/1/1/4, Lakin to Vera, 25/7/1939.

[7] TNA, PREM 1/332 contains Lakin's official written account of the visit.

[8] TNL Archive, ST/ED/CL/1/1/4, Lakin diary of visit.

[9] TNA, PREM 1/332, 'Resume of Talks'.

[10] TNA, PREM 1/332, 'Resume of Talks'.

[11] Cyril Lakin, 'Some Personal Observations [of discussions]'. Document passed to author by Bridget Lakin.

[12] TNA, PREM 1/332, 'Resume of Talks'.

[13] TNA, PREM 1/332, 'Resume of Talks'.

[14] TNA, PREM 1/332, 'Resume of Talks'.

[15] This comment is from Lady Phipps, wife of Sir Eric Phipps, the British Ambassador when Mitford first arrived. Cited in David Pryce-Jones, *Unity Mitford: A Quest* (London: Book Club Associates/Weidenfeld and Nicolson, 1977), 99.

[16] TNA, PREM 1/332, 'Resume of Talks'.

[17] Phillips, *Fighting Churchill, Appeasing Hitler*, 315.

[18] Bouverie, *Appeasing Hitler*, 345.

[19] Otto Dietrich, *The Hitler I Knew* (London: Methuen, 1957), 45; Phillips, *Fighting Churchill, Appeasing Hitler*, 316.

[20] Pryce-Jones, *Unity Mitford: A Quest*, 99.

[21] Phillips, *Fighting Churchill, Appeasing Hitler*, 317.

[22] Cyril Lakin, 'Some Personal Observations'.

[23] *The Pearl of Days*, 213.

[24] *The Pearl of Days*, 214.

[25] Bouverie, *Appeasing Hitler*, 324.

[26] Andrew Roberts, *Eminent Churchillians* (London: Weidenfeld and Nicolson, 1995), 311. Roberts's chapter on Bryant is a brilliant exposé.

Chapter 11. BBC Broadcaster

[1] *The English Spirit*, ed. Anthony Weymouth (London: George Allen and Unwin, 1942) includes chapters based on radio talks on aspects of British life and culture from J. B. Priestley, Somerset Maugham, H. E. Bates and others, following Weymouth's introduction.

[2] BBC WA, Anthony Weymouth Talks file 2 (1939); Margery Wace, internal memo, 18/5/1939.

[3] Anthony Weymouth, *Journal of the War Years (1939–1945) and One Year Later, Volume 1* (Worcester: Littlebury and Co, 1948), 21.

[4] Noted by Anthony Eden in his diary. Cited in Nicholas Shakespeare, *Six Minutes in May: How Churchill Unexpectedly Became Prime Minister* (London: Harvill Secker, 2017), 62.

[5] BBC WA, Anthony Weymouth, Talks file 1; Margery Wace, internal memo, 23/3/1938.

[6] 'Lord Camrose Diary 3 May 1940', cited in Martin Gilbert, *The Churchill War Papers: At the Admiralty, Volume 1: September 1939 – May 1940* (London: Heinemann, 1993), 1190–91.

[7] BBC WA, Cyril Lakin Talks file 1940–1946, Barkway to Lakin 24/5/1940 and Lakin to Barkway 25/5/1940.

[8] Letter from F. A. Bracey to the *Western Mail*, 22/5/1942.

[9] Ivor Brown, 'The Empire Girdle', *The Listener*, 3/4/1941.

[10] See Olechnowicz, 'Liberal Anti-Fascism in the 1930s', 636–60.

[11] *The Pearl of Days*.

[12] TNL Archive, ST/ED/CL/3/1, 9/9/1940.

[13] BBC WA, Howard Marshall Talks file 7 (1940), internal memo, 21/5/1940.

[14] BBC WA, Cyril Lakin Talks file.

[15] Weymouth, *Journal of the War Years, Vol. 1*, 338.

[16] BBC WA, Cyril Lakin Talks file, internal memo.

[17] BBC WA BBC Script Library, 29/11/1940.

[18] BBC WA BBC Script Library, 8/12/1940.

[19] BBC WA BBC Script Library, 6/12/1940.

[20] BBC WA BBC Script Library, 22/12/1940.

[21] BBC WA BBC Script Library, 1/1/1941.

[22] BBC WA BBC Script Library, 3/1/1941.

[23] BBC WA BBC Script Library, 19/1/1941.

[24] BBC WA BBC Script Library, 22/1/1941.

[25] BBC WA BBC Script Library, 'Did You Hear That?', *The Listener*, 2/10/1941.

[26] Bridget Lakin, private correspondence, Brodrick to Lakin, 22/4/1941.

[27] BBC WA BBC Script Library, 'Did You Hear That?', *The Listener*, 2/10/1941.

[28] BBC WA, Cyril Lakin Talks file, internal memo, 24/4/1941.

[29] BBC WA, Cyril Lakin Talks file, internal memo, (Michael Barkway), 6/5/1942.

[30] BBC WA, Cyril Lakin Talks file, 1/2/1942.

[31] BBC WA, Cyril Lakin Talks file, internal memo, 10/2/1942.

[32] Dorian Lynskey, *The Ministry of Truth: A Biography of George Orwell's 1984* (London: Picador, 2019), 90.

[33] *The Times*, 4/5/1942.

Chapter 12. The Barry By-Election

[1] Stead, 'The Town That Had Come of Age', 368.

[2] Stan Awbery, *Let Us Talk of Barry* (Barry: self-published, 1954), 77.

[3] Stead, 'The Town That Had Come of Age', 389.

[4] Peter Stead, 'Barry since 1939: war-time prosperity and post-war uncertainty', in *Barry: The Centenary Book*, 434–5.

[5] *Daily Telegraph*, 25/5/1942.

[6] *Manchester Guardian*, 'Rank and File Labour Helping Mr Mackay', 9/6/1942.

[7] TNL Archive, ST/ED/CL/1/1/1/95, West to Lakin, (undated, but 1940).

[8] Victor Gollancz, letter to Harold Laski, 8/5/1942, cited in Ruth Dudley Edwards, *Victor Gollancz: A Biography* (London: Victor Gollancz Ltd, 1987), 369. However, as Dudley Edwards points out, within months Gollancz became disenchanted with Common Wealth.

[9] Noreen Branson, *History of the Communist Party of Great Britain 1941–1951* (London: Lawrence and Wishart, 1997), 5.

[10] *Western Mail*, 5/6/1942.

[11] TNL Archive, ST/ED/CL/2/1, Zoe Longdon to Lakin, 24/5/1942.

[12] TNL Archive, ST/ED/CL/2/1, Mafydd Morgan to Lakin, 21/5/1942.

[13] TNL Archive, ST/ED/CL/2/1, Hadley to Lakin, 19/5/1942.

[14] *Western Mail*, 30/5/1942.

[15] HFP. The letter was widely publicized in the press.

[16] Bridget Lakin, interview with author.

[17] *Western Mail*, 29/5/1942.

[18] *Western Mail*, 30/5/1942.

[19] Hadley Cantril, *Public Opinion, 1935–1946* (Princeton: Princeton University

Press, 1951), 195, cited in Paul Addison, 'By-Elections of the Second World War', in Chris Cook and John Ramsden, eds., *By-Elections in British Politics* (London and Basingstoke: Macmillan, 1973), 169. Addison discusses Mackay and the impact of the Common Wealth Party but oddly makes no mention of Llandaff and Barry.

20 Mackay later wrote a short book arguing this point: *Coupon or Free?: A Study in Electoral Reform and Representative Government* (London: Secker and Warburg, 1944).

21 *Manchester Guardian*, 30/5/1942.

22 *Western Mail*, 2/6/1942.

23 Rhys Evans, *Gwynfor Evans: A Portrait of a Patriot* (Ceredigion: Y Lolfa, 2008), 61.

24 Evans, *Gwynfor Evans: A Portrait of a Patriot*, 67; NLW, G1/1, Gwynfor Evans Papers, Idris Evans to Gwynfor Evans, 14/5/1940.

25 TNL Archive, ST/ED/CL/2/1, Sinclair to Lakin, 4/6/1942.

26 Bridget Lakin, interview with author.

27 Bridget Lakin, interview with author.

28 *Western Mail*, 8/9/1942.

29 *Manchester Guardian*, 30/5/1942.

30 *Daily Herald*, 9/6/1942; *Daily Mirror*, 9/6/1942.

31 TNL Archive, ST/ED/CL/2/1, Camrose to Lakin, 12/6/1942.

32 TNL Archive, ST/ED/CL/2/1, Pearn to Lakin, 16/6/1942.

33 TNL Archive, ST/ED/CL/2/1, James Palmer to Lakin, 14/6/1942.

34 TNL Archive, ST/ED/CL/2/1, Watson to Lakin, 15/6/1942.

Chapter 13. Politician

1 This arrangement continued until October 1950. Between 1940 and 1941 the business of Parliament was conducted in Church House, Westminster because of fears of bombing. See Sarah Tudor, 'Bombing of the Houses of Parliament: 75th Anniversary', House of Lords Library: In Focus (2016), https://researchbriefings.files.parliament.uk/documents/LIF-2016-0028/LIF-2016-0028.pdf, accessed 30 Apr. 2021.

2 Hansard, HC Deb 1 July 1942, vol 381, c224.

3 Hansard, HC Deb 2 July 1942, vol 381, c527.

4 Details of the debate are given in Hansard, HC Deb 7 July 1942, vol 381, cc652–742.

5 Richard Davenport-Hines, *Enemies Within: Communists, the Cambridge Spies and the Making of Modern Britain* (London: William Collins, 2018), 484.

6 Bartlett to Lakin (n.d.). Private correspondence held by author.

7 Hansard, HC Deb 7 July 1942, vol 381, cc652–742.

8 *Western Mail*, 8/7/1942.

9 *The Listener*, 24/9/1942.

[10] In 1945 he was elected Labour MP for Bradford Central and also served as chairman of the Parliamentary Labour Party before losing Bradford North (after his original seat was abolished) in the 1955 general election.

[11] *The Listener*, 1/10/1942.

[12] *The Observer*, 4/10/1942.

[13] *The Listener*, 12/11/1942.

[14] *Western Mail*, 23/10/1942.

[15] *The Listener*, 22/10/1942.

[16] 'Eric Blair to Norman Collins (Empire Talks Manager), 13/2/1943. In a letter headed "Approaching Distinguished or well-known people in regard to broadcast talks", Orwell (Blair) lists Lakin along with Dr Edith Summerskill and Will Lawson (sic).' George Orwell, *Keeping Our Little Corner Clean*, ed. Peter Davison (London: Secker and Warburg, 2001), 343–4.

[17] George Orwell, 'Eric Blair's resignation letter 24th September 1943', BBC Radio 4, The Real George Orwell: Orwell letters (2012), https://www.bbc.co.uk/programmes/p014cvms/p01465y2, accessed 5 May 2021.

[18] Reported in the *Western Mail*, 22/5/1943.

[19] *The Onlooker*, August 1943.

[20] Gary Love, 'Making a "New Conservatism": The Tory Reform Committee and Design for Freedom, 1942–1949', *The English Historical Review*, 135 (2020), 605.

[21] *The Times*, 17/5/1943.

[22] *Western Mail*, 11/6/1943.

[23] Hansard, HC Deb 29 July 1943, vol 391, cc1825–928.

[24] TNL Archive, ST/ED/CL/1/1/24, Lakin to Kemsley, 20/2/1943.

[25] *Western Mail*, 30/10/1943.

[26] *Western Mail*, 25/3/1943.

[27] *Western Mail*, 25/3/1943.

[28] *Western Mail*, 22/8/1944.

Chapter 14. The Lost Worlds of Cyril Lakin

[1] Bridget Lakin, interview with author.

[2] 'Winston Churchill's Declaration of Policy to the Electors', in *1945 Conservative Party General Election Manifesto* (1945), http://www.conservativemanifesto.com/1945/1945-conservative-manifesto.shtml, accessed 30 Apr. 2021.

[3] John Bew, *Citizen Clem: A Biography of Attlee* (London: riverrun, 2017), 334.

[4] *Daily Mail*, 9/6/1945, cited in Bew, *Citizen Clem*, 334.

[5] Kenneth O. Morgan, *Revolution to Devolution: Reflections on Welsh Democracy* (Cardiff: University of Wales Press, 2014), 230.

[6] *Western Mail*, 4/7/1945.

[7] *Western Mail*, 6/7/1945.

[8] NLW, GB 0210 CARCON 11/10/1945, Welsh Political Archive, Llandaff and Barry Conservative Association minutes.

[9] Weymouth, *Journal of the War Years, Vol. 2*, 396–7.

[10] Paul Addison, *The Road to 1945: British Politics and the Second World War* (rev. edn, London: Pimlico, 1994), 273.

[11] Johnes, *Wales Since 1939*, 36.

[12] Stead, 'Barry Since 1939', 450.

[13] *The Pearl of Days*, 241.

[14] Bridget Lakin, private papers, Lambert to Lakin, 15/5/1946.

[15] HFP, Cyril Lakin to Stan and Annie Lakin, 10/7/1946.

[16] David Kynaston, 'A Brief History of the *Financial Times*', *Financial Times Historical Archive* (2010), https://www.gale.com/intl/essays/david-kynaston-brief-history-financial-times, accessed 30 Apr. 2021.

[17] David Kynaston, *The Financial Times: A Centenary History* (London: Viking, 1988), 142.

[18] TNL Archive, ST/ED/CL/1/3/1, Lakin to Camrose, 5/5/1948.

[19] TNL Archive, ST/ED/CL/3/4.

[20] Geraint Thomas, 'The Conservative Party and Welsh Politics in the Inter-War Years', *The English Historical Review*, 128 (2013), 877–913.

[21] Matthew Cragoe, 'Conservatives, "Englishness" and "Civic Nationalism" Between the Wars', in Duncan Tanner, Chris Williams, Andrew Edwards and W. P. Griffith, eds., *Debating Nationhood and Governance in Britain, 1885–1939: Perspectives from the 'Four Nations'* (Manchester: Manchester University Press, 2006), 192–210.

Note on Sources

The book draws on the Cyril Lakin papers held in the archive of Times Newspapers Ltd (TNL), notably correspondence from his time at the *Sunday Times* and the *Daily Telegraph*. For his early life in Barry, it includes material from the Glamorgan Archives (GA); for his time at Oxford, the diaries of his contemporaries Ernest Willmore and William Watkin Davies are held in the St John's College Archive (SJCA) and the National Library of Wales (NLW), respectively. His BBC scripts and correspondence related to his time as a broadcaster are held in the BBC Written Archives Centre in Caversham (BBC WA). Information on Lakin's service in the First World War can be found in the war diaries held at the National Archives (TNA), which also holds his written report of the visit to Germany in 1939. A range of miscellaneous material covering different parts of his life, the First World War, working for the Berry brothers, the Barry by-election and Lakin family correspondence have been held at Highlight Farm (HFP). Following publication of this book, these papers, together with material held by Bridget Lakin and correspondence obtained by the author, will constitute a new Cyril Lakin collection in the Welsh Political Archive at the National Library of Wales.

Select Bibliography

Addison, Paul, *The Road to 1945: British Politics and the Second World War* (rev. edn, London: Pimlico, 1994).

Awbery, Stan, *Let Us Talk of Barry* (Barry: self-published, 1954).

Barker, Ernest, *Age and Youth: Memories of Three Universities and Father of the Man* (Oxford: Oxford University Press, 1953).

Beckett, Francis, *Fascist in the Family: The Tragedy of John Beckett M.P.* (Abingdon: Routledge, 2017).

Bew, John, *Citizen Clem: A Biography of Attlee* (London: riverrun, 2017).

Bonfiglioli, Margaret, and James Munson, eds., *Full of Hope and Fear: The Great War Letters of an Oxford Family* (Oxford: Oxford University Press, 2014).

Bouverie, Tim, *Appeasing Hitler: Chamberlain, Churchill and the Road to War* (London: The Bodley Head, 2019).

Brittain, Vera, *Chronicle of Youth: War Diary 1913–1917*, ed. Alan Bishop (London: Victor Gollancz, 1981).

Channon, Chips, *Henry 'Chips' Channon: The Diaries 1918–1938*, ed. Simon Heffer (London: Hutchinson, 2021).

Colley, Margaret Siriol, *More Than a Grain of Truth: The Biography of Gareth Richard Vaughan Jones* (Newark: Nigel Colley, 2005).

Cook, Chris, and John Ramsden, eds., *By-Elections in British Politics* (London and Basingstoke: Macmillan, 1973).

Croll, Andy, *Barry Island: The Making of a Seaside Playground, c.1790–c.1965* (Cardiff: University of Wales Press, 2020).

Hart-Davis, Duff, *The House the Berrys Built: Inside the Telegraph, 1928–1986* (London: Hodder and Stoughton, 1990).

Dickie, John, *The Craft: How the Freemasons Made the Modern World* (London: Hodder and Stoughton, 2020).

England, Joe, *Merthyr: The Crucible of Modern Wales* (Cardigan: Parthian, 2017).

Evans, Rhys, *Gwynfor Evans: A Portrait of a Patriot* (Ceredigion: Y Lolfa, 2008).

Francis, Hywel, *Miners Against Fascism: Wales and the Spanish Civil War* (London: Lawrence and Wishart, 2012).

Francis, Hywel, and Dai Smith, *The Fed: A History of the South Wales Miners in the Twentieth Century* (Cardiff: University of Wales Press, 1998).

Fishman, Nina, *Arthur Horner: A Political Biography, Volume 1: 1894–1944* (London: Lawrence and Wishart, 2010).

Gilbert, Martin, *The Churchill War Papers: At the Admiralty, Volume 1: September 1939 – May 1940* (London: Heinemann, 1993).

Griffiths, Richard, *Patriotism Perverted: Captain Ramsay, the Right Club, and British Anti-Semitism, 1939–1940* (London: Faber and Faber, 2010).

Hadley, W. W., *Munich: Before and After* (London: Cassell and Company, 1944).

Hicks, Jonathan, *Barry and the Great War 1914–1918* (Barry: Fielding Publishing, 2007).

Hobson, Harold, Phillip Knightley and Leonard Russell, eds., *The Pearl of Days: An Intimate Memoir of the Sunday Times 1822–1972* (London: Hamish Hamilton, 1972)

Janner, Elsie, *Barnett Janner: A Personal Portrait* (London: Robson Books, 1984).

John, Angela, *Turning the Tide: The Life of Lady Rhondda* (Cardigan: Parthian, 2013).

Johnes, Martin, *Wales Since 1939* (Manchester: Manchester University Press, 2012).

Jones, Richard Wyn, *The Fascist Party in Wales?: Plaid Cymru, Welsh Nationalism and the Accusation of Fascism* (Cardiff: University of Wales Press, 2014).

Kenny, Mary, *Germany Calling: A Personal Biography of William Joyce, Lord Haw-Haw* (Dublin: New Island, 2003).

Leeworthy, Daryl, *Labour Country: Political Radicalism and Social Democracy in South Wales 1831–1985* (Cardigan: Parthian, 2018).

Lewis, Jeremy, *Cyril Connolly: A Life* (London: Jonathan Cape, 1997).

Lord Burnham, *Peterborough Court: The Story of the Daily Telegraph* (London: Cassell and Company, 1955).

Lycett, Andrew, *Dylan Thomas: A New Life* (London: Phoenix, 2003).

McCabe, Cameron [Ernst Julius Bornemann], *The Face on the Cutting-Room Floor* (Blackmask Online, 2005).

Masterman, C. F. G., *The Condition of England* (London: Faber and Faber, 2008).

Moore, Donald, ed., *Barry: The Centenary Book* (Barry: Barry Centenary Book Committee, 1984).

Morgan, Kenneth O., *Wales in British Politics 1868–1922* (Cardiff: University of Wales Press, 1963).

Moulton, Mo, *Mutual Admiration Society: How Dorothy L. Sayers and Her Oxford Circle Remade the World for Women* (London: Corsair, 2019).

Nicolson, Harold, *Diaries and Letters 1930–39*, ed. Nigel Nicolson (London: Collins, 1966).

Orwell, George, *Keeping Our Little Corner Clean: 1942–1943*, ed. Peter Davison (London: Secker and Warburg, 2001).

Parry-Jones, Cai, *The Jews of Wales: A History* (Cardiff: University of Wales Press, 2017).

Peake, Felicity, *Pure Chance* (Shrewsbury: Airlife Publishing Ltd, 1993).

Phillips, Adrian, *Fighting Churchill, Appeasing Hitler: How a British Civil Servant Helped Cause the Second World War* (London: Biteback, 2019).

Pryce-Jones, David, *Unity Mitford: A Quest* (London: Book Club Associates/Weidenfeld and Nicolson, 1977).

Shakespeare, Nicholas, *Six Minutes in May: How Churchill Unexpectedly Became Prime Minister* (London: Harvill Secker, 2017).

Smith, Dai, ed., *A People and a Proletariat: Essays in the History of Wales, 1780–1980* (London: Pluto Press, 1980).

Smith, Dai, *Aneurin Bevan and the World of South Wales* (Cardiff: University of Wales Press, 1993).

Stourton, Edward, *Auntie's War: The BBC during the Second World War* (London: Penguin Random House, 2017).

Taylor, D. J., *Orwell: The Life* (London: Vintage, 2004).

Taylor, D. J., *The Prose Factory: Literary Life in England Since 1918* (London: Chatto and Windus, 2016).

Weymouth, Anthony [Ivo Geikie-Cobb], *Journal of the War Years (1939–1945) and One Year Later*, 2 vols (Worcester: Littlebury and Co, 1948).

Wheeler, Michael, *The Athenaeum: More Than Just Another London Club* (New Haven and London: Yale University Press, 2020.

Acknowledgements

I could not have written the book without the help of Bridget Lakin, whose recollections of her father and mother and memories of his literary and political friends were always lucid and insightful. Each phone call brought witty anecdotes and prompted new ideas. Bridget and her husband Clifford were excellent hosts on the Isle of Wight and generous in sharing photos and letters. I am grateful to my cousin Chris Lakin and his wife Tina for giving me full access to the family archive at Highlight Farm, and for their hospitality and good humour.

I should like to thank Dai Smith, who commissioned the book for Parthian as part of its *Modern Wales* series, for sharing his knowledge as a historian of South Wales and for his thoughtful comments at all stages. Parthian's director, Richard Davies, has been very supportive in seeing the book through, and I benefited from the excellent copy-editing skills and literary interests of Robert Harries. I have enjoyed discussing Welsh history with Daryl Leeworthy and gained much from our conversations.

Early snippets of my research appeared in *The Oldie* and the *BBC History Magazine* (*HistoryExtra*) and I'm grateful to the editors for their interest, notably the late Jeremy Lewis, the biographer of Cyril Connolly. The archivists at the Glamorgan Archives in Cardiff were always helpful in answering my queries. I should like to thank Rob Phillips and Iwan ap Dafydd at the National Library of Wales for help with the William Watkin Davies and Gareth Jones papers. I am grateful to Michael Riordan, archivist at St John's College, Oxford for access to the Ernest Willmore diaries, and to the Oxford University Archives for providing the admission and examination details of Lakin and his contemporaries. Nicky Hammond, Special Collections Archivist at University of Wales Trinity Saint David, helpfully answered my queries on Ystrad Meurig Grammar School. I am grateful to Jennie De Protani, archivist at the Athenaeum, for answering queries and for carrying an early article in their members' newsletter. Once again, I should thank Kate O'Brien and colleagues at the BBC Written Archives Centre at Caversham for permission to cite script material and correspondence, and their colleagues in the BBC Photo Library. Nick Mays, archivist at News UK, which holds the Cyril Lakin papers in its *Sunday Times* archive, answered several queries and I am grateful for permission to cite the material. Ivo Geikie-Cobb told me more about his grandfather and generously answered all my questions. Robert Smyly, grandson of Lord Buckland (Seymour Berry), kindly allowed me to see private papers related to the Berry family. Lady (Ruth) Morris was generous in sharing information about her father, Barnett Janner. Thanks to my friend Lucy Gaster for telling me more about her grandparents, Robert and Sylvia Lynd.

I am fortunate to have benefited from the work of historians who have previously written about Barry, notably Peter Stead and Brian Luxton. The following helped in different ways along the way: Mo Moulton, D. J. Taylor (for conversations on Orwell and the literary world of the 1930s), Daniel Richards (for sharing his knowledge of Barry veterans of the First World War), Neil Evans, Gary Love, Christine James (née Lakin), Angela John, Peggy Andrews (for memories of Highlight Lane), Leighton Andrews, Lisa Olrichs at the National Portrait Gallery, staff at Oxford's Bodleian Library, the National Archives at Kew, and the library and archive at the Museum of Freemasonry in London. In Barry, Nic and Shirley Hodges have helped keep the history of the town alive through interesting talks and by sharing photo archives. The People's Collection Wales hold a range of historical images that are very helpful for researchers. I am lucky to work with supportive and stimulating colleagues in the Politics and International Studies department of The Open University. The book was completed during the COVID-19 pandemic and I'm especially grateful to the irreplaceable London Library for sending on books so that it could be finished on time. Finally, thanks to Anita, who reads everything and is always interested.

Index

Modern Wales by Parthian Books

The Modern Wales Series, edited by Dai Smith and supported by the Rhys Davies Trust, was launched in 2017. The Series offers an extensive list of biography, memoir, history and politics which reflect and analyse the development of Wales as a modernised society into contemporary times. It engages widely across places and people, encompasses imagery and the construction of iconography, dissects historiography and recounts plain stories, all in order to elucidate the kaleidoscopic pattern which has shaped and changed the complex culture and society of Wales and the Welsh.

The inaugural titles in the Series were *To Hear the Skylark's Song*, a haunting memoir of growing up in Aberfan by Huw Lewis, and Joe England's panoramic *Merthyr: The Crucible of Modern Wales*. The impressive list has continued with Angela John's *Rocking the Boat*, essays on Welsh women who pioneered the universal fight for equality and Daryl Leeworthy's landmark overview *Labour Country*, on the struggle through radical action and social democratic politics to ground Wales in the civics of common ownership. Myths and misapprehension, whether naïve or calculated, have been ruthlessly filleted in Martin Johnes' startling *Wales: England's Colony?* and a clutch of biographical studies will reintroduce us to the once seminal, now neglected, figures of Cyril Lakin, Minnie Pallister and Gwyn Thomas, whilst Meic Stehens' *Rhys Davies: A Writer's Life* and Dai *Smith's Raymond Williams: A Warrior's Tale* form part of an associated back catalogue from Parthian.

the RHYS DAVIES TRUST

PARTHIAN

WALES: ENGLAND'S COLONY?

Martin Johnes

From the very beginnings of Wales, its people have defined themselves against their large neighbour. This book tells the fascinating story of an uneasy and unequal relationship between two nations living side-by-side.

PB / £8.99
978-1-912681-41-9

RHYS DAVIES: A WRITER'S LIFE

Meic Stephens

Rhys Davies (1901-78) was among the most dedicated, prolific and accomplished of Welsh prose writers. This is his first full biography.

'This is a delightful book, which is itself a social history in its own right, and funny.'
– The Spectator

PB / £11.99
978-1-912109-96-8

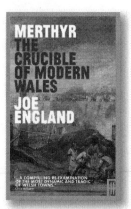

MERTHYR, THE CRUCIBLE OF MODERN WALES

Joe England

Merthyr Tydfil was the town where the future of a country was forged: a thriving, struggling surge of people, industry, democracy and ideas. This book assesses an epic history of Merthyr from 1760 to 1912 through the focus of a fresh and thoroughly convincing perspective.

PB / £18.99
978-1-913640-05-7

TO HEAR THE SKYLARK'S SONG

Huw Lewis

To Hear the Skylark's Song is a memoir about how Aberfan survived and eventually thrived after the terrible disaster of the 21st of October 1966.

'A thoughtful and passionate memoir, moving and respectful.'
– Tessa Hadley

PB / £8.99
978-1-912109-72-2

ROCKING THE BOAT

Angela V. John

This insightful and revealing collection of essays focuses on seven Welsh women who, in a range of imaginative ways, resisted the status quo in Wales, England and beyond during the nineteenth and twentieth centuries.

PB / £11.99
978-1-912681-44-0

TURNING THE TIDE

Angela V. John

This rich biography tells the remarkable tale of Margaret Haig Thomas (1883-1958) who became the second Viscountess Rhondda. She was a Welsh suffragette, held important posts during the First World War and survived the sinking of the *Lusitania*.

PB / £17.99
978-1-909844-72-8

BRENDA CHAMBERLAIN, ARTIST & WRITER

Jill Piercy

The first full-length biography of Brenda Chamberlain chronicles the life of an artist and writer whose work was strongly affected by the places she lived, most famously Bardsey Island and the Greek island of Hydra.

PB / £11.99
978-1-912681-06-8

PARTHIAN

MW MODERN WALES

RAYMOND WILLIAMS: A WARRIOR'S TALE

Dai Smith

Raymond Williams (1921-1998) was the most influential socialist writer and thinker in post-war Britain. Now, for the first time, making use of Williams' private and unpublished papers and by placing him in a wide social and cultural landscape, Dai Smith, in this highly original and much praised biography, uncovers how Williams' life to 1961 is an explanation of his immense intellectual achievement.

"Becomes at once the authoritative account... Smith has done all that we can ask the historian as biographer to do."
– Stefan Collini, *London Review of Books*

PB / £20
978-1-913640-08-8

BETWEEN WORLDS: A QUEER BOY FROM THE VALLEYS

Jeffrey Weeks

A man's own story from the Rhondda. Jeffrey Weeks was born in the Rhondda in 1945, of mining stock. As he grew up he increasingly felt an outsider in the intensely community-minded valleys, a feeling intensified as he became aware of his gayness. Escape came through education. He left for London, to university, and to realise his sexuality. He has been described as the 'most significant British intellectual working on sexuality to emerge from the radical sexual movements of the 1970s'.

HB / £20
978-1-912681-88-4